Evidence for the Crucifixion and Resurrection of Jesus Christ Examined through Islamic Law

Suheil Madanat

Langham
MONOGRAPHS

Published 2023 by Langham Monographs
An imprint of Langham Publishing
www.langhampublishing.org

Langham Publishing and its imprints are a ministry of Langham Partnership

Langham Partnership
PO Box 296, Carlisle, Cumbria, CA3 9WZ, UK
www.langham.org

ISBNs:
978-1-83973-790-9 Print
978-1-83973-900-2 ePub
978-1-83973-901-9 PDF

British Library Cataloguing-in-Publication Data
A catalogue record for this book is available from the British Library

ISBN: 978-1-83973-790-9

Cover & Book Design: projectluz.com

To Abeer,
the virtuous wife who is clothed in strength and dignity,
and our two sons, Layth and Louay

Contents

Preface xiii

Chapter 1 1

Introduction

The Evidentiary Challenge 2

Christian Claims and Islamic Denials 7

Thesis 10

Limitations and Delimitations 10

Significance 11

Why the Islamic World? 11

Why Evidential Historical Apologetics? 12

Apologetics vs. Polemics 22

Evaluating the Juridical Approach in the West 26

Why the Islamic Law? 29

Originality of the Study 32

A Brief Overview of the History of Juridical Apologetics in the West 33

Methodology 39

Personal Interest and Background 40

Chapter 2 43

An Overview of Islamic Law

Nature, Formation, and Features 44

Sources and Formation 46

Concluding the Formative Period and Closing *Ijtihād* Gates 56

Islamicity of the Law 59

Components of Islamic Law 61

The Islamic Law School Selected for This Study 62

The Tension between Stagnation and Development in Islamic Law 67

Attempted Solutions 67

Current Islamic Reactions 70

Conclusion 75

Introductory Overview of Court Procedure and Evidence 76

Court System 76

Admissibility of a Lawsuit 80
Penal Law 81
Standard of Proof 82
Burden of Proof 84
Categories of Evidence 85

Chapter 3 87
Authenticity of the New Testament Documents
De Jure Admissibility of Documentary Evidence 88
Documents between Theory and Practice 89
Rules for Admissibility of Documents 90
Broad Principles vs. New Testament Documents 91
The Evidence of *Istiṣḥāb* 92
De Facto Admissibility of Documentary Evidence 93
Compilation and Authentication of the Qur'ān 94
New Testament Authenticity vs. Qur'ān Authenticity 106
Compilation and Authentication of the Sunna 137
New Testament Authenticity vs. Sunna Authenticity 146
The Islamic Story of the Corruption of the New Testament 155
Conclusion 160

Chapter 4 161
Eyewitness Testimony and Confession
Eyewitness Testimony 161
Number and Gender of Eyewitnesses 162
Qualifications of Eyewitnesses 163
Consistency of Testimonies 182
Confession 199
Compliance with Confession under Islamic Law 201
Confession by Paul 203
Confession by James 205

Chapter 5 209
Expert Witness Testimony and Circumstantial Evidence
Expert Witness Testimony 209
Circumstantial Evidence 214
The Empty Tomb 218
The Origin of Christianity 223
Sunday Worship and the Eucharist 225
Archaeology and Ancient Literature 225

Miracles and Visions 232
Christianity and Civilization 233

Chapter 6 239
Conclusion

Bibliography 243

List of Figures

Preface

The resurrection of Jesus Christ captivates my entire being like no other reality. It is the dazzling ultimate evidence that he is the way, the truth, and the life, and it is the guarantee of my own resurrection. I see no surer evidence; no greater inheritance. At the same time, no deadlier lie has ever been devised after the serpent's lie in Eden than denying this reality and depriving billions of the life and glory that are in the crucified and risen Christ. This dissertation is another apologetic tool aimed at exposing this lie and opening their eyes.

I have been immensely blessed to have Dr. Ted Cabal as my doctoral supervisor and, before that, as my instructor during the coursework. His passionate encouragement and wise guidance were fuel and light throughout this wonderful journey. I thank Dr. Ayman Ibrahim and Dr. Tim Beougher for serving on the dissertation committee, and Dr. David Johnston for serving as the external reader. I also thank the now-retired Dr. James Parker for his effort during the coursework, and Dr. Albert Mohler for his distinguished leadership. To these godly and knowledgeable men, I will remain ever grateful. Graduating from The Southern Baptist Theological Seminary, this monumental institution in both its unwavering commitment to the truth and its highest academic standards, is an undeserved honor for which I thank the Lord.

Suheil Madanat

December 2019

CHAPTER 1

Introduction

The Christian faith is unique in possessing an unlikely combination of supernatural claims and historical verifiability. On the one hand, its supernatural and bold foundational claims challenge natural human understanding.[1] One God exists yet in three consubstantial divine persons: Father, Son, and Holy Spirit. The second person of the Trinity, God the Son, born of a virgin, took on at conception a human nature in addition to and inseparable from his divine nature.[2] The fully divine person became also fully human, without adding a second person or without ceasing for a moment to be fully God, thus "acknowledged in two natures, unconfusedly, unchangeably, indivisibly, inseparably."[3] He walked on this earth as a poor and meek man yet performed miracles like no other, including raising the dead and calming the sea. He suffered an excruciating death on a cross yet rose from the dead and ascended into heaven.

On the other hand, the Christian faith is verifiable like no other as its alleged foundational events, however strange and wondrous they may appear, happened in real history. They were witnessed by ordinary people, the Evangelists or their source eyewitnesses, who used their natural senses and

1. So much so that Christian existentialist philosopher Søren Kierkegaard, who rejects grounding faith on natural theology arguments or objective evidence, sees as evidence of the divine origin and truth of the Christian faith its very oddity and apparent implausibility, since no human would possibly invent it. See Kierkegaard, *Philosophical Fragments*, 21–22, 35–36, 51.

2. Erickson, *Christian Theology*, 361–364.

3. Excerpt from the Chalcedonian Creed, English translation by Schaff, *Creeds of Christendom*, 2:62–63.

then wrote or told the events from clear memory.[4] The apostle John's words are unequivocal: "What was from the beginning, what we have heard, what we have seen with our eyes, what we have looked at and touched with our hands, concerning the Word of Life . . . what we have seen and heard we proclaim to you also" (1 John 1:1–3).[5] Indeed, the very fact that the events were supernatural and so unusual makes them ever so memorable to their eyewitnesses.[6] Challengers of the Christian faith can therefore examine these claims objectively for themselves today by recognized historical inquiry. This historical testability is unique to Christianity.[7]

The Evidentiary Challenge

All other great world religions are based upon untestable claims that are unreliably subjective, inaccessibly metaphysical,[8] confusingly diversified, or speculatively philosophical. Such claims are neither falsifiable nor verifiable. Islam, the world's second largest religion, offers as its evidence to a divine origin the literary style of the qur'anic text, marked by its "intrinsic beauty, clarity, eloquence, and levels of meaning."[9] The Qur'ān asserts four times in four different *sūras* (chapters) that only God can possibly write such words: "If you are in doubt concerning what We have sent down unto Our servant [Muhammad], then bring a *sūra* like it, and call your witnesses apart from God if you are truthful" (Qur'ān 2:23). Another assertion reads, "Or do they say, 'He [Muhammad] has fabricated it'? Say, 'Then bring ten *sūras* like it, fabricated, and call upon whomsoever you can apart from God, if you are truthful.' But if they answer thee not, then know that it has been sent down with God's Knowledge and that there is no god but He" (Qur'ān 11:13–14).[10] Islamic scholars thus confidently claim that "the Quran is the central miracle

4. For modern methods of defending the ability of the Evangelists to remember both the sayings of Jesus and the witnessed events, see Blomberg, *Historical Reliability*, 53–62.

5. All biblical citations, unless otherwise noted, will be from the New American Standard Bible.

6. Bauckham, *Jesus and the Eyewitnesses*, 341–42.

7. Habermas and Licona, *Case for the Resurrection*, 27.

8. "Metaphysical" in the sense of referring to a reality that is beyond the perception of natural human senses.

9. Nasr, *Study Quran*, 18.

10. See also Qur'an 10:37–38 and 17:88.

of Islam in that it 'incapacitates' challengers' argument against it, as miracles do in general. That the Prophet was 'unlettered' forms the background of this challenge."[11] Such an assertion remains largely subjective and its evidentiary power too weak to underpin the entire edifice of a religion with its bold denials of the foundational claims of its predecessor, Christianity. Indeed, one can challenge the literary beauty of passages from the Qur'ān with other non-qur'anic passages. For example, one can argue that Psalm 19, with almost the same message of the first *sūra* of the Qur'ān, is "superior in almost every aspect."[12]

Muslims relate another miracle, the night travel, or *al-isrā'* of Muhammad from his home in Mecca to the Farthest Mosque (the site of the destroyed Jewish Temple, today the Dome of the Rock) in Jerusalem,[13] then his ascension from the Rock through the seven heavens, or *al-mi'rāj*.[14] There he talked to several Judeo-Christian prophets and proceeded on "till he was within two bows' length or nearer" (Qur'ān 53:1–11) from God himself, who made his faith firmer.[15] That same night he returned to his home in Mecca where, according to tradition, the door of his home through which he left was still swinging.[16] Allegedly, he was between sleeping and waking when the archangel Gabriel roused him and escorted him through the miraculous journey upon a winged horse named *al-Burāq*. No witnesses to this story exist, however. Indeed, the Qur'ān addresses this evidentiary challenge and rebukes those who ask Muhammad for a miracle as evidence of his prophethood: "We shall not believe in you till you make a spring gush forth for us from the earth, . . . or till you make the sky fall upon us in pieces, as you have claimed, or you bring God and the angels before us, or till you have a house of gold ornament, or you ascend to Heaven. And we shall not believe

11. Nasr, *Study Quran*, 18. See also Lings, *Muhammad: His Life*, 70.

12. Habermas and Licona, *Case for the Resurrection*, 27. They also note that "the Muslim who objects that the beauty of the Qur'an is only realized in Arabic should wonder at the soundness of this objection, since a Jew might argue for the superiority of the linguistic and structural beauty of the Hebrew Psalm." Habermas and Licona, 253.

13. "Glory be to him Who carried His servant by night from the Sacred Mosque to the Farthest Mosque" (Qur'an 17:1).

14. This is why Jerusalem is the third most sacred city to Muslims. Nasr, *Study Quran*, 695. Muslims celebrate this occasion, *al-isrā' wa al-mi'rāj*, every year.

15. Nasr, 693–94. Two-bows length in Arabic denotes a very close distance.

16. Nasr, 693–94.

in your ascension till you bring down unto us a book we can read" (Qur'ān 17:90–93).[17] Clearly, the best evidence proffered for the claims of Islam is subjective and inaccessible.

Hinduism, the world's third largest religion, has a plethora of gods exceeding hundreds, including kings, monkeys, hybrid beings, and stones, and taking part in the wildest of mythical tales.[18] With no creed, one can choose one's preferred gods and beliefs.[19] A truth-seeker finds it difficult even to start searching for evidence since "of all the great religions, Hinduism is the least dogmatic and the most diverse, . . . forever absorbing [new influences]. . . . Hinduism is what Hindus do and think, and what Hindus do and think is almost everything under the sun. . . . Under Hinduism's sacred canopy sit a dizzying variety of religious beliefs and behaviors."[20] Its influential *Advaita Vedanta* school holds that the ultimate reality, Brahman, is the sole reality, a nonpersonal absolute without qualities or characteristics. The phenomenal world with its substances, whether personal or physical, is illusion and seems to endure due to human ignorance. In reality, the enduring self, or *atman*, is identical to Brahman, and these facts are known only once one attains to the *moksha* esoteric experience.[21] Such alleged experience is too subjective to stand as evidence to the already unfalsifiable and unverifiable claims, including the promise of self-deification, which is at the heart of Hinduism.

Buddhism, the world's fourth largest religion, is more mundane, promising a this-worldly nirvana and freedom from suffering, ultimately the samsara cycle. Indeed, Buddhists can attain this freedom without depending on a divine being or divine revelation but on themselves.[22] More distinctively, no

17. Nasr, 693–94, 721–22.

18. For example, the most popular of their gods, Ganesha, has four arms and one tusk (having plucked the other to use as a pen and write a Hindu epic). His head, one story goes, was transplanted from an elephant after Ganesha, who was guarding his bathing mother, had been killed by her intruding husband. Prothero, *God Is Not One*, 131–34.

19. Of Hindus, C. S. Lewis asks in a letter, "But what do they deny? That has always been my trouble – . . . to find any proposition they [would] pronounce false. But truth must surely involve exclusions?" In another letter he notes that Hinduism is "ready to take any shape but able to retain none." Martindale and Root, *Quotable Lewis*, 620–21.

20. Prothero, *God Is Not One*, 134–35.

21. Netland, *Dissonant Voices*, 52–53.

22. Prothero, *God Is Not One*, 172, 177. The more recent Mahayana Buddhism encourages its adherents to seek help from any of their many gods. Prothero, 188–89.

real soul or self exists and the *I* is mere illusion.[23] The proof Buddhism offers to these claims is in personal experience.[24] Buddhism thus is a "religious philosophy which grounds its truth in non-historical legend and non-cognitive experience"[25] and is therefore unfalsifiable. Indeed, the historicity of Buddha's life and sayings, written centuries after his death, is itself in doubt.[26]

In stark contrast to all the above great world religions, the heart of Christianity is historical: "God's redemptive entrance into our history has created news. A deed has been done. The gospel (news) is an interpretation of history. At its core is an interpretative event: Christ died (event) for our sins (interpretation)."[27] The unique Christian claims, however strange or bold, stand or fail on the verifiability of specific historical events.[28] They are specific, objective, accessible, and therefore testable.

Indeed, this verifiable Christian evidence, made possible through God's unique "redemptive entrance into our history," would not have happened without the trinitarian nature of the one personal God as revealed in the Bible. Buddhism, with its mundane concern and "non-historical legend and non-cognitive experience" makes no explicit claims about ultimate reality. Hinduism, with its plethora of mythical gods, cannot possibly make claims of verifiable divine entrance into the world since its ultimate reality, Brahman, is non-personal and without qualities or characteristics, and the phenomenal world is itself mere illusion. The religion that one might imagine could come closest to the conception that its God could enter into history and leave verifiable evidence is Islam: God, after all, is personal and one, and the world is

---

23. Prothero, 179, 184.

24. Prothero, 183–84.

25. Moore, "Some Weaknesses," 155.

26. Moore, "Some Weaknesses," 146–47.

27. Cole, "Peril of a 'Historyless,'" 68.

28. Keith Yandell applies to religious claims the philosophy of science distinction between confirmationism (acceptable theories being those confirmable by evidence) and falsificationism (acceptable theories being those with explanatory power and not falsified). He joins both in one: "If monotheism has explanatory power regarding things hard to explain otherwise, monotheism has not been falsified, and there are experiences it is reasonable to think veridical that are veridical only if monotheism is true, then there is evidence that monotheism is true." He concludes that monotheism is true. Yandell, *Philosophy of Religion*, 352–57. One can replace "monotheism" with "Christianity" in his statement to the exclusion of Eastern religions and Islam in view of the explanatory problems inherent in non-Trinitarian theology and lack of veridical evidence.

real. But with its fundamental doctrine of the absolute oneness of God, such entrance proves to be just as impossible.

Absolute oneness means that the concept of relationship is irrelevant to God before creation. His entering into relationship with rational beings after creation, therefore, would mean a change in his attributes. To avoid such unacceptable conclusion, Muslim theologians, following extensive and long debates, settled on separating his attributes of actions, such as those related to his dealing with humans, from his attributes of essence, the former stemming from his absolute will and manifested in his power rather than describing him in his essence.[29] In his absolute free will, God is not bound by any principle or promise such that he can even decide to punish the righteous and reward the guilty. His actions in dealing with humans, which are what humans can see and experience, do not tell anything about his nature or essence.[30] This led to the oft quoted dismissive principle of "*bila kayf*" (without inquiring) and the associated principle (a rhyme in Arabic): "All what comes into your mind is perishing, and Allah is different from such thing."[31] God, therefore, remains absolutely transcendent and so unknowable, and an unknowable God cannot possibly reveal himself to humans or enter into genuine relationship with them.

In contrast, a Trinitarian God, as Father, Son, and Holy Spirit, enjoys an eternal relationship within himself from eternity past. Such relationship, as an attribute of actions, stems from God's nature, and is rooted in his attributes of essence with no change of attributes and no conflict whatsoever. Human can thus know God and understand his attributes of essence, which he has revealed to them in both his written revelation and his Son incarnate.[32] This also means that God can be immanent, living among humans as one of them and solving their predicament without ceasing to be the transcendent God:

> While God exists eternally as Trinity and is active in himself without creation, at the same time, in the abundance of his love and grace, he enters personally into time and space to establish a relationship with creation. He thus penetrates human history

29. Shehadeh, *God With Us*, 111–12.
30. Shehadeh, 116–17.
31. Shehadeh, 121.
32. Shehadeh, 146–47.

> in a personal, free and faithful way. He is able to be outside and inside creation at the same time, manifested supremely in the incarnation and redemption."[33]

God's absolute holiness and justice demanded that man's sin be punished by death. This predicament of humanity could only be solved when the one perfect, sinless man of infinite value, God the Son, entered human history and paid the wages of sin on the cross and was vindicated in his resurrection: "The fact that God exists as a Trinity makes it possible for him to justify sinners and at the same time remain righteous. For, being a Trinity, it is possible for God to remain seated on the throne of justice in heaven as God the Father, and at the same time bear the punishment of justice on earth as God the Son incarnate."[34] This redemption, rooted in the trinitarian God, gave man the salvation of his soul and at the same time gave his searching mind and his quest for certainty a sure and testable evidence, the historical event of the crucifixion and the resurrection of the man Jesus Christ.

Christian Claims and Islamic Denials

These claims, the Trinitarian nature of God including the divinity of Christ as God the Son incarnate, the crucifixion, and the resurrection, are the backbone of Christianity. Without them the Christian faith is nullified. They are the good news of salvation: "*Gospel* is defined by a minimum of three essential facts . . . (1) the deity of Jesus; (2) the death of Jesus in our place; and (3) the resurrection of Jesus."[35] Bruce Ware succinctly expresses the essentiality of the combination of the doctrine of Trinity and the deity of Jesus on the one hand, and the crucifixion event on the other, to Christianity:

> The doctrine of the Trinity is both *central and necessary for the Christian faith* to be what it is. Remove the Trinity, and the whole Christian faith disintegrates . . . In order for us sinners to be saved, one must see God at one and the same time as the one judging our sin (the Father), the one making the payment

33. Shehadeh, 527.

34. Shehadeh, 533.

35. Habermas and Licona, *Case for the Resurrection*, 25.

> of infinite value for our sin (the divine Son), and the one empowering and directing the incarnate – human – Son so that he lives and obeys the Father, going to the cross as the substitute for us (the Holy Spirit). The Christian God, to be savior, must then be Father, Son, and Holy Spirit.[36]

The resurrection, however, is the one sign upon which Jesus substantiated the truthfulness of all his claims, the validating stamp of all: "The Jews then said to Him, 'What sign do You show us as your authority for doing these things?' Jesus answered them, 'Destroy this temple, and in three days I will raise it up'" (John 2:18–19). The resurrection, therefore, "has been the spearhead of the Christian case. From it flows belief in the deity of Christ and all the other Christian truths."[37]

Today, the resurrection continues to be the test that validates the wondrous claims of Jesus.[38] In addition to its significance as the all-validating sign of the Christian faith, his resurrection is the first fruits of the promise of our own bodily resurrection and the consummation of our salvation at the second coming of Christ: "But now Christ has been raised from the dead, the first fruits of those who are asleep" (1 Cor 15:20). The apostle Paul therefore declares boldly that "if Christ has not been raised, your faith is worthless" (1 Cor 15:17). C. S. Lewis rightly argues that

> to preach Christianity meant primarily to preach the Resurrection. . . . The Resurrection is the central theme in every Christian sermon reported in the Acts. The Resurrection, and its consequences, were the "gospel" or good news which the Christians brought: what we call the "gospel", the narratives of Our Lord's life and death, were composed later for the benefit of those who had already accepted the gospel. They were in no sense the basis of Christianity: they were written for those already converted. The miracle of the Resurrection, and the

36. Ware, *Father, Son, & Holy Spirit*, 16–17. For theological and philosophical reflections on Christology in the context of Trinity see Sanders and Issler, *Jesus in Trinitarian Perspective*. On Islamic misconception about the doctrine of Trinity see George, "Trinity and the Challenge".

37. Wenham, *Easter Enigma*, 9.

38. Habermas and Licona, *Case for the Resurrection*, 27.

> theology of that miracle, comes first: the biography comes later as a comment on it.[39]

Islam is the one great world religion whose scripture expressly denies all three: the Trinity and Christ's divine nature, the crucifixion, and, by extension, the resurrection.[40] To be sure, the Qur'ān recognizes the Bible, including the books of the Torah, the Prophets, the Psalms, and the Gospel (New Testament)[41] as sent from God, and seems to equate them with the Qur'ān when it refers to God's promise of paradise to believers as recorded "in the Torah, the Gospel, and the Quran" (Qur'ān 9:111).[42] The Qur'ān, and with it Muslims all over the world, even recognize and highly revere Jesus Christ and believe in his virgin birth and miraculous deeds, including his raising the dead (Qur'ān 3:45–50). Yet they believe in Jesus, or *ʿĪsa*, as a mere human prophet, a distinguished one indeed, but not as the crucified and resurrected Redeemer (Qur'ān 4:157–58), and certainly not as the Son of God (Qur'an 112:3, 4:171). To Muslims, the extant Bible, the source of these beliefs, is inauthentic and substantially corrupted (Qur'ān 2:75, 3:78).[43] Crucifixion has always been at the center of the differences between Islam and Christianity. As expressed by the Muslim caliph al-Mahdi in a debate with Timothy, patriarch of Baghdad in the late eighth century, Muslims base their denial of the crucifixion on three arguments: first and foremost, the Qur'ān expressly denies the crucifixion: "They did not kill him nor crucify him, but so it was made to appear to them" (Qur'ān 4:157); second, God cannot possibly allow his righteous prophet to suffer such heinous murder at the hands of his

39. Lewis, *Miracles*, 234. Likewise, Kreeft and Tacelli note that "the gospel or "good news" means essentially the news of Christ's resurrection." Kreeft and Tacelli, *Handbook of Christian Apologetics*, 176.

40. Scriptures of the other great world religions do not deny these tenets because they precede Christ. For an overview of Islam's views on Christianity see *Encyclopedia of the Qur'ān*, s.v. "Christians and Christianity."

41. See footnote 41 in chapter 3 (page 93).

42. Griffith, *Bible in Arabic*, 54. Sydney Griffith is a leading scholar and professor of early Christian studies at the Catholic University of America. Torah is mentioned eighteen times (e.g., Qur'an 5:44), Psalms three times (e.g., Qur'an 17:55), and the Gospel twelve times (e.g., Qur'an 5:46). Some interpret "al-Ṣuḥuf al-ūlá, Ṣuḥuf Ibrahim wa-Mousa" in Qur'an 87:18–19, as sheets (suḥuf) given by God to Adam, Seth and Enoch. Albayrak, "People of the Book," 303.

43. Crook, *New Testament*, 3, 13. Jay Crook is a convert to Islam. One evangelist and Washington DC pastor who converted from Islam notes, "I cannot think of one conversation with a Muslim friend where the reliability and authority of the Bible were not in question." Anyabwile, *Gospel for Muslims*, 105.

enemies and look so shamefully weak; and third, the crucifixion of an allegedly divine Jesus means God's death and so damages the divine nature and threatens God's eternal character.[44]

The validating facts of the authenticity of the Bible and the central events of the crucifixion and the resurrection, however, are well established and accessible for Muslims to examine for themselves. The apostle Paul's words still echo to them today: "The word is near you" (Rom 10:8). Presenting these facts to them prayerfully, respectfully, and credibly through a trusted validating apparatus can be more convincing. No such apparatus seems more acceptable and trustworthy than the rules of evidence of their own Islamic law.

Thesis

This book argues that available evidence for the historicity of the crucifixion and bodily resurrection of Jesus Christ can pass the criteria of sound evidence set by the Islamic law. This includes authenticity of the New Testament documents, soundness of eyewitness testimony and confession, and the corroborative role of expert witness testimony and circumstantial evidence. Christian evidence is better vindicated to Muslims when it is examined through their Islamic law. Believed to be God-given, Islamic law provides to the Muslim a trustworthy, objective, and stable arbiter of evidential truth.

Limitations and Delimitations

Islamic law is a wide and well-researched field that has attracted an increasing interest among scholars in the West in the last four decades or so.[45] The introduction of chapter 2 is thus only meant to give those new to Islamic law a general idea rather than cover every aspect of it. Likewise, in examining the already well-researched topic of Christian evidence, this study does not purport to give a comprehensive account, which can be sought in referenced works. And since this study is an exercise in evidential apologetics, the focus will be on factual evidence rather than theological debate. Moreover, this

44. Beaumont, "Debating the Cross," 56, 59, 61.

45. Hallaq, *Origins and Evolution of Islamic Law*, 1.

study will not refer to works on legal apologetics employing the Islamic law as apparently no such works exist.

Islamic law is to Muslims God's right path to be followed through obeying the "commands, prohibitions, guidance and principles that God has addressed to mankind pertaining to their conduct in this world and salvation in the next."[46] It thus encompasses the two broad categories of worship/rituals and civil transactions. The latter concerns enforceable juridical matters, including the law of evidence.[47] Insofar as examining Christian evidence, the term "Islamic law" is used in this study in its narrower, juridical sense, following the *Ḥanafī* school of Islamic jurisprudence.[48] And in following the *Ḥanafī* school, this study will resist the temptation of making comparisons with the other schools on a certain topic as this can be distracting and time-consuming.

Significance

This book aims at making a worthwhile contribution to the interactive and overlapping fields of Christian apologetics, evangelism, and Christian life. The overall significance of the study lies in vindicating the Christian faith by examining its evidence through the authoritative law that stems from the very scripture of the one great world religion that denies the divinity, crucifixion, and resurrection of Jesus Christ.

Why the Islamic World?

This study targets the Islamic world by subjecting Christian evidence to the tests of Islamic law, for good reasons. First, I live, work, and minister, and will continue to do so in the predominantly Muslim Middle East. Second, Islam is the second great world religion after Christianity. About 1.8 billion Muslims inhabit the globe, almost one quarter of humanity. Indeed, the American nonpartisan Pew Research Center, a think tank specialized in demographic trends in the world, asserts that Islam is now the fastest growing religion in the world, mainly due to birth rate, and is projected to outnumber Christianity

46. Kamali, *Shari'ah Law*, 14.

47. Kamali, 17.

48. Chapter 2 provides an introductory explanation of the Islamic law, including its main four Sunni schools and why the *Ḥanafī* school is selected for this study.

in about fifty years.[49] Size and expansion are coupled with the fact that the vast majority of Muslims in the world are religious, staunchly rejecting the fundamental tenets of the Christian faith and utterly challenging not only the resurrection, but the crucifixion of our Redeemer in the first place. To be sure, Muslim countries, except for Saudi Arabia and Afghanistan, do not follow strict Islamic law. Rather, they follow hybrid legal systems thanks to the European colonization starting with the British who favored in mid-nineteenth century a modern legal system that facilitates an open economic market that maximizes profit.[50] The Islamic law, nevertheless, is still revered today by almost all Muslims, with calls by the religious even to re-enforce it.[51] Moreover, positive apologetics is more acceptable to Muslims than antagonizing polemics, as will be shown. The apologetic and evangelistic significance of this study is therefore evident in effectively defending and respectfully communicating the gospel to Muslims through their authoritative and trusted means, the Islamic law.

This study has other, secondary benefits. Vindicating the Christian faith through the Islamic law and exposing the inconsistency of those who reject Christian truth yet revere their Islamic law should help bolster the confident faith and Christian life of new Muslim-background believers. Finally, this study lends support to the juridical approach to apologetics by directing it to the firmer foundation of religion-based legal systems, such as the Islamic law and the Jewish law, rather than changing secular systems.

Why Evidential Historical Apologetics?

Apologists are not agreed on a standard classification for the various approaches to apologetics. One helpful system provides a comprehensive mapping that covers as many as ten approaches, starting on the far left of the continuum with fideism, and moving to the right with more emphasis on

---

49. Lipka and Hackett, "Why Muslims Are,". The same article attributes the fast expansion of Islam to birth rate: "Muslims have more children than members of the seven other major religious groups analyzed in the study. Muslim women have an average of 2.9 children, significantly above the next-highest group (Christians at 2.6) and the average of all non-Muslims (2.2). In all major regions where there is a sizable Muslim population, Muslim fertility exceeds non-Muslim fertility."

50. Hallaq, *Introduction to Islamic Law*, 85.

51. Hallaq, *Impossible State*, x.

"objective, independently existing evidence."[52] These approaches include fideism, presuppositionalism, Reformed epistemology, experientialism, pragmatism, veridicalism, combinationalism, classical apologetics, evidential apologetics, and Cartesian rationalism.[53] Following the same left-to-right continuum, the common approaches that will be surveyed below are fideism, presuppositionalism, Reformed epistemology, experiential/narrative approaches, combinationalism (integrative, or cumulative case apologetics), classical apologetics, and evidential apologetics.[54] Though each of these approaches has its avowed advocates, what determines the suitability of an approach is its ability to respond to the specific need of an audience.[55] These approaches will be briefly examined for their suitability as apologetics to Muslims.[56]

Fideism. Fideists call for mere faith, without evidence or rational arguments, since faith and evidence are mutually exclusive: "If we have faith, we have no reasons to believe; if we have reasons to believe, we do not need faith."[57] In its extreme case it is not an overstatement that "fideism is . . . a denial of apologetics."[58] Apologists of all other schools regard fideism as "diametrically opposed to the very idea of apologetics – and fideists themselves

52. Morley, *Mapping Apologetics*, 14–15.

53. Morley, 14–15.

54. For example, Morley settles on five main approaches as the focus of his survey: Presuppositionalism, Reformed epistemology, combinationalism, classical apologetics, and evidentialism. See Morley, *Mapping Apologetics*. Boa and Bowman consider for their survey classical apologetics, evidentialism, Reformed apologetics (Reformed epistemology and presuppositionalism), and fideism. See Boa and Bowman, *Faith Has Its Reasons*. Cowan selects for his edited volume classical apologetics, evidentialism, cumulative case apologetics, and presuppositionalism, which he terms "the Big Four." He adds to them the then-new method, Reformed apologetics. See Cowan, *Five Views on Apologetics*. More recently, Chatraw and Allen selected for their 2018 work classical apologetics, evidential apologetics, presuppositional apologetics, and experiential/narrative apologetics. See Chatraw and Allen, *Apologetics at the Cross*. Common to all the works above that span from 2000 to 2018 are presuppositionalism, classical apologetics, and evidentialism.

55. See the discussion of Boa and Bowman at the end of their valuable survey of the different approaches to apologetics, where they call for tailoring an apologetic to the specific need of a targeted person and give a helpful matrix of the various cases. Boa and Bowman, *Faith Has Its Reasons*, 516–19.

56. Another form of apologetics is dialogical. See Mascord, "Apologetics as Dialogue," 49–64.

57. Morley, *Mapping Apologetics*, 13.

58. Morley, 16.

would agree."[59] Yet fideism has some arguments to offer to apologetics, though of a different kind,[60] mainly existential and experiential. Muslims, however, need external evidence to break through centuries of indoctrination against the authenticity of the Bible, the incarnation of God, and his crucifixion. Indeed, this need of a breakthrough explains why Christ is appearing today to many Muslims in dreams and visions, a fact that is well attested.[61] These persons only believe upon such powerful sensory evidence. According to a consistent view of fideism, their resulting faith cannot be true faith.

Presuppositional apologetics. This approach contends that the atheistic worldview and sinful presuppositions of a non-Christian prevent a neutral interpretation of proffered Christian rational arguments or even evidence.[62] Moreover, atheists "self-deceivingly relied on borrowed presuppositions" from theism in their very use of the otherwise inexplicable language, logic, history, ethics, or experience.[63] Presuppositional apologists therefore first aim at disarming and refuting the bankrupt worldview of atheists and exposing their "borrowed capital," and only then invite them to presuppose the authority of the Bible in order to understand its message.[64] Muslims, however, already reject the atheism that presuppositional apologists aim to undermine, and stumble in the very beliefs that these apologists want them to presuppose, i.e. the authority of a "corrupt" Bible. Presuppositional apologetics is therefore not an effective approach to Muslims, if not irrelevant altogether. A Muslim's first need is for external evidence that the Bible today is the same uncorrupted scripture recognized in the Qur'ān fourteen centuries ago. Avid presuppositional apologist Greg Bahnsen, however, argues that the Bible "is not externally verified at all, for *it* has absolute authority inherent to itself; its *self*-attesting nature is of utmost apologetical significance."[65] The Bible was indeed self-attesting to many Muslims through the special work of the Holy Spirit, yet even those who so believe would need evidence to understand and dispel shadows of lingering doubt. A Muslim in general has a justified

59. Boa and Bowman, *Faith Has Its Reasons*, 339.
60. Boa and Bowman, 339.
61. Butts, "Role of Dreams," iv.
62. Bahnsen, *Presuppositional Apologetics*, 14–15.
63. Bahnsen, 18.
64. Chatraw and Allen, *Apologetics at the Cross*, 117–18.
65. Bahnsen, *Presuppositional Apologetics*, 9.

need for evidential help to counter charges of a corrupted Bible and accept its absolute authority. Denying the legitimacy of providing such basic evidence is denying apologetics to Muslims.

Reformed epistemology. An offshoot of presuppositionalism, this approach builds on John Calvin's *sensus divinitatis*, the idea that the "natural knowledge of God is not arrived by inference of argument . . . but in a much more immediate way."[66] Philosopher Alvin Plantinga argues that belief in God "resembles perception, memory, and *a priori* belief."[67] A believer can consider it a rational "properly basic belief" in the sense that "it is indeed basic for him (he doesn't accept it on the evidential basis of other propositions) and, furthermore, he is *justified* in holding it in the basic way: he is within his epistemic rights, is not irresponsible, is violating no epistemic or other duties in holding that belief in that way."[68] Again, a Muslim already believes in God's existence and even believes in the notion of a *sensus divinitatatis*, known in Islam as *fiṭra*: "Man knows God through *fiṭra*, without discursive reasoning."[69] Moreover, what is at issue in presenting the Gospel to a Muslim is not defending the epistemic rights of the Christian but rather removing obstacles to belief by presenting evidence and refuting factual errors regarding the Bible and the nature and work of Christ.[70]

Experiential/narrative apologetics. The narrative apologetics part of this hybrid approach is a relatively recent approach that addresses postmodernism and has something in common with fideism. It rejects arguments from reason and evidence, and instead invites the non-Christian to view the Christian faith as a story in which one is involved and then to experience it for himself.[71] Such invitation to evidence-by-experience is not unique to Christianity but is also extended by other religions, such as Buddhism and Mormonism. However, this approach is hardly relevant to a non-postmodern Islamic world. More importantly, in rejecting evidence this approach fails to

66. Plantinga, *Warranted Christian Belief*, 175.

67. Plantinga, 175.

68. Plantinga, 177–78.

69. Shihadeh, "Existence of God," 198.

70. On the tension between advocates of academic knowledge and advocates of practical, simple faith, particularly evangelists, and the importance of both, with emphasis on the acquisition of knowledge, see Machen, "Scientific Preparation."

71. Chatraw and Allen, *Apologetics at the Cross*, 121–23. N. T. Wright's soft approach, which briefly appeals to evidence, is an exception. Chatraw and Allen, 126.

solve the main problem of unbelief in the authenticity of Scripture, the deity of Christ, and his crucifixion and resurrection.

Integrative apologetics. Seeing strength in each approach, an increasing number of apologists are following integrative approaches that benefit from more than one approach in cumulative case arguments, also known as combinationalism. One of the first to adopt this approach is Edward J. Carnell who integrates the presuppositional, classical, evidential, and fideist approaches. He starts with a presupposition of Christianity and allows it to be tested "rationally (for consistency), empirically (for its fit with the facts) and existentially (for its livability).[72] Together, these tests show that Christianity best explains the world we live in. Integrationists differ as to how many approaches they deem useful to employ, with most seeking to integrate the classical and the evidential on the one hand with the presuppositional on the other. Integrative apologists note that the great premodern apologists, long before modern classifications were coined, employed more than one approach, and that even today most apologists unwittingly resort to more than one approach.[73] The prime need and interest of the theistic Muslim, however, is empirical historical evidence, though experiential arguments can have a complementary role.

Classical apologetics. Classical apologists employ a two-stage approach. They start with philosophical arguments for theism and then align with evidential apologists to argue for Christian theism through presenting evidence for the truthfulness of the Bible and the historicity of Jesus and the resurrection.[74] Indeed, even in their first stage of arguing for theism, classical apologists corroborate the cosmological and teleological philosophical arguments with scientific evidence before moving to the second stage of giving historical evidence for the resurrection.[75] Classical apologists argue that the non-theist needs first to accept the existence of God before being presented with Christian evidence of God acting supernaturally in history. They note that a naturalist would seek naturalistic explanations for the miraculous and

72. Morley, *Mapping Apologetics*, 176. See also Boa and Bowman, *Faith Has Its Reasons*, 427–38.

73. Boa and Bowman, 425–26.

74. Morley, *Mapping Apologetics*, 107.

75. Craig, *Reasonable Faith*, 23–24. See also Craig's concluding remarks *ad* Kelly James Clark in Craig, "Classical Apologist's Closing Remarks," 320–21.

may well reject the supernatural indicator. Establishing theism first would make the non-Christian more likely to accept the resurrection as God's supernatural vindication of Jesus's self-claims and so "Christian evidence will be most effective when combined with arguments of natural theology."[76] This may be true for non-theists. A Muslim, however, is already a theist. Indeed, apologist William Lane Craig builds his classical apologetic for theism on the *kalam* cosmological argument, developed by medieval Muslims.[77] This first stage of proving theism is therefore unnecessary to a Muslim. It is what differentiates classical from evidential apologetics.

Evidential apologetics. The evidential approach sees nothing wrong in classical apologetics' first stage of proving theism but sees it as unnecessary once the second stage of giving historical evidence for the resurrection is accepted by the targeted audience; the resurrection event is "an indication of God's existence and activity" and so proves theism as a matter of course.[78] Apologetics to Muslims is thus primarily evidential, proceeding directly with the presentation of evidential arguments for the truthfulness of the Bible, the source of Christian beliefs, and then the historicity of the crucifixion and the resurrection.[79] Islam is a monotheistic religion and therefore does not need apologetical approaches that aim at defending theism, viz., presuppositionalism, Reformed epistemology, the non-evidential components in integrative approaches, and the first stage of classical apologetics. Existential and experiential approaches may be of help to some, yet the evidential approach is what establishes the objective foundations of the Christian faith.

Evidential apologists deal with inductive conclusions based upon factual and historical matters, and so, like historians, most of them claim probabilistic conclusions.[80] For this they are strongly criticized by presuppositional

76. Craig, "Classical Apologist's Response," 127–28.

77. Craig, *Reasonable Faith*, 96.

78. Habermas, "Evidential Apologetics," 94.

79. Not all evangelists agree. For example, Thabiti Anyabwile notes that the Qur'an itself does not teach that the Bible is corrupt but that some misunderstood its meaning, and so an "intellectually honest" Muslim should readily accept it as trustworthy. Anyabwile's advice: Just share the gospel confidently and it will speak for its authenticity. Anyabwile, *Gospel for Muslims*, 20, 105–15. Almost all Muslims interpret the Qur'ān as teaching that the Bible is corrupt. Although the gospel, as God's Word, has its own power that is aided by the work of the Holy Spirit, Muslims need evidence to dispel this deeply-held belief. Evidence works alongside, not instead of, the power of the Word and the work of the Spirit.

80. Montgomery, *Shape of the Past*, 237.

apologists who claim certainty based upon biblical authority: "If the defender of the Christian system . . . presents [biblical] truth as only probable he forfeits his argumentative strength and he drops Christianity to the level of any other 'probability.'"[81] However, if certainty in factual and historical matters is taken to mean the same as mathematical certainty, one would be confusing two categories in one equivocal and undifferentiated term. Matters of daily life are only judged by mathematical probability, yet when such probability is so high it amounts to what can be termed factual, or moral, certainty.[82] With this understanding, the fact that historians claim probabilistic conclusions "does not preclude [their] achieving certainty in matters of well-established historical findings. Events that are validated by careful historical research (and especially those established for long periods of time) in the absence of viable contrary findings are proven facts."[83]

Another criticism levelled against the evidential approach is that it "can lack an appreciation for human situatedness."[84] What sounds like common sense or reason to a Westerner may not all seem so from an Eastern worldview and so what a certain worldview recognizes as normative historical method may not be acceptable to another.[85] In response, the evidential apologist should understand the worldview and cultural differences of a targeted audience and adapt his or her assumptions and tools while maintaining the unadulterated truth. Evidentialist apologist Habermas acknowledges that

> historical occurrences are not brute facts that interpret themselves. While the event itself is objective, . . . evidentialists recognize that crucial factors always enter historiography. Events must be chosen for study, and since there is more than one perspective on what has happened, there is almost always more than one point of view. Personal preferences and prejudices can substantially color our interpretations, not to mention the affect of our worldviews on our research.[86]

---

81. Bahnsen, *Presuppositional Apologetics*, 224.
82. Montgomery, *Tractatus Logico-Theologicus*, 106.
83. Habermas, *Historical Jesus*, 263.
84. Chatraw and Allen, *Apologetics at the Cross*, 111.
85. Chatraw and Allen, 112–14.
86. Habermas, "Evidential Apologetics," 94.

Such concerns, however, do not detract from the historical method, as otherwise one should dismiss all human history as subjective. Habermas deals with this challenge:

> It is for reasons such as these that the careful application of historical principles, tempered by various sorts of critical analyses, are necessary in order to recognize and offset as much as possible the subjective element. Although such biases can never be completely eliminated, it is still possible to reach sturdy conclusions within the canons of historical research. . . . Historiography is certainly capable of determining the past. We just must be careful not to read biases into the accounts.[87]

Habermas criticizes fellow evidentialist John Warwick Montgomery for failing to recognize this challenge in his juridical-historical apologetic.[88] Elsewhere he notes that historiography is concerned with the actual events and their recording and interpretation by the historian, and a scholar's duty is to recognize such prejudices and biases and isolate the recorded events to determine what really happened.[89] The historian arrives at objective data if he has "accurately performed his investigation, applied the appropriate standards of criticism, and determined the outcome according to the canons of reliability."[90]

The real historiographical dispute, however, is not as much scientific and objective as philosophical when it comes to the Gospels. The point of departure is whether the possibility of divine intervention in history is recognized or not.[91] While historical criticism of the Gospels, including the so-called quest for the historical Jesus is gaining momentum today,[92] it is not a new development. In 1440 Lorenzo Valla used external and internal evidence to show that the Decree of Gratian document, largely accepted as authentic, was forged. This discovery prompted further examination of ancient documents by employing careful criteria.[93] Historical criticism of the New Testament

87. Habermas, 95.
88. Habermas, 94–95.
89. Habermas, *Historical Jesus*, 262.
90. Habermas, 264.
91. Bock, *Studying the Historical Jesus*, 161.
92. Bauckham, *Jesus and the Eyewitnesses*, 1.
93. Bock, *Studying the Historical Jesus*, 154.

thus emerged in the Renaissance and became a formal discipline in the eighteenth century. Soon, however, it was partly tainted by the naturalistic and rationalistic commitments of the Enlightenment thinkers, the way having been paved by deists of the seventeenth century.[94] Historical criticism thus worked from two opposing worldviews: those holding Enlightenment deistic presuppositions sought to undermine the historicity of the Gospel accounts of the miracles and teachings of Jesus, while Christians sought a better understanding of Scripture in the light of its historical background.[95] Yet in examining historical material, Christians have followed the same historical methods used by their opponents albeit after ridding them of non-theistic biases,[96] or the "extra-historical commitments" that tended to relativize history and keep secularists from seeing divine history objectively.[97]

More recently, historians increasingly acknowledge an inevitable objective-subjective synthesis, yet without succumbing to historical relativism. They therefore seek more objective tools for their research while also dealing with the subjective factor.[98] Such tools include, inter alia, documents, eyewitnesses, and archaeological remains.[99] Ancient documents should be examined externally for originality, background, authorship, date and place of writing, reliability, and correspondence to facts, and internally for the ability and credibility of their authors.[100] When the author is himself an eyewitness, his testimony gains paramount importance. Indeed, Richard Bauckham's seminal work, *Jesus and the Eyewitnesses*, aims at showing that eyewitness testimony is the key to wedding the work of the theologian with the historian. The aim is to establish the historical Jesus, the one presented in the Gospels rather than the reductionist one reconstructed by modern historians through their attempts to deconstruct the Gospels.[101]

The difference in viewing history between Christianity and Islam, however, differs from that between Christianity and non-theists in the West in that

94. Hughes, "Truth of Scripture," 177.

95. Bock, *Studying the Historical Jesus*, 156–57.

96. Bock, 161.

97. Montgomery, *Where Is History Going*, 166.

98. Habermas, *Historical Jesus*, 265.

99. Habermas, 270.

100. Habermas, 272–73.

101. Bauckham, *Jesus and the Eyewitnesses*, 4–5.

the latter is historiographical and philosophical whereas the former is simply factual and historical. Muslims already believe in divine intervention in history as the Qur'ān relates several Old and New Testament supernatural events, including the virgin birth of Jesus and his miraculous deeds. Theological differences over the nature and work of Jesus aside,[102] historical differences between Christians and Muslims center on the authenticity of the extant Bible and the *factuality* of the crucifixion and resurrection event rather than the *possibility* of such happening. The historical tools and methods, nevertheless, should be largely like those in the West except that the possibility of the supernatural is not at issue, thus reducing the debate from evidential *and* philosophical to evidential. The evidential argument in this study will therefore follow the common standards and consider the caveats of modern historiography. Importantly, it will also tend to interact and align with the principles and practices of Islamic historiography.

In brief, the Christian faith is based upon God's acting in human history, and this through the historical and identifiable God-man Jesus Christ. The Christian faith is therefore verifiable. "Unlike the gods of other religions, the Christian God did not just send a messenger to speak his revelation into human history; he himself entered into human history as the revelation!"[103] As already said, the other great world religions are based upon untestable claims that are unreliably subjective, inaccessibly metaphysical, confusingly diversified, or speculatively philosophical. If the Christian faith is uniquely historical, its vindication should also be uniquely historical, no matter what other defenses may also be employed. Christianity's unique historicity is its unique evidentiary strength.

Indeed, evidence has been central to Christianity from its beginning, as evident in the New Testament. It was meant to be tested by ordinary audiences using their natural senses. The apostle John states that the purpose of writing his Gospel with its selection of signs performed by Jesus is to give evidence so his readers may believe (John 20:30–31). Luke assures his addressee, Theophilus, that he has carefully investigated and obtained his information from eyewitnesses so Theophilus may "know the exact truth" (Luke 1:1–4) about Jesus who presented himself alive by "many convincing

102. Theological differences are subsumed in the historical ones.

103. Chatraw and Allen, *Apologetics at the Cross*, 109.

proofs" (Acts 1:3). Indeed, much of what Jesus said and did, culminating in the resurrection, was aimed at giving evidence to his wondrous identity.[104] Objective testable evidence is therefore an essential ingredient to Christian apologetics. To Muslims, it is the paramount apologetic.

Apologetics vs. Polemics

Kreeft and Tacelli call for contextualizing an argument to cater to the psychological state of the two persons in dialogue and their relationship, as well as their immediate situation and the larger social, cultural, historical, political, and racial context. They argue that "the arguer's tone, sincerity, care, concern, listening and respect matter as much as his or her logic – probably more."[105] In an essay on the importance of communicating Christian truth to Muslims as grand narrative, one scholar concludes with this "word of caution":

> One might be tempted to . . . construct philosophical arguments against Islam. There is a place for that, particularly on the campuses of Western universities and in the media, but this type of approach is generally ineffective for evangelizing Muslims and can create a certain animosity that obscures Gospel comprehension. This is especially true in the Muslim world where the use of critical scholarship to examine one's faith is foreign.[106]

Although he stops short of mentioning the root cause, his word of caution is in order. Polemics against Islam can be especially antagonizing to Muslims as Islam is not just a religion with a set of beliefs. It is a most cherished identity that deeply infiltrates and shapes their personal lives, familial and social relationships, dress, food, habits, idioms, politics, and their entire culture. This identity is clearly felt and witnessed in both the Muslim world and the diaspora.[107] In her study of the political understanding of Muslim identity in the United States, a Muslim American scholar sheds a helpful light on Muslim

---

104. See, for example, John 2:19, 4:36, and 14:11.

105. Kreeft and Tacelli, *Handbook of Christian Apologetics*, 23.

106. Curry, "Mission to Muslims," 237. Theodore A. Curry is pseudonym for J. Scott Bridger, a professor of global studies and world religions. See also Schlorff, "Muslim Ideology," 181.

107. Confirmed by my life experience in living and interacting with Muslims in Jerusalem, Jordan, Iraq, Yemen, Nigeria, Turkey, England, and the U.S.

identity. It is basically "shaped within a religious mold,"[108] yet also exceeds the religious with closely related areligious aspects. She names for her study "three significant [non-conclusive] ways in which one may understand one's Muslim identity beyond the theological criteria: (i) belonging to a Muslim community (*ummah*), (ii) occupying a Muslim body, and (iii) habituating oneself through practices associated with the religion."[109] Thus, the concept of *ummah* "signifies a strong idea of pan-Muslim unity, of all of us holding tight to the rope of God (Qur'ān 3:103)."[110] Muslims consider that they constitute one *ummah* all over the world, yet "the idea of *ummah* does not transcend race, nationalities, and ethnicities, rather works with them based on the shared axis of faith in God (Qur'an 49:13)."[111] She gives one example: "The rich Kuwaiti oil sheikh and the poor Somali woman do not share race, nationality, social class, gender, and more importantly, possibly any imaginable experience of oppression based on their identity as a Muslim, yet both ought to count under the umbrella of *ummah*. Faith serves as the shared axis."[112]

Muslim identity tends to linger on for generations in Muslims living in non-Muslim cultures even as they try to adapt and establish their lives there permanently. Studies show that second and consecutive generations of Muslims in the West, even those considered progressive Muslims, do not trade their Muslim identity for their European or American identity but rather see it working alongside it.[113] In one case, second-generation Muslim founders of a charitable clinic in Southern California were keen on highlighting the Muslim identity of their law-abiding clinic through architecture, interior decorations, and verses from the Qur'ān, even with a governing board largely composed of non-Muslims.[114] They say that they see their clinic "as an institution not necessarily religious, but [that] has its identity found in the Muslim community."[115]

---

108. Fatima, "Who," 339. Fatima is associate professor in the Philosophy Department at Southern Illinois University Edwardsville.

109. Fatima, 343.

110. Fatima, 343.

111. Fatima, 343.

112. Fatima, 343. By "Muslim body" she means features that distinguish the appearance of a Muslim, such as the beard, turban or hijab for women, and the darker skin.

113. Duderija, "Progressive Muslims," 128.

114. Caird and Cadge, "Constructing American Muslim Identity," 270–71.

115. Caird and Cadge, 287.

More to the point, Muslim identity can even be defiant in anti-Muslim and hostile cultures. One study among Muslim American women during the challenging college adjustment period shows that their feeling of Muslim identity and Islamic dress adherence are inversely proportional, contrary to common belief.[116] This indicates that Islamic dress is an expression of strong identity even though the woman herself may not be religious; she sees this expression of identity as "more empowering than debilitating."[117] Another study among Muslim pupils in Finland shows that "when interviewed by a Christian researcher they emphasised their Muslim identity, but in the classroom they positioned themselves more as outsiders. The absence of out-group pressure seemed to allow room for critical identity deliberations and also highlighted the social tensions inside the group."[118] The same study stresses that "if religious beliefs are intimately connected to identity and self-esteem, they are very persistent and can function as an 'identity maintenance system', giving unity and meaning to the [young Muslims]."[119] One study on young Muslims in Switzerland notes that they "socialize in a lay, non-Muslim environment, very often within a framework which envisages their professional future. Yet in most cases their private life, family life, and their life story probably remain marked by a universal culture characterized by Islamic traditions and values."[120] The researcher then explains that "Islam is often expressed as a fundamental point of reference in the identity of the individual; in their relationship with their family and family circle; or more simply it forms an element of their human, spiritual, and personal development."[121]

Another study on Muslim women in Canada shows that "Muslim women indicate that they wear the hijab as a symbol of Muslim identity and even as a symbol of resistance against the discrimination and demonization efforts evidenced in Western media and society. . . . [They] intentionally and consciously [try] to publicize their identity despite discrimination."[122] Likewise, in the aftermath of the 9/11 attacks in the United States and the angry reaction

116. Rangoonwala, Sy, and Epinoza, "Muslim Identity," 240.

117. Rangoonwala, Sy, and Epinoza, 240.

118. Rissanen, "Developing Religious Identities," 130.

119. Rissanen, 126.

120. Lathion, "Muslims in Switzerland," 56.

121. Lathion, 56.

122. Mohammadi, "Becoming a Hijabi Now," 14–15.

of non-Muslim Americans, "many donned beards where none were before or wore *hijab* to own up to their heritage, their religion as a sign of resistance and subversive defiance."[123] Indeed, the strong sense of identity is particularly seen in the all too common observation that even a secular Muslim who feels free to criticize Islam and its practices in a conversation would feel deeply offended if the same criticism is made, or is even consented to, by a Christian friend, even a close friend, minutes later.[124]

One may object that the above studies took place in the context of Muslims in the West as minorities, and so one may attribute the observed strong feeling of identity to a "reactive religious awakening," where "'total identification' with Islam seems to fill the 'identity void' resulting of the perceived rejection by the [Western] majority."[125] Yet the same is true of Muslims living in the Islamic world. They react to the perceived superiority of the developed West with a strong sense of Islamic identity born out of such "identity void" and feeling of alienation in a globalized world that is increasingly influenced by the Western lifestyle. Similarly, one may also object that some of the above observations may not be limited to Muslim identity bearers but may also apply to other minority social groups facing identity challenges. The point to be made, however, is that Islam constitutes to the Muslim a strong and deeply ingrained personal and cultural *identity* rather than just a system of beliefs that can be freely and objectively criticized and debated.

The conclusion is evident. Engaging in polemics would antagonize the Muslim and is a non-starter.[126] "Apologetics is giving the reasons for one's own faith. This is quite justified and right. On the other hand, controversy is to

123. Fatima, "Who Counts as a Muslim," 345.

124. Personal observation that is shared by other Christians living in the Middle East.

125. Holtz, Dahinden, and Wagner, "German Muslims," 243.

126. Exceptions always exist, but this is the prevailing observation. "Polemics" here means hostile attacks against the other's beliefs. Renowned Hyde Park evangelist to Muslims Jay Smith, responding to calls to show love in evangelizing Muslims rather than confrontation, argues that Muslims despise weakness: "Why should Muslims respect any Christian who distances himself from what he believes?" He therefore argues that the best way to evangelize Muslims is direct confrontation: "True love confronts friends when they go wrong. Paul certainly argued. Jesus certainly argued. That's the kind of love Muslims need to hear." Alford, "Unapologetic Apologist," 36. This study does not call the Christian to distance himself or herself from what he or she believes but to first make the Muslim a friend through presenting objective non-confrontational evidence and then engaging in polemics and confrontation if need be. "True love confronts friends when they go wrong" – but they must become friends first.

attack the faith of another, and this usually leads to ill-feeling and bitterness."[127] Presenting positive evidence for the crucifixion and resurrection, however, is a non-aggressive defense of historical facts that can be better received by a Muslim even though it ultimately implicates the Qur'ān in serious error. The ultimate polemic conclusion is quietly yet clearly implied and does not have to be spelled out, at least not in the early stages of engagement.

Another reason, a common one, favors positive apologetics over polemics. While the result of positive apologetics may imply the sought conclusion of a polemic, the opposite is not necessarily true. Polemics may succeed in undermining the other's position, but the conclusion does not necessarily vindicate the polemist's faith; there are always competitors. To be sure, engaging in polemics may prove useful, even necessary, in subsequent, developed stages of an argument in response to sincere questions and in the course of the positive apologetic. The reaction would be different.

In conclusion, this study advocates taking the shortcut of vindicating the Christian faith to Muslims through presenting factual evidence and avoiding, to the extent possible, needless argumentation and the resulting hostility. Uniquely equipped with sound factual evidence, the Christian should present the truth clearly and confidently, "yet with gentleness and reverence" (1 Pet 3:15). One should deal sensitively with their deeply held beliefs and give due regard to their strong identity factor, "connecting with their feelings and frustrations."[128] One can always present Christian evidence with respect, sensitivity, confidence, and clarity by directly appealing to reason and history. This approach can be further enhanced by presenting the same evidence in a juridical framework, through the Islamic law. As will be shown below, law can help validate the evidence that validates Christian claims.

Evaluating the Juridical Approach in the West

Factual evidence, meant to be the objective means to establish a claim, is not always evaluated equally, and conflicting evaluations may well reduce fact to opinion in the mind of a seeker. No matter how strong a piece of evidence is, it may be rejected as irrelevant, inauthentic, non-credible, or even nonexistent. The institution of law provides an evaluative filter that can help

127. Levonian, "Christian Apologetics," 10.

128. Moreau, Corwin, and McGee, *Introducing World Missions*, 302–303.

address such concerns. Men and women around the globe entrust law with their societies and most important affairs, even their lives. Indeed, rejecting the authority of legal process "risks melting the very glue that holds society together."[129] Law is the product of accumulated wisdom and power of discernment gained through ages of human interaction. It is "the consequence of a logical process," such that logic is "the chief stabilizing bulwark of the law."[130] Law, therefore, is man's recognized arbiter that legitimizes proffered judicial evidence. No wonder Christian apologists from the seventeenth century onward have appealed to jurisprudence to vindicate Christian evidence, mostly through Anglo-American common law.[131]

Though this may have worked well for a time, apologists now raise concerns over the efficacy of the juridical method. Lawyer Ross Clifford, legal apologist and student of John Warwick Montgomery, the lawyer apologist who lately revived the juridical approach, makes the worthwhile observation that Montgomery did not bother to justify the juridical method. He notes that "the appropriateness of the legal apologetic has not been fully assessed *from within the boundaries of law itself*."[132] Having discussed this concern with several lawyers, Clifford refers to three objections to the juridical method. First, law is irrelevant to arbitrate the supernatural, to which it would suffice to mention Simon Greenleaf's response that, although the resurrection itself is supernatural, it could be witnessed and verified by natural human senses.[133] Second, the resurrection event does not prove the eternal revivification of Christ's body, to which the response is that legal apologists rest their case on proving the resurrection event itself, leaving inferences to extra-law sources.[134]

The third and, to this study, the most important objection questions the real objectivity and universal reliability of law. Though associated with postmodernist thought, the concern is not quite philosophical as much as factual. The common law, home to Western legal apologetics, is a precedence system continuously evolving throughout centuries of rulings on actual cases and

129. Montgomery, *Tractatus Logico-Theologicus*, 70.

130. Patterson, "Logic in the Law," 876, 882.

131. See "A Brief Overview of the History of Juridical Apologetics in the West" on page 33 of this book.

132. Clifford, *John Warwick Montgomery's*, 248–49.

133. Greenleaf, *Testimony of the Evangelists*, 38.

134. Clifford, *John Warwick Montgomery's*, 256.

reform that has been "piecemeal, sporadic, slow, and usually limited to one specific area of the law, with little or no consideration of the impact of change on other related areas of the subject."[135] One example is the many exclusions to admissible evidence, including hearsay,[136] which in the past posed a challenge to Christian legal apologetics. A nineteenth-century lawyer decrying these exclusions concluded that a judge, deprived of evidence, would be "compelled to resort either to lot or to arbitrary will."[137] Another admits that some exclusions were tools for political punishment,[138] and laments the fact that, despite all improvement, law still has defects, imperfections, and faults.[139]

Today, postmodernist Richard Matasar, prominent scholar and professor of law,[140] rejects claims of objectivity and notes that "legal scholars rarely are scientists who deal with abstractions and who have no stake in any particular outcome. . . . Legal scholarship has never really been objective."[141] He even calls forcefully for "making personal experience, ideology, and values explicit in scholarship and teaching."[142] He notes that, influenced by culture and ideology, "law is a reflection of very personal matters," and that the entire enterprise of law "rests on a subjective foundation."[143] He also notes, "I present no false picture of stability or inevitability to law. . . . Law is variable and can be constructed to fit multiple patterns."[144]

Other philosophers of law in the West also stress the non-objective aspect of law and are not without factual merit. Adherents of legal realism, a century-old product of empirical social sciences, for example, reject basing legal principles and rules on the stability and autonomy of a universal natural law concept. Rather, law is a variable that is subject to the forces of social and political influences and interests and thus governed by empirical evidence

135. Keane and McKeown, *Modern Law of Evidence*, 4.

136. Hearsay in evidence law is any statement given as evidence with the witness not standing before the court to be examined and cross-examined. Keane and McKeown, 12.

137. Appleton, *Rules of Evidence*, 13.

138. Best, *Principles of the Law*, 124.

139. Best, 102.

140. Author, former dean of the Chicago-Kent College of Law, former dean of the University of Florida College of Law, and former dean and president of New York Law School.

141. Matasar, "Storytelling and Legal Scholarship," 353.

142. Matasar, 353.

143. Matasar, 355.

144. Matasar, 359.

on a par with social sciences. They insist therefore that law lacks the three epistemic conditions that classical doctrinalists require of a modern autonomous law: objectivity, neutrality, and coherence.[145] In response, others stress the role of human freedom in effecting such epistemic conditions as part of legal reform. In both views, however, the subjective factor is still evident.[146] Law is clearly not infallible, not quite objective, and certainly not stable. One version of a legal system may uphold certain evidence at a certain time under a certain system, yet an altered version of the same law, let alone another legal system, may reject the same evidence altogether.

Why the Islamic Law?

In stark contrast, Muslims have their own legal system, the Islamic law, or *Sharīʿa*, ultimately derived from the Qurʾān, their God-inspired source, and *Sunna*, which mainly consists of *Ḥadīth*, the sayings and exemplary actions of Muhammad believed to be authorized by God.[147] To a Muslim, therefore, the Islamic law is ultimately God-given and thus an intrinsic part of religion, carrying divine authority that sets it above all other fallible and changeable secular legal systems. Indeed, "to say that Islamic law originates in divine revelation implies that adherence to its rules is at once a legal and a religious duty of Muslims."[148] The five pillars of Islam, the double testimony (that no god exists but God and that Muhammad is the Messenger of God), prayer, payment of alms, pilgrimage, and fasting are called the "*legal* pillars of religion." They are at once religious and legal, thus "melding the theological with the legal."[149] In line with this understanding and somewhat like the law for the Jews, the Islamic law "comprises in its scope not only law, but also theology and moral teaching."[150] The vast majority of Muslims thus revere it as God's ordained way that covers all aspects of their daily life. The term *Sharīʿa* means

---

145. Kahn, "Freedom, Autonomy," 158.

146. Kahn, 181–83.

147. Kamali, *Shariʿah Law*, 23–24. *Sunna* includes, in addition to *Ḥadīth*, the *sīra-maghāzī*, or the biographies and epics of Muḥammad. Unless the context suggests otherwise, the term "*Sunna*" will be used in this study to denote *Ḥadīth*.

148. Kamali, *Shariʿah Law*, 46.

149. Hallaq, *Sharīʿa: Theory, Practice, Transformations*, 225.

150. Kamali, *Shariʿah Law*, 41.

the "correct standard of living" and is "a global concept that is able to answer every moral, legal, religious, or other question."[151]

Islamic law scholar Joseph Schacht notes that "the sacred Law of Islam is an all-embracing body of religious duties, the totality of Allah's commands that regulate the life of every Muslim in all its aspects; it comprises on an equal footing ordinances regarding worship and ritual, as well as political and (in the narrow sense) legal rules."[152] He adds that the "legal subject-matter forms part of a system of religious and ethical rules."[153] This integrality within a sacred framework gives the Islamic law its elevated status, authority, and respect, ensuring that the Muslim heartily embraces it as a divine guide to virtuous life rather than an unwanted imposition. Such embrace is significant to this study and underlines the credibility of the Islamic law as trustworthy arbiter of Christian evidence to the Muslim. Leading Islamic law scholar and Columbia University professor Wael Hallaq notes that the Islamic law enters the private abode of one's personal status to such a degree that *Sharīʿa* is accused by colonialist Europeans of failing to differentiate between law and morality, thus undermining its efficacy as law.[154] He admits that the term *law* is "*a priori* problematic," imposed by linguistic limitations and superimposes on the *Sharīʿa* alien concepts of European nation-state punitive laws. But then he unequivocally asserts,

> It turns out that Islamic law's presumed "failure" to distinguish between law and morality equipped it with efficient, communally based, socially embedded, bottom-top methods of control that rendered it remarkably efficient in commanding willing obedience and – as one consequence – less coercive than any imperial law Europe had known since the fall of the Roman Empire.[155]

Others defend Islamic law against the said charge by noting that Muslim jurists have "recognized a *functional* distinction between law, morality and religion [italics mine]."[156] Nevertheless they caution that "a total separation

151. Burns, *Introduction to Islamic Law*, 24.
152. Schacht, *Introduction to Islamic Law*, 1.
153. Schacht, 1.
154. Hallaq, *Sharīʿa*, 2.
155. Hallaq, 2.
156. Kamali, *Shariʿah Law*, 44.

between law and morality is neither feasible nor recommended."[157] This indistinguishability between the legal and the personal religious-moral nature of Islamic law sets it apart from secular Western legal systems and is the source of its strength.

In line with the divine origins attributed to Islamic law, the status of an Islamic law judge, or *qadi*, is paramount. Muslims consider Muhammad to be the first Muslim judge, and so an Islamic judge continues in the same office.[158] Thus, many consider the office of the judge as higher than any other secular state office, even that of a minister.[159] A jurist of the third Hijri century described the status of the judge in clear terms: "Know that the cadi's [judge's] office enjoys in God's sight an importance exceeding any other. This is because it is God's balance, by means of which the affairs of everything in the world are regulated."[160] During caliphate states, the judge was appointed directly by the caliph and would outlast him and consecrate the installing of a new caliph. His tasks exceeded judging disputes to humanitarian and religious roles such as acting as the guardian of the orphans, and leading Friday prayers.[161] Considered as the "guardian of the welfare of Muslims," they see him not only a judge but also as a religious leader,[162] and so his rulings carry religious authority. Even more, early Islam drew an analogy between the earthly court and the heavenly eschatological court such that "the analogy between the Judge and the judge made it possible that judges were on occasion thought to preenact God's justice on the Day of Judgment."[163]

Caliphs, or successors to Muhammad as rulers of the Islamic world saw themselves as subject to Islamic law. They could not overrule the legal scholar or *qadi*, at least not in the formative period, and their interference with the work of *qadis* was more consultative.[164] Both rulers and the public saw legal scholars and judges as the guardians of religion and the "locus of legitimacy

157. Kamali, 44.
158. Baʿyoun, *Nithām al-qaḍāʾ fī al-ʿahd al-nabawī*, 157.
159. ʿAlia, *Al-dawlah al-fāḍilah fī al-Islām*, 272–73.
160. Masud, Peters, and Powers, "Qadis and their Courts," 1.
161. Hallaq, *Sharīʿa*, 54.
162. Surty, "Ethical Code," 153.
163. Lange, "Judge and the judge," 107–108.
164. Hallaq, *Introduction to Islamic Law*, 39–40.

and of religious and moral authority."[165] They were the defenders of the lower classes against the interests of the rulers, and so the caliph derived his legitimacy and had access to the masses through associating with the legal profession as an intrinsic part of his royal court. Jurists interpreted the law of God, and the caliph and his government were, like all Muslims, subject to that law, and their *raison d'etre* was to "enforce the religious law not to make it."[166] This submission to the fairness and knowledge of jurists as legitimizers to rulers continued throughout Islamic regimes.[167] Indeed, this moral-religious authority and social status of an Islamic judge continues to this day in Muslim communities, and with it the status of Islamic law.

To Muslims, Islamic law originates from the God-given Qur'ān, the God-authorized *Sunna*,[168] and the Prophet-approved *ijtihād*,[169] or independent human reasoning by jurists to interpret and apply the Qur'ān and *Sunna* to everyday life. Muslims scholars see their Islamic law at once divine insofar as it originates from the Qur'ān and *Sunna*, and human insofar as it represents their interpretation through the authoritative *ijtihād* of jurists, and so they consider it as ultimately divine.[170] Muslims in general therefore intimately cherish and revere it as God's gift to direct, organize, and adjudicate their lives. One can hardly think of a better and more trustworthy means for vindicating Christian evidence to a Muslim than examining it through the evidentiary rules and principles of the Islamic law.

Originality of the Study

Writings in legal apologetics employing the common law abound.[171] To the best of my knowledge, however, no legal apologist so far has employed Islamic law to verify Christian evidence. One might expect to find such work in the contribution of the late Sir Norman Anderson, British missionary to Libya and Egypt, legal apologist, and renowned professor of Islamic law at the

165. Hallaq, 43.
166. Hallaq, 43.
167. Hallaq, 44–45.
168. Kamali, *Shari'ah Law*, 23–24.
169. Kamali, 25–26.
170. Kamali, 40, 46.
171. See "Methodology" on page 39 of this book.

University of Cambridge and the University of London. His work on juridical apologetics, however, is limited to the common law.

A Brief Overview of the History of Juridical Apologetics in the West

Christians have appealed to law from the outset. Paul, for example, resorted to the typical legal speech of the day before the Roman authorities.[172] Juridical arguments in apologetics were evident in the early patristic era by such apologists as Justin Martyr and Athenagoras in the second century, and Tertullian in the third. They engaged in juridical reasoning to defend Christians against contemporary charges, such as atheism, infanticide, and sexual promiscuity, and to argue against coercion to worship the gods of the Roman Empire. This is particularly true with Tertullian. Himself a lawyer, he had "extraordinary forensic talents" that he utilized in his defense.[173] His magnum opus, *Apology*, "shows a first-rate ability in Roman juridical philosophy" as he criticized the ruling magistrates of the Empire for their alleged pluralism that excluded Christians alone.[174] Strictly speaking, these apologists, epitomized by Tertullian, employed juridical reasoning and rhetoric to defend Christians rather than Christianity. Insofar as they pleaded for state toleration, they are better called political apologists rather than legal apologists.[175]

The father of modern juridical apologetics is the prominent Protestant Dutch jurist Hugo Grotius (1583–1645), who also co-founded the modern legal theory based on natural law.[176] Indeed, some consider him the father of the entire field of modern apologetics.[177] His main work, *The Truth of the Christian Religion*,[178] was written in 1621 and is considered "the first formal Protestant apologetics textbook."[179] Despite appealing to jurisprudence, he

172. McGrath, "Apologetics to the Romans," 390.
173. Dulles, *History of Apologetics*, 49–50.
174. Edgar and Oliphant, *Christian Apologetics*, 1:117.
175. Boa and Bowman, *Faith Has Its Reasons*, 14.
176. Edgar and Oliphant, *Christian Apologetics*, 1:299.
177. Craig, "Classical Apologetics," 28.
178. Grotius, *Truth of the Christian*.
179. Edgar and Oliphant, *Christian Apologetics*, 1:299.

wrote in a clear and easy style, originally in poetic verse for the use of sailors travelling to non-Christian territories.[180]

The juridical approach, however, was to take its express form and thrive in the Anglo-American world. The beginning was with Thomas Sherlock (1678–1761) in his 1729 main work, *Trial of the Witnesses of the Resurrection of Jesus.*[181] Himself not a lawyer, he seems to have obtained his legal knowledge while pastoring a congregation of lawyers. He creatively set up a mock trial in his said book to respond to deist theologian Thomas Woolston's denial of the miracles of Christ, with Woolston's counsel acting as prosecutor and the apostles' counsel as defense.

A more systematic and technical defense based on common law principles was laid down by Simon Greenleaf (1783–1853), Harvard law professor and renowned authority on evidence law, in his short yet seminal 1846 work, *The Testimony of the Evangelists.* Greenleaf starts with the reasonableness of expecting from God a special revelation of his nature to humans, and then employs the principles of evidence law to vindicate the testimony of the four Evangelists. He argues first for the genuineness of the writings as we have them today and appeals to the principle that "every document, apparently ancient, coming from the proper repository or custody, and bearing on its face no evident marks of forgery, the law presumes to be genuine, and devolves on the opposing party the burden of proving it to be otherwise."[182] The Gospels have always been where they ought to be, i.e. the church, and have been used in worship by all denominations. The multiplication of their copies makes it difficult to forge all and, anyway, they lack evident signs of forgery. Greenleaf deems this enough to prove that the Gospels are genuine and spends little effort in presenting historical evidence for the dating, authorship, and transmission of the manuscripts. He then moves to the question of the truthfulness of the contents of the Gospels and starts with the standard of proof normally sought in factual matters, i.e. probability rather than mathematical certainty. Thus, "in trials of fact, by oral testimony, the proper inquiry is not whether

180. Dulles, *History of Apologetics*, 173–74.

181. Sherlock, *Tryal of the Witnesses.*

182. Greenleaf, *Testimony of the Evangelists*, 16.

it is possible that the testimony may be false, but whether there is sufficient probability that it is true."[183]

Greenleaf then examines the credibility of the witnesses themselves and their testimony. He first sets a solid legal ground: "In the absence of circumstances which generate suspicious, every witness is to be presumed credible, until the contrary is shown; the burden of impeaching his credibility lying on the objector."[184] Greenleaf here laments the injustice done to the Christian cause, where opponents reverse the burden of proof to devolve on the Christian, yet he accepts the challenge.[185] He employs and quotes a rule expressed by "a legal text-writer of the highest repute," his contemporaneous English lawyer of the Inner Temple and Queen's Counsel, Thomas Starkie: "The credit due to the testimony of witnesses depends upon, firstly, their integrity and honesty; secondly, their ability; thirdly, their number, and the consistency of their testimony; fourthly, the conformity of their testimony with experience; and fifthly, the coincidence of their testimony with collateral circumstances."[186] Greenleaf then subjects the Evangelists and their writings to each of the above credibility tests. His work has since influenced several prominent apologists as a main reference.[187]

The short work by judge and Harvard lecturer Edmund H. Bennett (1824–1898), *The Four Gospels from a Lawyer's Standpoint* was published posthumously in 1899.[188] He calls the reader to treat the Gospels with an unprejudiced mind as any other historical work by applying the same rules of evidence and judging on the preponderance of evidence rather than mathematical certainty. An ancient letter describing some event and found long after the writer and the eyewitnesses have vanished would be taken as prima facie authentic. How much more should a historical account be accepted when written by four different witnesses with some limited variations that rule out the possibility of collusion?[189] Bennett then explores the Gospels for pointers to truthfulness, inter-explanatory agreements, complementary

183. Greenleaf, 28.

184. Greenleaf, 29.

185. Greenleaf, 30–31.

186. Greenleaf, 31. See also Starkie, *Practical Treatise*, 864.

187. Clifford, *John Warwick Montgomery's*, 23.

188. Bennett, *Four Gospels*.

189. Bennett, 2–4.

variations, and reconcilable inconsistencies, while citing a few cases to show how courts address similar matters in daily life.

The juridical approach continued into the twentieth century with the 1943 work of lawyer Irvin H. Linton (1879–1962), *A Lawyer Examines the Bible: A Defense of the Christian Faith.*[190] His account is technical and makes frequent references to Simon Greenleaf. He starts with a poignant plea to fellow lawyers to use their legal skills and test Christian evidence, at least once before they die, for their own benefit and salvation.[191] He then argues that Christianity is based on historical events that can be verified with certainty, and responds to barriers to the faith, such as the problem of pain and the God of the Old Testament. He supplements his evidential argument with his personal conversion experience as well as others'.

One notable contribution comes from academic lawyer Norman Anderson (1908–1994).[192] In his 1973 work, *A Lawyer among Theologians*, he confronts liberal theologians and biblical scholars who deny the supernatural. As a lawyer, he warns that they "impose their preconceived ideas on the evidence rather than assess the evidence as it stands and see where it leads them."[193] He then appeals to legal principles to call for exegesis rather than eisegesis in interpreting documentary evidence and asks them to seek a reasonable standard of evidentiary proof. After arguing that the Jesus of history is the same Christ of faith, he considers at length the evidence for the resurrection. He first answers Rudolf Bultmann's denial of the historicity of the resurrection and focuses on the otherwise inexplicable transformation of the apostles. He then addresses at length the different accounts of the resurrection event and notes that those who attempt extreme harmonization are prompted by the principle of inerrancy, while those who exaggerate the differences are influenced by liberal bias. Though he sides more with harmonization, he vows as a lawyer to "do [his] best to weigh the evidence impartially . . . on [its] intrinsic merits."[194] In fact, Anderson argues more from commonsense than from specific legal principles, and his work reflects more the mentality

190. Linton, *Lawyer Examines the Bible*, 13.

191. Linton, 13.

192. Also known as J. N. D. Anderson.

193. Anderson, *Lawyer among the Theologians*, 13.

194. Anderson, 108–109.

of an academic lawyer than the practice of a professional lawyer, which he never claims.[195]

Another notable contribution comes from former Lord Chancellor of Britain, Lord Hailsham (1907–2001). In the early part of his 1975 autobiography, *The Door Wherein I Went*, he discusses the reasons that led him to theism and on to the Christian faith. Of particular relevance is his defense of the Christ of history, where he appeals to extra-biblical and manuscript evidence.[196] In defending the authenticity of New Testament accounts he cites an interesting court case in which he was involved to show the difficulty of a faker to conceal his deception.[197] His brief contribution to juridical apologetics is significant due to his stature, as he is "arguably the most influential legal figure and political philosopher in recent British history."[198] His witty and confident style is reminiscent of C. S. Lewis.

In the same year, 1975, Don Gutteridge, a corporate lawyer and evangelist wrote a short book, *The Defense Rests Its Case*. He starts with a confident note: "I feel I can say with some expertise that the available evidence surrounding the person and claims of Jesus Christ is absolutely irrefutable."[199] He refers to the right of a litigant to testify for himself and calls both fact and expert witnesses to testify. His references to legal principles, though, are scarce and hardly technical.

The recent revival of the juridical approach and evidential apologetics in general is partly owed to John Warwick Montgomery, a theologian, historian, and lawyer, himself influenced by Simon Greenleaf.[200] His work in the 1960's and 1970's helped bolster the faith of several then-young Christians, some of whom were to become prominent scholars and leaders: "Indeed, some of us would have veered off the path of truth but for God's grace working through Montgomery."[201] His earlier works showed signs of interest in the juridical

195. Anderson, 10.

196. Hailsham, *Door Wherein I Went*, 28–30.

197. Hailsham, 32–33.

198. Clifford, *Leading Lawyers' Case*, 72.

199. Gutteridge, *Defense Rests Its Case*, 7.

200. Montgomery even reproduces Greenleaf's work, *The Testimony of the Evangelists*, in his own book, *The Law Above the Law*.

201. Dembski and Schirrmacher, *Tough-minded Christianity*, xviii.

approach.[202] After obtaining academic degrees in law he developed his own juridical apologetic in a 1991 article.[203] In it he seeks to answer whether the Gospels are reliable as historical records, whether their testimony is reliable to know Jesus's claims about himself, whether the resurrection accounts establish these claims, and whether the proven deity of Jesus vindicates the entire Bible. After quoting expert legal arguments to show that the Gospels are genuine, he addresses the testimonial question. He employs a recognized criminal law method to expose perjury by testing the witnesses for internal defects in their characters and for external motives for them to lie. He then tests their recorded testimonies for internal defects and inconsistencies, and for external defects vs. known historical facts. He also employs legal literature to show the complexity of deception and the difficulty of concealing it, citing Lord Hailsham's aforesaid case. Finally, he defends the resurrection evidence by focusing on the missing body of Jesus, and underlines the far-reaching, life-changing consequences of this proven fact.

As the methods and legal expertise of the various juridical apologists vary, lawyer Ross Clifford suggests a helpful categorization. Under category one he includes "lawyer apologists using an evidential approach that often includes general legal principles."[204] This approach helps in testing the credibility of a witness, the reliability of the Gospels, and circumstantial evidence, while also bringing down legal arguments to the popular, easy-to-understand level. This category includes, inter alia, Hugo Grotius, Sir Norman Anderson, Edmund Bennett, Herbert Casteel, and Lord Hailsham.[205] Category two includes "lawyer apologists using a technical legal approach,"[206] adding to the first category the use of such legal principles as the admissibility of the Gospels and the hearsay charge, thus subjecting the Gospels to more stringent legal constraints. This category includes lawyers like Simon Greenleaf, Irwin Linton, John Warwick Montgomery, Clarence Barlett, Ross Clifford,

202. See, for example, his article "The Legal Reasoning and Christian Apologetics" in his work *The Law Above the Law*.

203. Montgomery, "Jury Returns," 319. This article constitutes also a chapter in his book, *History, Law and Christianity*, and a chapter in his book *Human Rights and Human Dignity*.

204. Clifford, *John Warwick Montgomery's*, 32.

205. Clifford, 32–36.

206. Clifford, 32–33.

and Pamela Binnings Ewen.[207] Category three is for "lawyer apologists citing a non-technical legal apologetic in support of their argument and/or arguing a non-technical apologetic themselves,"[208] such as Paul Barnett, Kenneth Boa, Wilbur Smith, C. Stephen Evans, and Lee Strobel. Category four goes to "non-lawyer apologists using a technical legal apologetic,"[209] such as Thomas Sherlock, Josh McDowell, and Michael Licona.[210]

Methodology

This study considers Christian evidence according to the main relevant categories under Islamic law: documentary evidence, eyewitness testimony, confession, expert witness testimony, and circumstantial evidence. Evidence under each category will be examined individually according to the criteria set by the Islamic law, while also addressing Islamic objections or would-be objections to such evidence. Some evidence may fall under more than one categorization. For example, Paul falls under both eyewitness testimony and confession. The examination of documentary evidence will primarily interact with modern studies of Islamic historiography as the process of the transmission of each of the very sources of Islamic law, Qur'ān and *Sunna*, provides a *de facto* standard for documentary transmission, in addition to the recognized *de jure* rules and principles.

Works employed in this study can be divided into five groups. The first includes works on Islamic law in general rather than the law of evidence, such as introductions, formation history, and relevant distinguishing features. These are modern works in English by both Muslim and non-Muslim scholars. The second group covers works addressing evidence in Islamic law in particular. Apart from a few works in English, most works in this category are in Arabic. This is because the law of evidence is "a largely neglected subject in the study of Islamic law . . . [and] little has been written in European languages to which the student of the field can refer."[211] The third group

207. Clifford, 35–37.

208. Clifford, 33.

209. Clifford, 33.

210. Clifford, 37–39.

211. Haykel, "Theme Issue," 129. Though works on Islamic law in general, including its formation history and legal theory abound (see, for example, chapter 2), works on the law of

includes non-juridical works that nevertheless relate to this study, such as the place of biblical books in the Qur'ān, and Islamic historiography and history including the transmission of *Ḥadīth* and *Sunna* and the compilation and canonization of the Qur'ān. The study sometimes refers to the common law for comparing and placing Islamic law in perspective, especially for a Westerner. The fourth group thus includes works on the common law, both old and modern. Finally, the fifth group includes leading works on Christian evidence, including dating, authorship, transmission, provenance, and the inerrancy of the Bible. These works will be employed in interaction with the principles used to defend the authenticity of the Qur'an and *Sunna* in chapter 3. This group also includes leading works on the historicity of the crucifixion and the resurrection as sources of Christian evidences to be examined by the relevant principles of the Islamic law of evidence.

Personal Interest and Background

My interest in apologetics, without then knowing the term or that such a thing exists, goes back to my early teen years when my atheist teachers at my British Anglican school in Jerusalem exposed us, young and unarmed students, to claims of atheistic science. Although my father was pastoring the Christian and Missionary Alliance church there, I did not have access to any resources to investigate and respond. My home faith, though, by God's grace did not falter, and I started looking earnestly for answers, both philosophical and scientific. It was, quite literally, faith seeking understanding. After decades of a professional career in engineering and lay ministry I was able to support myself financially, resign my profession, and pursue theological studies and apologetics at Biola University, followed by a doctoral program at Southern Seminary. Here I read Montgomery's *History, Law and Christianity*, which ushered me into the field of legal apologetics. My initial research interest was the standard of evidential proof required by the common law and its effect on the certainty – probability debate in apologetics. I also wanted to explore, for comparison, the standard of proof in Islamic law and philosophy. At this point, however, my supervisor, Dr. Ted Cabal, suggested that I shift my entire

evidence are limited and mostly appear in single chapters that form small parts of introductions to Islamic law.

focus to the area of Islamic law. I discovered that works in legal apologetics were limited to Western laws and that the law revered by one fourth of humanity who stumble in the Gospels on evidential grounds is ignored; hence this dissertation.

CHAPTER 2

An Overview of Islamic Law

To understand and appreciate the law of evidence under Islamic law and its relevance, its applicability, and the limitations to this study, one should first form a general idea of the special theocratic yet communal nature of Islamic law that sets it apart from other legal systems, and the process of its evolvement and synthesis in ancient Arab culture. Muslims acknowledge that its sources are both divine and human, yet ultimately hold it as divinely authoritative, hence its fitness for the purpose of this study. While Western scholars charge the formation of Islamic law with falling under the influence of neighboring legal systems, Muslims insist that it is Islamic through and through. The above, with a brief description of the components of Islamic law and the law school selected for this study, is covered under the first section of this chapter: *Nature, Formation, and Features.*

The next section, *The Tension between Stagnation and Development in Islamic Law*, shows that despite being solidified since the fourth Hijri century and so hardly applicable today, Islamic law is still seen by most Muslims as fully authoritative and applicable in its original form, with a minority calling for modernizing it while keeping the divine kernel intact. To all, it is still God's authoritative law and their sacred ideal.

The chapter ends by introducing the law of evidence under Islamic law, including its court system, penal law, case admissibility, burden of proof, standard of proof, and types of evidence. Details of the latter will be left to the next chapters where they will be discussed and applied in the relevant contexts of examining actual Christian evidence.

Nature, Formation, and Features

"Islam, unless eviscerated, stands or falls on the Sharīʿa."[1] *Sharīʿa*, or Islamic law, is more than an "enforceable body of rules that govern [a] society."[2] To Muslims, it is God's prescribed way of every aspect of life equally, between humans and God, between humans and the state, and among humans.[3] This is because Muhammad arguably aimed at showing his people God's way rather than inventing a new legal system per se, and so he brought the ritual, moral, and legal (in the narrow sense) "under the authority of the same religious command."[4] At the same time, the new community with its religious identity needed a legal system to organize its life and saw that it must be judged by the law of God, the best judge, rather than following a foreign legal system.[5]

Thus one definition of Islamic law is "that which answers the following query: What should the conduct of man be in his individual and collective life, in his relationship to God, to others and to himself in a universal community of mankind for the fulfillment of man's dual purpose: life on earth and life in the hereafter?"[6] This is why the system of punishment in Islamic law, for example, is essentially moral rather than penal.[7] It follows that the Western separation between state law and church law, or between the legal and the moral cannot be imposed on Islamic law without distorting its nature and misrepresenting many of its features.[8] To Muslim jurists, law "was not in fact an independent or empirical study. It was the practical aspect of the religious and social doctrine preached by Mohammed. For the early Muslims there was little or no distinction between 'legal' and 'religious.' In the Koran the two aspects are found side by side, or rather interwoven one with the other."[9] This connection between the legal and the religious persisted

1. Hallaq, *Impossible State*, 49.

2. Oxford Dictionary of Law, s.v. "Law."

3. Schacht, *Introduction to Islamic Law*, 1.

4. Schacht, 11. Some conservative Muslim scholars, like M. Mustafa al-Azami, do not agree that Muhammad did not intend to found a new legal system, arguing that this legal role was authorized by the Qur'an itself. Al-Azami, *On Schacht's Origins*, 15–17.

5. Hallaq, *Sharīʿa*, 31.

6. Bassiouni, "Sources of Islamic Law," 12.

7. Schacht, *Introduction to Islamic Law*, 13.

8. Hallaq, *Sharīʿa*, 86.

9. Gibb, *Mohammedanism*, 89.

throughout the history of Islam.[10] Thus, theology to a Muslim is what God wants him or her to believe, and law is how God wants him or her to behave.[11] Islamic law is therefore the "product of the private efforts of Muslim scholars to capture the divine commands and prohibitions inherent in revelation and to articulate these in the form of detailed legal rulings covering all aspects of a believer's ritual and social life."[12] It is the comprehensive and authoritative law to Muslims. Islamic law scholar Joseph Schacht goes to the extent of describing it as "the epitome of Islamic thought, the most typical manifestation of the Islamic way of life, the core and kernel of Islam itself."[13]

Islamic law as we know it today is the product of some three centuries of legal reasoning that culminated in the classical legal theory of Islam. This theory, or *ūṣūl al-fiqh*, sets the criteria and determines the sources of Islamic law, their order of priority, and the methods by which legal rules may be deducted from them.[14] *Fiqh* is the legal science of understanding *Sharīʿa*, where *Sharīʿa* in its wider meaning encompasses the entirety of God's way for human interaction, or the entire corpus of Islamic law, theology, and moral teachings.[15] *Sharīʿa* and *fiqh*, however, are often used synonymously. The theory's positive law consists of principles and rules aimed at defining and organizing the individual and communal aspects of life that reflect its distinct Islamic identity.[16]

Designed for a theocracy, Islamic law considers the state "not [as] an alien power but the political expression of the same religion."[17] Yet it was not the state that undertook the development of Islamic law but legal specialists who were versed in the Qur'ān and *Sunna*.[18] Indeed, the modern concept of state with its legislative, executive, and judicial powers did not exist in early Muslim communities, who had to regulate and manage their daily lives by

10. Gibb, 90.
11. Anderson, *Islamic Law*, 19.
12. El Shamsy, *Canonization of Islamic Law*, 3.
13. Schacht, *Introduction to Islamic Law*, 1.
14. Kamali, *Principles of Islamic Jurisprudence*, 1.
15. Kamali, *Shariʿah Law*, 16, 40–41.
16. El Shamsy, *Canonization of Islamic Law*, 3.
17. Schacht, *Introduction to Islamic Law*, 2.
18. Schacht, 5.

themselves.[19] In their military expansion, the nascent Muslim communities were mainly garrisons rather than major towns, and the judge was often himself their governor, military commander, and tax-collector.[20]

Sources and Formation

The sources of Islamic law can be categorized according to whether they are considered to be revealed or of human origin, or according to the degree of consensus they enjoy. Some limit the primary sources to revealed texts, the Qur'ān and *Sunna*, but most consider as primary those sources that enjoy consensus by the major schools of law, including revealed texts.

Primary revealed sources

To draw up a legal system, early Muslim communities had to start with what they possessed: the Qur'ān, the basic source of Islamic law. The ultimate drive behind adopting it was

> metaphysical and a priori. It is a conviction of the imperfection of human reason and its inability to apprehend by its sole powers the real nature of the Good or indeed any reality whatsoever. Absolute good and evil can therefore be known to men only through a divine revelation mediated through Prophets.[21]

Muslims believe that the Qur'ān is "the *ipsissima verba* of God, written from eternity in Arabic in heaven, and vouchsafed to the Prophet, as the need arose, through the agency of the Angel Gabriel."[22] The earlier part of the Qur'ān was revealed in Mecca and includes mostly theological and ethical matters. The latter part, however, contains the bulk of legal content: it was revealed in Medina where Muhammad had migrated with his followers out of resistant Mecca upon the invitation of two of its tribes.[23] This migration (*hijra*) to Medina in 622 CE marked the establishment of the new Muslim

19. Hallaq, *Introduction to Islamic Law*, 7–8.
20. Masud, Peters, and Powers, "Qadis and their Courts," 8–9.
21. Gibb, *Mohammedanism*, 91.
22. Anderson, *Islamic Law*, 10–11.
23. Masud, Peters, and Powers, "Qadis and their Courts," 6.

community (*ummah*) under Muhammad's leadership, and the beginning of the Hijri calendar.[24]

The Qur'ān is limited, however, in its direct coverage of detailed positive law. Its verses that can be regarded as legal are by some estimates five hundred,[25] and by others six hundred, most related to worship rituals.[26] Those that can be considered as strictly substantive law or from which specific laws can be inferred (excluding matters of devotional rituals and religious duties) are little over two hundred out of its 6,237 verses.[27] Of these, around seventy verses address matrimonial and inheritance matters, seventy address commercial matters, thirty address crime and penal matters, thirty address justice and evidence, and ten verses address other economic concerns.[28] These are scattered throughout the Qur'ān rather than codified in discrete sections as in the Pentateuch: most came in response to problematic incidents that Muhammad encountered in the course of his mission.[29]

Despite that, and though some of these legal verses are in the form of specific rules on specific matters, the Qur'ān is replete with general principles that underpin almost all major issues of Islamic law.[30] Leading Islamic law scholar Wael Hallaq, while agreeing that the legal verses are limited and address selective issues,[31] stresses the overriding legal significance of the Qur'ān:

> In comparison to the overall bulk of Quranic material, the legal verses appear exiguous, giving the erroneous impression that the Quran's concern with legal matters is merely incidental. At the same time, it has frequently been noted by Islamicists that the Quran often repeats itself both thematically and verbatim. If we accept this to be the case, . . . it means that the proportion of the legal subject matter (in which repetition is virtually absent) to non-legal subject matter is larger than is generally thought. And if we consider the fact that the average length of

24. Masud, Peters, and Powers, 6–7.
25. Hallaq, *Introduction to Islamic Law*, 16.
26. Nyazee, *Outlines of Islamic Jurisprudence*, 154.
27. Lippman, McConville, and Yerushalmi, *Islamic Criminal Law*, 29.
28. Kamali, *Shariʿah Law*, 19–20.
29. Kamali, 19.
30. Kamali, *Principles of Islamic Jurisprudence*, 37.
31. Hallaq, *History of Islamic Legal Theories*, 10.

> legal verses is twice or even thrice that of the non-legal verses, it would not be difficult to argue . . . that the Quran contains no less legal material than does the Torah, which is commonly known as "The Law."[32]

Around half a century after Muhammad's death, judges and legal scholars began referring to his transmitted sayings and exemplary acts (*Ḥadīth*).[33] Muslims considered him to be the ideal and exemplary judge.[34] Collectively known as *Sunna*,[35] this second basic source of law was established in obedience to the clear saying of the Qur'ān: "He who obeys the Messenger [Muhammad] obeys God" (Qur'ān 4:80), and the direct instruction: "Whatsoever the Messenger ordains, you should accept, and whatsoever he forbids, you should abstain from" (Qur'ān 59:7).[36] Muslims therefore consider Mohammad's *Ḥadīth* part of the divinely revealed texts.[37] The prominent Islamic philosopher in the fifth Hijri century, al-Ghazali, considers that, just as God revealed the Qur'ān to Muhammad, so he revealed the *Ḥadīth/Sunna*, such that God's revelation to Muhammad falls into two categories, the Qur'ān and *Sunna*.[38] Yet the Qur'ān remains the first source, and in case of conflict between a *Ḥadīth* and Qur'ān, the Qur'ān prevails. This is because the Qur'ān is direct revelation while *Ḥadīth* comes as part of stories told by narrators. Moreover, the Qur'ān enjoys absolute authenticity, whereas parts of the *Ḥadīth* enjoy only probable authenticity. In addition, *Ḥadīth* explains the Qur'ān, and so it naturally comes second in priority.[39]

Sunna acts alongside the Qur'ān in three ways: it reiterates a qur'anic ruling and principle; or it explains qur'anic verses in the sense of "clarify[ing] the ambivalent, qualify[ing] the absolute, or specify]ing] the general"; or it

32. Hallaq, 3–4.

33. Hallaq, *Origins and Evolution*, 56.

34. Masud, Peters, and Powers, "Qadis and their Courts," 7.

35. Although *Ḥadīth* literally means speech, it came to include both the sayings of Muhammad and his deeds, or *sīra*. *Ḥadīth*, therefore, will be used synonymously with *Sunna* unless otherwise indicated.

36. Hallaq, *Sharīʿa*, 41.

37. Kamali, *Shariʿah* Law, 23.

38. Kamali, *Principles of Islamic Jurisprudence*, 63.

39. Kamali, 79.

introduces new rulings not addressed in the Qur'ān.[40] Like the Qur'ān, *Sunna* is not a comprehensive source of law. Though Muhammad was highly skilled in drafting legal documents and was himself an arbitrating judge,[41] *Sunna* mostly represents his spontaneous responses to day-to-day encountered events and simple cases that reflect the primitive and nomadic desert culture.[42]

Ḥadīth was compiled and integrated as a distinct body into Islamic law only in the second Hijri century. Western scholarship therefore questions the authenticity of the traditions that comprise *Sunna* and considers them as a second Hijri-century forgery. Cambridge Islamic law scholar J. N. D. Anderson believes that "most of them [are], beyond question, fabricated."[43] Prominent Islamic studies scholar Ignaz Goldziher notes that "whatever Islam produced on its own or borrowed from the outside was dressed up as ḥadīth."[44] Muslim scholars, however, while agreeing that much of what had been attributed to Muhammad was forgery, note that early Muslim scholars devised methods that can differentiate the authentic from the forgery, rendering the present corpus of *Sunna* authentic.[45] Regardless of Western views and the actual authenticity of *Ḥadīth*, what matters to this study, it must be noted, is what Muslim scholars and Muslims in general believe their *Ḥadīth* to be. It consists of the authentic sayings and acts of Muhammad and is therefore the second revealed basis of their sacred law and a trusted tool for examining Christian evidence.

Primary non-revealed sources and ijtihād

The rest of the Islamic law had to be formed by *ijtihād*, a long evolving process of authoritative independent legal reasoning consisting of interpretations and inferences for matters not directly covered by the two revealed primary sources.[46] Of the quality of such reasoning Gibb argues that "for Muslims [Islamic law's] proof-texts were to be found in the Koran and Prophetic Tradition; and on this assumption the jurists and theologians of the second century

40. Kamali, *Shari'ah Law*, 24–25.
41. Hallaq, *History of Islamic Legal*, 4.
42. Ba'youn, *Nithām al-qaḍā' fī al-'ahd al-nabawī*, 123.
43. Anderson, *Islamic Law*, 12.
44. Goldziher, *Introduction to Islamic Theology*, 40.
45. More on this in chapter 3.
46. Hallaq, *Introduction to Islamic Law*, 27.

elaborated a structure of law that is, from the point of view of logical perfection, one of the most brilliant essays of human reasoning."[47] *Ijtihād* basically interprets and projects revealed texts and applies them to the various changing conditions of daily life.[48] It is the authority of adjudicating a new case not directly addressed by the Qur'ān, *Sunna*, or an authoritative precedent, and is based on the concept that "human intellectual faculty mediates between God's will and human reality."[49]

According to Muslim jurists, the reasoning process of *ijtihād* was sanctioned by the Prophet himself.[50] It started on a personal level by the *mufti*, a jurisconsult versed in the legal interpretation of the Qur'ān and *Sunna*. In this process he "exercises his utmost effort in extracting a rule from the subject matter of revelation while following the principles and procedures established in legal theory."[51] To be accepted as authoritative, such reasoning had to be ultimately rooted in divine or prophetic textual evidence, i.e. the Qur'ān and *Sunna*, rather than human authority.[52] The *mufti* would form informal circular gatherings to teach his opinions and interpretations to his students, thus passing the tradition on to the next generation.[53] Ordinary people, leaders, and judges sought his *fatwa* (opinion) and upheld it as decisive and authoritative; it was overturned only by a better *fatwa* of another senior *mufti*.[54]

Those circles gradually produced the ancient schools of Islamic law by the early second Hijri century, identified by their geographical centers: Kūfa and Basra in Iraq, Medina and Mecca in Hijaz, and Syria. Their main contribution was ensuring that the nascent corpus of Islamic law, including its independent reasoning and any external influences, was built on the essence of qur'anic religious and ethical norms and principles.[55] As many as nineteen different

47. Gibb, *Mohammedanism*, 90.
48. Kamali, *Shari'ah Law*, 25.
49. Hallaq, *Sharī'a*, 110.
50. Kamali, *Shari'ah Law*, 25–26.
51. Hallaq, *History of Islamic Legal Theories*, 117.
52. Hallaq, *Sharī'a*, 49.
53. Hallaq, *Introduction to Islamic Law*, 12.
54. Hallaq, 8–9.
55. Schacht, *Introduction to Islamic Law*, 28–29.

schools are known to have emerged during the first three Hijri centuries.[56] Others put the number at thirty in the first two centuries.[57]

By the middle of the third Hijri century, however, the schools changed their identity from geographical to personal, with allegiance to individual master-jurists, such as *Abū Ḥanīfa* in Kūfa, Iraq and *Malik* in Medina, Hijaz.[58] The real maturation of a legal school, however, was marked by loyalty to its distinguishing doctrine rather than the person of its eponym master-jurist.[59] Only four of the personal schools were able to mature to doctrinal,[60] following the general thought and methodology of the eponym and subsequent development by his followers, while keeping his name.[61] This doctrinal rather than mere personal loyalty enabled a school to survive the death of its founder.[62] Thus, by the end of the seventh Hijri century the four surviving schools in Sunnī or orthodox Islam were the *Ḥanafī*, the *Mālikī*, the *Shāfiʿī*, and the *Ḥanbalī*, all named after their founders,[63] and in the same chronological order.[64] They continue to survive today.

The school's founding *mufti*, also known as *imam*, was an authoritative and absolute master-jurist whose "doctrine laid claim to originality not only because it derived directly from the revealed texts [i.e. Qur'ān and *Sunna*], but also, and equally importantly, because it was gleaned systematically from the texts by means of clearly identifiable interpretive principles."[65] His outstanding virtuous character and, most importantly, his unique epistemic ability were seen as special gifts from God making him "the ultimate source of legal knowledge and moral authority."[66] Legal authority was therefore vested in a gifted person who was versed in legal epistemology rather than

56. Lippman, McConville, and Yerushalmi, *Islamic Criminal Law*, 26. The other main school is the Shiite *Jafari* school.

57. Abou El Fadl, *Great Theft*, 32.

58. Schacht, *Introduction to Islamic Law*, 57.

59. Hallaq, *Introduction to Islamic Law*, 32.

60. Hallaq, *Origins and Evolution*, 168–169.

61. Hallaq, *Introduction to Islamic Law*, 34–35.

62. Hallaq, 34–35.

63. Schacht, *Introduction to Islamic Law*, 65.

64. Hallaq, *Sharīʿa*, 66.

65. Hallaq, *Introduction to Islamic Law*, 34–35.

66. Hallaq, 35.

in some political or military position.[67] Around this axis figure, the defining legal doctrines of each of the respective four major formative schools evolved through the process of *ijtihād*.[68] Though the ultimate corpus of law was indebted in part to the contributions of the eponym's predecessors and successors,[69] what gave authority and recognition to their contribution was its grounding in the eponym, the axis of authority, sometimes retrospectively.[70] Such grounding of authority in one person was necessary to both the maturation and the stability of the school.[71] *Ijtihād* produced the two other primary sources and several secondary sources.

*Ijmā*ʿ, or consensus of the jurists, is the third primary source of Islamic law after the Qur'ān and *Sunna*. It may be defined as "a sanctioning instrument whereby the creative jurists . . . representing the community at large, are considered to have reached an agreement, known retrospectively, on a technical legal ruling, thereby rendering it as conclusive and as epistemically certain as any verse of the Quran and the Sunna of the Prophet."[72] It is the infallible agreement of the *ijtihād* (reasoning) of the entire community of major legal scholars on a body of juristic conclusions that are based on otherwise probable textual evidence, bestowing on them the authoritative status of epistemic certainty and extending to guarantee the entire structure of Islamic law.[73] This unanimity of consensus must cover all jurists (but not necessarily laypersons) in all geographical areas, of all schools of law, and of all theological denominations of Islam including both Sunnī and Shīʿi faiths.[74] *Ijmā*ʿ is considered infallible based on Muhammad's saying: "My community shall never agree on a falsehood."[75] Conclusions are considered

67. Hallaq, 35.

68. Hallaq, 35.

69. Hallaq, *Sharīʿa*, 67.

70. Hallaq, *Authority, Continuity and Change*, 29. Hallaq addresses in chapter 2 at length the grounding of legal authority *ex post facto* in the eponym of a school, such as Abū Ḥanīfa, rather than in any of his contributing predecessors or successors, some of which he may never had held.

71. Hallaq, *Authority, Continuity and Change*, 238.

72. Hallaq, *History of Islamic Legal Theories*, 1.

73. Hallaq, *Sharīʿa*, 97–98, 100. See also Hallaq, *Introduction to Islamic Law*, 21.

74. Kamali, *Principles of Islamic Jurisprudence*, 233.

75. Hallaq, *Introduction to Islamic Law*, 21. See also Hallaq, *Origins and Evolution*, 138.

certain despite being reached and agreed through the utilization of inferential methods.[76] Moreover, they cannot be abrogated by subsequent scholars.[77]

Ijmāʿ is so significant that it is the authority that determines the transmission of even the Qur'ān itself as wholly certain, or whether a *Ḥadīth* is authentic.[78] For this reason, Anderson notes that "consensus has proved in history the most important source of all – for even the Koran stood in need of interpretation, while the traditions [*Sunna*] stood in need of authentication."[79] He then adds that "it was the consensus alone which in the final analysis was in a position to give an authoritative ruling."[80] *Ijmāʿ* thus "occurs at the highest echelon of the Islamic society on rare occasions."[81] Indeed, opinions authorized by *ijmāʿ* form no more than 1 percent of the corpus of Islamic law, yet they remain significant due to this "extraordinary instrument" of authorizing them.[82] The rest of *ijtihād* (reasoning) process thus excludes legal rules that are directly, unambiguously, and unequivocally stated in the Qur'ān or *Sunna*, or that are already sanctioned by *ijmāʿ* (consensus) and so have acquired the status of finality and certainty.[83]

Qiyās is the fourth primary source of Islamic law. It is a process of "disciplined and systematic reasoning on the basis of revealed text, the Quran and *ḥadīth*."[84] It is thus a product of *ijtihād* and employs several inferential methods, and is used by some jurists synonymously with *ijtihād*. The predominant method of *qiyās* is analogical reasoning whereby an emerging case is deemed analogous to, and so treated as similar to, a previous case ruled by one of the three established prior sources, Qur'ān, *Sunna*, or *ijmāʿ*.[85] The key to analogical reasoning thus is to determine the *ratio legis*, the common denominator between the original reference case and the new case.[86] Another method is

76. Hallaq, *Sharīʿa*, 100.
77. Auda, *Maqasid al-Shariah*, 111.
78. Hallaq, *Introduction to Islamic Law*, 17.
79. Anderson, *Islamic Law in the Modern World*, 13–14.
80. Anderson, 14.
81. Burns, *Introduction to Islamic Law*, 28–29.
82. Hallaq, *Introduction to Islamic Law*, 22.
83. Hallaq, *History of Islamic Legal Theories*, 117.
84. Hallaq, *Origins and Evolution of Islamic Law*, 114.
85. Hallaq, *Introduction to Islamic Law*, 22–23.
86. Hallaq, 23.

the *reductio ad absurdum*, which here means determining a rule by showing that its converse is false. An even more important method is the *argumentum a fortiori* whereby a new rule is determined based on the strength of a fixed one and includes both *a maiore ad minus* (determining a smaller scale on the strength of a major one), and *a minore ad maius* (determining a larger scale on the strength of a minor one).[87]

In all these methods, *qiyās* is legitimate only if based on a prior primary source, the Qur'ān, *Sunna*, or *ijmā'*/consensus.[88] Its authoritativeness carries certainty, just as the prior primary sources do.[89] Unlike the Qur'ān and *Sunna*, however, *qiyās* is more of a method than a substantive source.[90] It is a source "only insofar as it leads, as a method of reasoning, to the discovery of God's law on the basis of the revealed texts and of consensus."[91]

Secondary sources

The above four primary sources of law, Qur'ān, *Sunna*, *ijmā'*, and *qiyās*, are adopted by all the four schools of Islamic law. *Istiḥsān* (juristic preference) is another product of *ijtihād* yet a disputed one and so is a secondary source. It is adopted by the *Ḥanafī*, *Mālikī*, and *Ḥanbalī* schools, and rejected by the *Shāfi'ī*.[92] It is a process of free opinion whereby a judge, faced with necessity, sanctions departure from a relevant strict principle that would cause unjustified hardship.[93] *Istiḥsān* is similar to the principle of equity in Western legal systems in that both are based on the principle of fairness, except that in *istiḥsān* the principle of equity is that of Islamic law.[94]

Istiṣlāḥ (public interest) is another disputed product of free opinion and reasoning/*ijtihād* whereby the prevailing factor in determining a verdict is consideration of public interest.[95] It is adopted as an independent source by

87. Hallaq, *Sharī'a*, 101–106.
88. Hallaq, *Origins and Evolution of Islamic Law*, 120.
89. Hallaq, *History of Islamic Legal Theories*, 105.
90. Hallaq, *Introduction to Islamic Law*, 22.
91. Hallaq, *History of Islamic Legal Theories*, 83.
92. Kamali, *Principles of Islamic Jurisprudence*, 324.
93. Hallaq, *Introduction to Islamic Law*, 22, 26.
94. Kamali, *Principles of Islamic Jurisprudence*, 322.
95. Hallaq, *Introduction to Islamic Law*, 22, 26.

the *Mālikī* and *Ḥanbalī* schools,[96] whereas the *Ḥanafī* school subsumes it under *istiḥsān* and the *Shāfi ʿī* accepts it only as part of the process of *qiyās*. Though in the second Hijri century both *istiḥsān* and *istiṣlāḥ* were based on free reasoning, their adherents insisted, after the third Hijri century, on basing them on revealed text.[97]

Another secondary source is *istiṣḥāb*, the presumption of continuity of the existence or non-existence of something (a state of affairs, an attribute, or a rule of law) proven to be so in the past unless and until proven otherwise.[98] It may be used only when no other sources are available. Both the *Shāfi ʿī* and *Ḥanbalī* schools accept it without qualification as a source of law. The *Ḥanafī* and *Mālikī* schools, however, accept only one kind of its scope, the continuity of attributes.[99] Moreover, they accept it only "as a means of defense, that is, to defend the continued existence of an attribute, but not as a means of proving new rights and new attributes."[100]

Finally, *ʿurf*, or custom, is a standalone secondary source to both the *Ḥanafī* and *Mālikī* schools and considered implicitly by the other schools,[101] and *sadd al-dhara'i ʿ*, or blocking lawful means to an unlawful end (such as selling grapes to a winemaker), is adopted by the *Mālikī* and *Ḥanbalī* schools.[102]

96. Kamali, *Principles of Islamic Jurisprudence*, 363–65.

97. Hallaq, *Sharī ʿa*, 107, 109.

98. Kamali, *Principles of Islamic Jurisprudence*, 384, 387–88.

99. Kamali, 388.

100. Kamali, 388–89.

101. Auda, *Maqasid al-Shariah*, 130–31.

102. Kamali, *Shari ʿah Law*, 75–76. See also Nyazee, *Outlines of Islamic Jurisprudence*, 184.

Primary (largely agreed)		**Secondary** (disputed)	**Adopted by**
Revealed	**Non-revealed** (by Ijtihad, or legal reasoning, sanctioned by Muhammad)		
Qur'ān			All
Sunna			All
	***Ijmā*ʿ** (consensus)		All
	qiyās (analogical reasoning)		All
		Istiḥsān (juristic preference)	*Ḥanafī; Mālikī; Ḥanbalī*
		Istiṣlāḥ (public interest)	*Mālikī; Ḥanbalī*
		Istiṣḥāb (presumption of continuity)	*Shāfiʿī; Ḥanbalī* (partially by others)
		ʿ*Urf* (custom)	*Mālikī Ḥanafī*
		***Sadd al-dhara'i*ʿ** (blocking lawful means to unlawful end)	*Mālikī; Ḥanbalī*
Ultimately Divine			

Figure 1. Sources of Islamic law

Concluding the Formative Period and Closing *Ijtihād* Gates

The progressive process of *ijtihād*, coupled with the progressive discovery and documentation of *Ḥadīth*, created a long period of tension over the role of reason vis-à-vis revealed text, with traditionalists restricting themselves to the Qur'ān and *Sunna*, and rationalists giving priority to human reason.[103] *Ijtihād* thus had to be regulated and *Ḥadīth* incorporated, and both had to be consolidated into one coherent body under one theory.[104] A process of

103. Hallaq, *Sharīʿa*, 57. The term "rationalists" here is not philosophical but simply referring to those with "an attitude towards legal issues that is dictated by rational, pragmatic and practical considerations." Hallaq, *Origins and Evolution*, 74. Both parties recognized the Qur'an as the ultimate source though extreme rationalists questioned its divine source. Hallaq, *Sharīʿa*, 57.

104. Kamali, *Principles of Islamic Jurisprudence*, 5–6.

synthesis thus began at the end of the second Hijri century until what Hallaq terms "the Great Synthesis" eventually prevailed, though more in favor of traditionalism.[105] It was a gradual process of rapprochement that culminated in "the acceptance of juristic reasoning by the [traditionalists] and the integration of the Hadith sciences into jurisprudence by the [rationalists]."[106] By the end of the third century, the synthesis had achieved mainstream status to most Muslims, including followers of the *Ḥanafī* school.[107] Determined extremists risked extinction; most Muslims saw extreme traditionalism as too rigid to deal with all aspects of daily life and rationalism as too libertarian and humanist.[108] This Great Synthesis was so important that "on both the ideological and legal levels, the history of Islam between 150 and 350 AH (ca. 770 and 960 CE) can be characterized as a process of synthesis."[109] It defined Islamic law and paved the way for the emergence of orthodox Sunnī Islam, followed today by most Muslims around the world.[110]

Around the same time, legal scholars of all recognized schools became gradually convinced that all important questions have been settled, leaving no further need for reasoning. They therefore decided in the early fourth Hijri century to close the gate of *ijtihād*, or independent reasoning, thus marking the solidification of Islamic law.[111]

The process of establishing Islamic law, also known as "the formative period," occupied on average the first three Hijri centuries. Schacht believes that it ended in the middle of the third Hijri century.[112] Hallaq disagrees and argues that recent research shows that, though the essential features of the judiciary system and legal doctrine had developed by early third century, the science of legal methodology and hermeneutics finally developed into

105. Hallaq, *Sharīʿa*, 58–59.

106. El-Shamsy, *Canonization of Islamic Law*, 195.

107. Hallaq, *Sharīʿa*, 58–59.

108. Hallaq, 57–58.

109. Hallaq, *Origins and Evolution*, 124. Note that AH stands for the Latin *Anno Hegirae*, or "Year of the Hijrah".

110. Hallaq, *Sharīʿa*, 57, 59.

111. Schacht, *Introduction to Islamic Law*, 70–71. Hallaq rejects as myth the common belief that closing the gate of *ijtihād* took place at the end of the formative period as some jurists continued to come up with their own doctrines though within the structure and confines of their respective schools. He also argues that the full maturation of the legal schools took two to three centuries beyond the formative period. Hallaq, *Authority, Continuity and Change*, 62–63, 65.

112. Schacht, *Introduction to Islamic Law*, 70.

a comprehensive legal theory in the middle of the fourth century, a time when the doctrinal legal schools matured.[113] The first century of the formative period, however, remains the most important, having given Islamic law its distinctive features and established its own institutions.[114]

Adopted by the recognized schools of law, the final form of the classical theory of Islamic law, or *ūṣūl al-fiqh*, recognizes four official and fundamental sources of Islamic law: Qur'ān, then *Sunna*, then *ijmā ʿ* (consensus), and lastly *qiyās* (analogical reasoning).[115] The Qur'ān and *Sunna* are the material sources while *ijmā ʿ* and *qiyās* are procedural sources drawing on the first two.[116] Schacht describes *ijmā ʿ* as the decisive method that establishes the authenticity of the two material sources and their interpretation, and *qiyās* as a "declaratory authority."[117] It is "a source only insofar as it provides a set of methods *through* which the jurist arrives at legal norms."[118]

Hallaq argues that *ijmā ʿ* and *qiyās* are no less important than the Qur'ān and *Sunna* in forming the fundamental assumptions of legal theory.[119] All Muslims should accept these two primary sources of law with unqualified certainty just as they accept the Qur'ān and *Sunna*.[120] This certainty, however, is necessary insofar as they are accepted as the four fundamental sources *qua* sources and does not necessarily extend to the process of drawing legal inferences.[121] Thus, the Qur'ān, *Sunna*, *ijmā ʿ*, and *qiyās* are all certain in themselves, though opinions and conclusions inferred from them and so staying outside them can be probable. All, however, are considered as equally correct inferences from their certain sources.[122] These four primary sources became the perpetual fixed tradition of Islamic law that all true Muslims are

113. Hallaq, *Origins and Evolution*, 2, 122.

114. Schacht, *Introduction to Islamic Law*, 15.

115. Schacht, 114.

116. Hallaq, *Origins and Evolution*, 119.

117. Schacht, *Introduction to Islamic Law*, 114–15.

118. Hallaq, *Sharī ʿa*, 101.

119. Hallaq, *History of Islamic Legal*, 126.

120. Hallaq, *Origins and Evolution*, 130.

121. Hallaq, *Sharī ʿa*, 94. The Qur'an is accepted as source *qua* source and content. *Sunna*, however, must be accepted as a fundamental source *qua* source, without necessarily extending to certainty about the authenticity of its content. This will be discussed in chapter 4.

122. Hallaq, *Origins and Evolution*, 130.

supposed to accept as authoritative.[123] Schacht notes that this "traditionalism of Islamic law, typical of a 'sacred law', is perhaps its most essential feature."[124]

Islamicity of the Law

Western Islamic law scholars note that, notwithstanding the purported origins and constituents of the Islamic law, the process of *ijtihād* (independent reasoning) during the first Hijri century admitted into Islamic law some pre-Islamic legal concepts and maxims.[125] Schacht notes that the early interaction of the Islamic world with its neighboring civilizations opened the door to import other legal concepts and maxims into the Islamic law from Roman law, Eastern Church canon law, Persian Sassanian law, and Jewish law.[126] He speaks of a "thorough process of Islamicizing the existing customary law" during the first and early second Hijri centuries.[127] Anderson agrees: "Pre-Islamic customary law, and the administrative practice of early Islam, provided the raw material out of which a great part of the Shari'a evolved."[128] Hallaq rejects this view and insists that such customary law was Islamic from the beginning.[129] Early Muslim legal scholars, it is true, resorted to *ijtihād* (independent reasoning) in addition to the revealed sources of Qur'ān and *Sunna*, and even made use of pre-Islamic laws, themselves having been tribal arbitrators (Muhammad himself was a prominent arbitrator before founding Islam).[130] Yet the developing law, Hallaq insists, was still Islamic through and through and continued to be so throughout its formative period:

> From the beginning, the Qur'an provided the framework for legal thinking, bringing its contents to bear upon as many situations as nominally could be justified. Generally speaking, any matter that could be conceived of as falling within its juristic

123. Hallaq, *Sharīʿa*, 81–82.

124. Schacht, *Introduction to Islamic Law*, 5.

125. Schacht, 19–21.

126. Schacht, 19–21. For example, Schacht believes that the third source of Islamic law, *ijmāʿ*, seems to have been inspired by the Roman law principle of *opinio prudentium*.

127. Schacht, 26.

128. Anderson, *Islamic Law*, 19.

129. Hallaq, *Sharīʿa*, 45–46. See also Hallaq, "Use and Abuse," 79–91.

130. Hallaq, *Sharīʿa*, 33.

> purview, even through expansive reasoning, was dealt with in Quranic terms or an extension thereof.[131]

Thus, it was emphasized from the beginning that *qiyās* (analogical reasoning) discovers legal rules and maxims from the Qur'ān and *Sunna* rather than invents them.[132] This is even true of the secondary sources, though not shared by all schools. For example, Hallaq notes that jurists who have accepted them "insisted that no argument of *istiḥsān* can rest on any grounds other than the texts of revelation."[133]

Regardless of the degree of support that the views of Schacht, Anderson, or other Western scholars may have among Islamic scholars, and even regardless of the degree of truth of these opinions, what matters to this study is not what non-Muslim scholars believe but rather what Muslims themselves believe the sources and constituents of their sacred law are. To them, it is God-given, and so trustworthy and infallible. It is the authoritative and trusted regulator of the entire life to Muslims. They believe it to be given by God in the Qur'ān, interpreted and practiced by Muhammad in the *Sunna*, and further interpreted and expanded by *ijtihād*/reasoning to cover all aspects of daily life by authoritative master-jurists within the confines of their major schools. Its role in Islam even surmounts theology:

> Law rather than theology came to constitute the central arena of Sunni Muslim thought. . . . By justifying itself as an interpretative effort based on the textual remains of revelation, Islamic law gained the status of an authorized discourse. In contrast to theology, where differences of opinion represented an insurmountable theoretical conundrum, law was able to accommodate and legitimize differences as the natural outcome of the process of interpretation.[134]

131. Hallaq, 36.

132. Hallaq, 51.

133. Hallaq, 107.

134. El Shamsy, *Canonization of Islamic Law*, 63.

Components of Islamic Law

Islamic law, or *Sharīʿa*, is meant to regulate the entire life of a Muslim with both its religious and secular aspects. As it is rooted in revelation, compliance by its rules and principles is both a legal and religious obligation of all Muslims in fulfilment of their duty towards God and fellow humans.[135] The Arabic word *Sharīʿa* means right path. Schacht notes that

> none of the modern systematic distinctions, between private and "public" law, or between civil and penal law, or between substantive and adjective law, exists within the religious law of Islam; there is no clear separation of worship, ethics, and law proper. The single chapters of the works of Islamic law fall, it is true, in the main under one or the other of those headings as far as the subject-matter is concerned, but there is continual overlapping and, above all, the concept of any systematic distinction is lacking.[136]

In a footnote he adds that distinctions made by the Ottoman *Mejelle* or by modern scholars are irrelevant, being a product of modernist thought.

With this understanding in mind, Islamic law is categorized in the *Ḥanafī* school into three divisions. The first, rituals, covers purity and dietary laws, obligatory prayer, fasting, pilgrimage, alms, and holy struggle/*jihād*, and constitutes one third of the *corpus juris*. The second division, civil transactions, covers matrimonial laws, exchange of valuables, equity and trusts, civil litigation, and estates, and occupies almost one half of the *corpus juris*. The third division, penal law, which is most relevant to this study, covers tort, illicit sexual acts, theft, alcohol drinking, courts and judges, evidence, testimonies, etc., and occupies one sixth of the law. The *Shāfiʿī* school dedicates a separate division for matrimonial laws and so has four divisions. The *Mālikī* school arranges all subject matters under two broad divisions, rituals, and transactions. Finally, the *Ḥanbalī* school follows the same *Shāfiʿī* divisions with some differences in the subdivisions.[137]

---

135. Kamali, *Shariʿah Law: An Introduction*, 46.

136. Schacht, *Introduction to Islamic Law*, 113.

137. Kamali, *Shariʿah Law: An Introduction*, 43–45. For relative sizes of divisions see Hallaq, *Sharīʿa*, 553–55.

The Islamic Law School Selected for This Study

The first major school, the *Ḥanafī*, was founded in Iraq by Abū Ḥanīfa al-Nuʿmān Ibn Thābit (d. 150 AH/767 CE). He lectured a small circle of students in Kūfa, Iraq, and left only a small volume of his doctrine. His student Abū Yūsuf (d. 182 AH/798 CE) recorded his works, and al-Shaybānī (d. 189 AH/805 CE), student of both Abū Ḥanīfa and Abū Yūsuf, compiled the full *corpus juris* of the *Ḥanafī* school.[138] Abū Ḥanīfa is renowned for having developed a "high degree of reasoning,"[139] and is the "unrivaled master" of legal reasoning, or *ijtihād*.[140] This achievement, coupled with the fact that *ijtihād* is "a cornerstone of Islamic law,"[141] gives Abū Ḥanīfa a prominent place among the founders of the Islamic law schools. He was, however, accused of placing heavy reliance on reason at the expense of revealed text, yet it seems that he was wary of excesses as evidenced by his leading statement: "No one may issue a *fatwa* [a reasoning-based rule] on the basis of what we have said unless he ascertains the [revealed] source of our statement."[142] He is also distinguished in illustrating his principles with a large number of real and hypothetical cases and issues, all organized in an instructive manner.[143] Nevertheless, any over-reliance on reasoning rather than revealed text had to be balanced after his death by his student Abū Yūsuf, probably due to the discovery of more *Ḥadīth* by then.[144] Al-Shaybānī, however, is the one who is credited with expanding and systematizing the *Ḥanafī* doctrine and building a body of highly developed analogical and systematic reasoning.[145] Moreover, his debates with Shāfiʿī (d. 204 AH/820 CE),[146] the main advocate of *Ḥadīth*-based law and eponym of the yet unfounded third school, played a crucial role in balancing and integrating the *Ḥanafī* legal tradition with the available corpus of *Ḥadīth*.[147] This balancing also affected traditionalist Shāfiʿī himself

138. Kamali, 70.
139. Schacht, *Introduction to Islamic Law*, 44–45.
140. El Shamsy, *Canonization of Islamic Law*, 45.
141. Hallaq, *Sharīʿa*, 70.
142. Kamali, *Shariʿah Law: An Introduction*, 72.
143. Nyazee, *Outlines of Islamic Jurisprudence*, 529–31.
144. Schacht, *Introduction to Islamic Law*, 44–45.
145. Schacht, 45.
146. El Shamsy, *Canonization of Islamic Law*, 46.
147. El Shamsy, 201.

who came to appreciate the indispensable role of independent reasoning as ministerial to revealed text and necessary for building a theory of law based on a synthesis between revealed texts and reasoning.[148] These rather early developments culminated in the Great Synthesis at the end of the third Hijri century. The *Ḥanafī* school is credited with being the first to develop the Islamic law systematically as we know it today, long before the other schools existed or before Shāfiʿī developed the legal theory, *ūṣūl al-fiqh*.[149] *Ḥanafīsm* is also credited with introducing into Islamic law the primary source of *qiyās* (analogical reasoning) and the secondary yet important pragmatic sources of *istiḥsān* (juristic preference) and *ʿurf* (custom).[150] The other schools based their systems on the work of Abū Ḥanīfa, whether by way of reacting, objecting, or responding.[151] After Abū Ḥanīfa's death, *Ḥanafīsm* was adopted by the Abbasid dynasty, where his students Abū Yūsuf and al-Shaybānī were prominent, with Abū Yūsuf appointed as the chief judge of the capital, Baghdad.[152] Abū Yūsuf is also among the foremost jurists credited with developing the Islamic criminal justice system.[153]

In general, the *Ḥanafī* school is formalistic and meticulous on religious duties, yet the most practical among all schools. In addition to developing pragmatic secondary sources, it tolerated the *ḥiyal* maneuver to circumvent inconvenient qur'anic prohibitions.[154] In *ta'azir* crimes, the only ones where punishment is subject to the judge's discretion rather than imposed by *Sharīʿa*, Abū Ḥanīfa used to opt for the most lenient penalties based on the maxim ascribed to Muhammad that "it is better that the Imam be wrong in his forgiving than to err in imposing the penalty."[155] The *Ḥanafī* school is also the "most humanitarian among all schools concerning the treatment of non-Muslims and war captives, and its penal law is considered to be more

148. El Shamsy, 53–55.

149. Nyazee, *Outlines of Islamic Jurisprudence*, 530–33.

150. Kamali, *Shariʿah Law*, 61.

151. Nyazee, *Outlines of Islamic Jurisprudence*, 533.

152. El Shamsy, *Canonization of Islamic Law*, 45–46.

153. Bassiouni, *Introduction to the Islamic*, xvi–xvii.

154. Lippman, McConville, and Yerushalmi, *Islamic Criminal Law*, 26.

155. Al-Saleh, "Right of the Individual," 61.

lenient."[156] Likewise, it has higher regard for individual freedom and women's rights, limiting personal restrictions to the minimum necessary.[157]

The *Ḥanafī* school is today the largest of all schools of law, probably because it was the exclusive school of law for the entire Ottoman Empire. It is predominant today in Jordan, Palestine, Syria, Lebanon, Turkey, Pakistan, Afghanistan, and India.[158] It is also followed in Sunnī Iraq where it started, Turkish Central Asia, and Bangladesh,[159] as well as among the Muslims of China.[160]

Next came the *Mālikī* school whose founder, Mālik (d. 179 AH/795 CE) lived in Medina, the second hometown of Muhammad. It is the most conservative in adhering to *Sunna*,[161] yet also "the most dynamic and comprehensive of all schools . . . [having] validated literally the entire range of proofs [validating sources] that are upheld by the other three schools."[162] Moreover, it alone adds to its sources the consensus of Medina, and *isṭiṣlāḥ* (consideration of public interest) as an independent source or proof when the other schools merely give it a dependent auxiliary role. It has also added *sadd al-dhara'i'* (blocking lawful means to an unlawful end).[163] *Mālikī* is the second largest school with substantial following today in Morocco, Algeria, Tunisia, Upper (southern) Egypt, Sudan, Bahrain, and Kuwait.[164] It was also the school of medieval Andalusia in Spain.[165]

The *Shāfi'ī* school started in Egypt after its eponym, Shāfi'ī (d. 204 AH/820 CE), a student of Mālik who split from him in his keenness to honor and keep the pure prophetic tradition of *Ḥadīth* to the exclusion of the tradition of the Prophet's Companions. He did engage in systematic reasoning yet synthetized it with prophetic tradition in a marked zeal that distinguished

156. Kamali, *Shari'ah Law: An Introduction*, 70.

157. Kamali, 71.

158. Kamali, 73.

159. Hallaq, *Introduction to Islamic Law*, 37.

160. Lippman, McConville, and Yerushalmi, *Islamic Criminal Law*, 27–28.

161. Lippman, McConville, and Yerushalmi, 26.

162. Kamali, *Shari'ah Law*, 75. Proofs here mean the revealed sources legitimizing a certain legal rule. Kamali, *Principles of Islamic Jurisprudence*, 11.

163. Nyazee, *Outlines of Islamic Jurisprudence*, 184.

164. Kamali, *Shari'ah Law: An Introduction*, 73.

165. Schacht, *Introduction to Islamic Law*, 65.

his legal thought.[166] He accepted *qiyās* (analogical reasoning) and rejected *istiḥsān* (judicial preference) thus distinguishing his school from the others.[167] He rejected any tenet of law that would override the tradition of the Prophet, rendering his thought inflexible vis-à-vis progressive development.[168] He believed in adhering to the apparent meaning of a written text rather than the subjective discovery of hidden meanings, intents, and motives behind the words.[169] Shāfiʿī is most credited with formulating the Islamic legal theory, or *ūṣūl al-fiqh*, known for its coherence, and his traditionalism influenced the ancient schools.[170] Nevertheless, Shāfiʿī is criticized for having frequently changed his views on several issues, though some see this as "indicative of his assiduous pursuit of new solutions and his dynamic intellect, [which] show his persistent quest for the truth."[171] The *Shāfiʿī* school is the third major school and is predominant in Lower (northern) Egypt, southern Arabia, East Africa, Indonesia, and Malaysia.[172]

Finally, the *Ḥanbalī* school, the last surviving, is named after Aḥmad Ibn Ḥanbal (d. 241 AH/855 CE), "the orthodox opponent of rationalists."[173] He wanted to limit Islamic law to the Qur'ān and *Sunna* and exclude any form of human reasoning. In their quest to formulate a comprehensive legal system, however, his followers had to accept a limited form of reasoning including both *ijmāʿ* (consensus) and *qiyās* (analogical reasoning), and accept the classical legal theory.[174] Ironically, the *Ḥanbalī* school is unique in having always rejected the closing of the gate of *ijtihād*, contending that it should remain open to any competent jurist.[175] Though once enjoying wide following, the *Ḥanbalī* school almost vanished after the fourteenth century only to be revived in the eighteenth by the *Wahhābī* movement in what is today Saudi

166. Schacht, 46–47.

167. Schacht, 46.

168. Schacht, 46–47.

169. Kamali, *Shariʿah Law: An Introduction*, 81–83. He quotes a *Ḥadīth* in which Muhammad says: "I adjudicate on the basis of what I hear." (Cf. Isa 11:3–4 and John 7:24.)

170. Schacht, *Introduction to Islamic Law*, 48.

171. Kamali, *Shariʿah Law: An Introduction*, 83.

172. Hallaq, *Introduction to Islamic Law*, 37.

173. Kamali, *Shariʿah Law: An Introduction*, 83.

174. Schacht, *Introduction to Islamic Law*, 62–63.

175. Kamali, *Shariʿah Law: An Introduction*, 85.

Arabia. It also has some following in Oman, Qatar, Bahrain, and Kuwait,[176] and is by far the smallest of the four schools.

This study will follow the *Ḥanafī* school of law, primarily because it is the school followed in Islamic courts in Jordan, my country,[177] and because it has the widest following in the Islamic world and is the oldest. Schacht notes that he has chosen the *Ḥanafī* school for his important work *An Introduction to Islamic Law* "because of its historical importance and wide distribution."[178]

Nonetheless, it is important to note that all of the four major Sunnī schools share much in principle and differ only in details and the degree of conservatism,[179] with each school distinguishing itself in legal assumptions and methodology.[180] Sunnī Muslims consider them as equally valid and legitimate interpretations of the Qur'ān and *Sunna*, and followers of one school do not accuse other schools of error.[181] Rather, "they mutually recognize each other's orthodoxy."[182] Collectively, all recognized schools comprise the *Sharī'a*.[183] Moreover, an individual Muslim is generally free to choose his or her preferred school and change to another without formalities. One can even select *ad hoc* a school other than one's own for a specific legal case if such move would ensure convenient results.[184] This commonality runs across legal differences, which are hardly governed by theological concerns. Islamic scholar Khaled Abou El Fadl notes that, "despite the significant theological differences between Shī'ī and Sunnī Muslims, . . . Shī'ī and Sunnī laws are remarkably similar both in terms of their methodologies and positive determinations. In fact, Shī'ī *Ja'farī* law is very similar to Sunnī *Shāfi'ī* law, and Shī'ī *Zaidī* law is very similar to Sunnī *Ḥanbalī* law."[185] Muslims see their law as their collective effort to understand God's will and so it "functioned like the symbolic glue that held the diverse Muslim nation together, despite its many

176. Kamali, 83–84.

177. In matters of worship and rituals (*'ibādāt*), Jordan follows the *Shāfi'ī* school, but these are irrelevant to this study.

178. Schacht, *Introduction to Islamic Law*, 112.

179. Lippman, McConville, and Yerushalmi, *Islamic Criminal Law*, 26.

180. Hallaq, *Introduction to Islamic Law*, 34.

181. Schacht, *Introduction to Islamic Law*, 67.

182. Anderson, *Islamic Law*, 15.

183. Abou El Fadl, *Great Theft*, 32.

184. Schacht, *Introduction to Islamic Law*, 68.

185. Abou El Fadl, *Speaking in God's Name*, 154.

different ethnicities, nationalities, and political entities."[186] It seems from the above that examining Christian evidence under one of the four Sunnī schools of law should not be expected to yield major differences from examination under another Sunnī, or even Shi'ite, school.

The Tension between Stagnation and Development in Islamic Law

The strength of the absolute authority of Islamic law gained by the divine origin attributed to it also creates its own challenges. Law is meant to organize and adjudicate a people's daily life and affairs, which obviously change with time. Islamic law, however, became rigid and "set in final mould" ever since the closing of the gate of *ijtihād* at the end of the formative period.[187] Made to fit life conditions that prevailed until then, it became increasingly difficult to apply and unable to address life developments amid growing tensions between theory and practice.

Attempted Solutions

Muslims have struggled since the early Hijri centuries to address the widening gap between the ideal and often strict theoretical demands of law and the exigencies of practice. Their solutions, often creative, varied with the ever-changing realities of social and political life.

Legal devices. To solve the tension, Muslim jurists resorted to *ḥiyal*, or legal devices that would enable one to evade the spirit and real intent of an undesired legal rule while giving lip service to the letter, thus obtaining the desired outcome without breaking the rule. This *ḥiyal* creative solution was thus a "*modus vivendi* between theory and practice: the maximum that custom could concede, and the minimum (that is to say, formal acknowledgement) that the theory had to demand."[188] Legal devices were applied to almost every aspect of daily life, including familial, penal, and commercial

186. Abou El Fadl, *Great Theft*, 34.

187. Schacht, *Introduction to Islamic Law*, 75.

188. Schacht, 80.

laws.[189] The *Ḥanafī* school has been the strongest advocate of *ḥiyal*, followed by both the *Shāfi ʿī* and the *Mālikī* schools, and last by the *Ḥanbalī* school.[190]

Custom. Islamic law thus has hardly been applied purely, letter and spirit. It also had to be combined with administrative and customary laws by successive Islamic states, and later by European colonialists. Attempts by reformists to rule exclusively by sacred law failed or were short-lived.[191] Indeed, the role of custom in Islamic law vis-à-vis revealed texts created tension since the era of the founding jurists, as illustrated in the failure of the foremost *Ḥanafī* jurist Abū Yūsuf to include custom as a source to Islamic law in the second Hijri century.[192] Though attempts to incorporate custom continued, the centrality of anchoring legal rules in revealed texts continued to be sacrosanct, and jurists had to find a way to deal with tensions by either circumventing revealed texts, or re-defining custom, or qualifying its use. Thus, though the *Ḥanafī* jurist Sarakhsī of the fifth Hijri century accepted the maxim, "What is known through custom is equivalent to that which is stipulated by the clear texts of revelation," he restricted the use of custom to a case-by-case basis.[193] *Ḥanafī* jurist Ibn Nujaym of the tenth Hijri century recognized universal custom that was not contradicted by an authoritative *Ḥanafī* doctrine, yet also acknowledged that it is an extraneous source.[194] Likewise, the last major *Ḥanafī* jurist Ibn ʿĀbidīn reiterated in the thirteenth Hijri century Ibn Nujaym's principle that custom may be considered except where a clear revealed text addresses the subject case.[195]

Ottoman hybrid codified laws. The Ottomans, "the most state-like dynasty of Islam,"[196] started with a puritan religious zeal, yet in supplementing Islamic law with state laws they unwittingly superseded its undesired parts

189. For example, the Qur'an prohibits usury. One device of *hiyal* to circumvent the prohibition is the double sale whereby the prospective debtor sells a slave to the prospective creditor and immediately buys the slave back for a higher price payable after an agreed time. Thus, the debtor gets the loan (slave's price), the creditor gets the interest (the price difference) and the security (the slave). Schacht, *Introduction to Islamic Law*, 79. Islamic banks today use similar devices in their transactions.

190. Schacht, 81.

191. Schacht, 85–86.

192. Hallaq, *Authority, Continuity and Change in Islamic Law*, 215–16.

193. Hallaq, 216–17.

194. Hallaq, 218–19.

195. Hallaq, 223.

196. Hallaq, *Sharīʿa*, 361.

and weakened it.[197] Eventually, the Ottoman Empire became the first Islamic entity to codify a hybrid state-Islamic legal system, known as the *Mejelle*. Yet it was, "strictly speaking, not an Islamic but a secular code, . . . and it contains certain modifications of the strict doctrine of Islamic law, particularly in the rules containing evidence."[198] Similarly, all subsequent attempts by modern states to codify the Islamic law in the Western style had to sacrifice its very nature. Codes of law are such that rules are neatly arranged in a systematic order whereby topics are delineated and indexed for quick access. Islamic law, in contrast, consists of the hermeneutic compilations of the individualistic *ijtihād* (reasoning) of scholars of a school in the context of custom and practice.[199] It claims to recognize the unique nature of individual and particular circumstances, hence the context-specific *ijtihād* rather than the blind and mechanistic rules of justice.[200] Moreover, "strict Islamic law is by its nature not suitable for codification because it possesses authoritative character only in so far as it is taught in the traditional way by one of the recognized schools."[201]

Colonial hybrid codified laws. In the second half of the nineteenth century, and with the rise of the Western model of the modern nation-state and the resolve of Western powers to control the laws of their colonies, the rule of Islamic law faced a survival challenge. Hallaq notes that "there is virtually no problem or issue in [the legal history of the modern Muslim world] that does not hark back to the conceptual, structural and institutional discord that exists between the thoroughly indigenous Islamic/customary laws, and the European-grown imports that were the inevitable concomitant of the nation-state and its modern legal system."[202] As a result, Islamic law lost its millennium-long prominence, with its use limited to religious rituals and personal status in most modern Islamic countries.[203]

The widely common culprit for such alienation as seen by Western and reformist Islamic scholars is the stagnation of Islamic law ever since the closing of the gate of *ijtihād* at the end of the third Hijri century. Schacht notes

197. Schacht, *Introduction to Islamic Law*, 91.

198. Schacht, 92–93.

199. Hallaq, *Sharīʿa*, 368.

200. Hallaq, 546.

201. Schacht, *Introduction to Islamic Law*, 92.

202. Hallaq, *Sharīʿa*, 359–60.

203. Hallaq, 443, 445.

that, while this stagnation gave it stability over the centuries, the Islamic law was left to fit the social and economic life of the third Hijri century, rendering it out of touch with the modern world.[204] Anderson goes further: "It was thus that until recently [before the start of modern reform] Sunni Islam had become largely moribund."[205] Hallaq, however, vehemently rejects this charge and blames the alienation of Islamic law on Western colonial powers in their quest to control their Islamic colonies and exercise unbridled material exploitation. Their tool was the "conquest of the mind [which], the colonial powers well understood, was more important than the conquest of the body: for whereas the latter enabled a partial control, the former yielded a totalistic dominance."[206] The Western-state legal model succeeded eventually in its project of legal transformation, displacing the indigenous Islamic law with such modern state elements as "centralization, codification, bureaucratization, [and] jural homogenization."[207]

Current Islamic Reactions

The persistent failure to achieve a rule of true Islamic law that can successfully address the exigencies of modern life is disquieting to most Muslims today, both reformists and traditionalists. Between charges of serving the interests of Western powers at the expense of true religion and countercharges of unrealistic reactionary demands in a modern world, the debate continues unabated.

Reformists. Mostly lawyers by profession, modern reformists aim at adapting the traditional aspects in Islamic law rather than its religiousness such that it fits modern times.[208] In their daunting attempt to claim both orthodoxy and reform, they insist that what they are calling for is a return to *Sharīʿa* as their valued heritage yet a *Sharīʿa* that is able to address the actual living conditions of Muslims today through "imaginative reconstruction" and modification of the rules to fit modern life.[209] Reformists also stress that classical *fiqh* writings cannot address the complexities of modern life and so call for codifying the Islamic law into a hybrid system combining the best of every

204. Schacht, *Introduction to Islamic Law*, 75.
205. Anderson, *Islamic Law*, 14.
206. Hallaq, *Sharīʿa*, 445–46.
207. Hallaq, 547.
208. Schacht, *Introduction to Islamic Law*, 100.
209. Kamali, *Shariʿah Law: An Introduction*, 37.

school rather than maintaining the rigidity of a single school.[210] Moreover, they call for moderation and balance aiming at relieving people from heavy burdens and hardships, and quote qur'anic verses in support.[211] Notably, they differentiate between unchangeable revealed sources of the Qur'ān and *Sunna* on the one hand and the fallible products of human *ijtihād/fiqh* on the other, and blame failure to differentiate on the inflexibility and resistance to renewal.[212] They insist that Islamic law is still relevant since it is flexible enough to accept development. It can be adapted to modernity without weakening by returning from the "fixed and unimaginative body of medieval law" to its original sources.[213] One way is to overstep the confines of the "scholastic traditionalism" of the traditional schools and rather flexibly and freely utilize their principles and reasoning as auxiliary arguments to modern theories.[214]

Other modernist Islamic voices are even bolder. Prominent Muslim American Islamic law scholar Khaled Abou El Fadl attempts to combine bold reform with faithfulness to revealed texts by questioning the authenticity and thus the authority of transmitted revealed texts, not just their ancient *ijtihādic* interpretation into legal rules. He insists that the image of the violent sword-wielding and women-demeaning Islam is not true Islam and that "the most emphatic moral values taught by Islam . . . would have to be mercy, compassion, and peace."[215] In his call for moderation, however, he must deal with a wealth of qur'anic and prophetic texts that expressly call otherwise. His approach is to uphold the Qur'ān as the "immutable and uncorrupted Word of God . . . [that is] not subject to reproach," yet dismiss much of *Sunna*.[216] It arrived to Muslims today through a long chain of human transmission, with "the intriguing problem of the possibility of multiple authorship."[217] There is the "possibility of fabrication, . . . creative selection and recollection . . . [such that] each tradition attributed to the Prophet is the end-product of an

210. Kamali, 250.
211. Kamali, 288, 294.
212. Auda, *Maqasid al-Shariah*, 59–60.
213. Bassiouni, "Sources of Islamic Law," 19.
214. Auda, *Maqasid al-Shariah*, 144–45.
215. Abou El Fadl, *The Great Theft*, 11.
216. Abou El Fadl, *Speaking in God's Name*, 87.
217. Abou El Fadl, 87.

authorial enterprise."[218] This enterprise means "a considerable degree of creative subjectivity in the process of authenticating, documenting, organizing, and transmitting the reports attributed to the Prophet and the Companions."[219] Abou El Fadl defends his bold claim by noting that "Muslim dogma does not assert that the *ḥadīth* literature is immutable or Divinely protected from the possibility of corruption."[220] Even when a report is authentic, questions remain about the role and intent of the Prophet since "not everything that the Prophet said or did was legislative in nature because not all Prophetic acts were intended to represent the Divine Will."[221]

Abou El Fadl then questions the authority of jurists to determine the meaning of revealed text in terms of their subjective influence and the limitations of language and the shaping of meaning.[222] Thus, much of Islamic law is the product of questionable *ijtihād* (reasoning). According to one school, the *mukhatti'ah*, no one will know whether his *ijtihād* is right or wrong until the Day of Judgement when God will reward him fully if correct, and partially if wrong provided he has done his best. According to the second school, the *musawwibah*, one cannot describe a determination as right or wrong; the process of diligent search is what God is after since if a correct determination exists, God would have spelled it out clearly in revealed texts.[223] Abou El Fadl argues that either theory means that no one can close the gate of *ijtihād*, which should be subject to development and adaptation. He calls for a "conscientious pause" at textual determinations handed down by jurists of the past and sealed against a re-examination vis-à-vis revealed text that would enable one to decide in good conscience whether to accept a determination or reject and revise it.[224]

In his most recent award-winning work, however, Hallaq seems to turn the tables on the entire debate on a reformed Islamic law in a modern Islamic state: "The 'Islamic state' . . . is both an impossibility and a contradiction in

218. Abou El Fadl, 88.
219. Abou El Fadl, 105.
220. Abou El Fadl, 105.
221. Abou El Fadl, 88.
222. Abou El Fadl, 89–91.
223. Abou El Fadl, 91, 147–48.
224. Abou El Fadl, 94.

terms."[225] He insists that there never was an Islamic "state" but an Islamic community, or *umma*, where the sovereign is God rather than the state, and his divine moral will is expressed in the moral-legal principles of Islamic law.[226] He notes that "there can be no Islam without a moral-legal system anchored in . . . divine sovereignty; and, at the same time, there can be no modern state without its own sovereignty and sovereign will, for no one . . . can reasonably argue that the modern state can do without this *essential* form-property of sovereignty."[227] He concludes that "the modern state can no more be Islamic than Islam can come to possess a modern state."[228]

Optimists. Others find some solace and hope in the present scene. Islamic law scholar Iza Hussin sees in the colonial marginalizing of Islamic law and relegating it to the private sphere of family law a positive paradox that underlines the unquenchable power of Islamic law and identity in Islamdom. While agreeing with Hallaq that colonialism did "impoverish Islamic law, erode its epistemic integrity, and rob its scholars of their protection and dignity," she warns that "there are reasons to be cautious about calling it moribund."[229] She notes that "each of the processes by which Islamic law . . . was marginalized by the colonial state – its circumscription into the domain of rituals, personal status, and the family; its textualization and codification – also had the opposite effect of centralizing Islamic law."[230] This circumscription, she explains, provided for the Muslim political elite a symbol of religious identity that they dearly held and defended against further Western encroachments, and the reification into a codified text gave Muslims an Islamic reference in their court proceedings.[231] She also notes that the surviving legacy of colonialization, the present-day independent Muslim state, "is a contradictory phenomenon, its institutional Islamic content marginal but playing a central role in authorizing the state."[232] She adds that "the contemporary Muslim state . . . finds itself in a double bind, in that it governs through many of the durable legacies of

225. Hallaq, *Impossible State*, ix.
226. Hallaq, 48–49.
227. Hallaq, 51.
228. Hallaq, 51.
229. Hussin, *Politics of Islamic Law*, 106.
230. Hussin, 33.
231. Hussin, 33.
232. Hussin, 33–34.

colonial statehood, including the institutional marginalization of Islam, but relies for its authority upon Islam's symbolic centrality."[233] She then concludes that "there is a politics of Islamic law . . . [that is] dynamic . . . [and] continuous, driven by deep individual beliefs in the law that, even as it frustrates desires for a simple justice, holds out the promise of a divinely inspired good."[234]

Traditionalists. Advocates of traditional Islamic law today argue that, as affixed by the end of the formative period, it was indeed effectively applicable during the ensuing centuries. Jurists insisted on abiding by the recognized sources and the literal interpretation of revealed texts, and any hermeneutic that tended to depart from tradition could not succeed in finding its way to the court system, the ultimate authority on admissibility.[235] Those advocates note that, while this traditionalism had survived and guarded the Islamic law throughout the pre-modern era,[236] modern reformers who see traditionalism as a stultifying obstacle think and act under the Western influences of religious utilitarianism and liberalism.[237]

Calls for reform of traditional Islamic law are clearly not well received in the Muslim world. Hallaq notes that "there is little question that dissatisfaction with the means and results of legal reform permeates many levels of Muslim society, particularly the educated elite."[238] Anderson accurately notes that the conservative Muslim remains defiant, preferring "to maintain the Shariʿa in its purity and entirety as the ideal law for the golden age, even if this meant abandoning it in practice for a secular law forced upon him by the exigencies of modern life, rather than to permit any profane meddling with its immutable provisions."[239] To conservatives, the general rule is that "it is far less heinous to ignore or disobey the divine law than to run any risk of questioning or denying it."[240]

Traditional Islamic law thus continues to claim victory today irrespective of the degree of its practical relevance. Hallaq notes that "to say that the

233. Hussin, 263.

234. Hussin, 265.

235. Hallaq, *History of Islamic*, 208–9.

236. Hallaq, 209–10.

237. Hallaq, 214.

238. Hallaq, 211.

239. Anderson, *Islamic Law*, 92.

240. Anderson, 92.

overwhelming majority of modern Muslims wish for the *Sharīʿa* to return in one form or another is to state what anyone with cursory knowledge of world affairs would readily acknowledge."[241] Islamic movements in the Middle East and worldwide today that call for a return to the traditional Islamic law claim the support of substantial segments of Muslims.[242] This claim is clearly witnessed by *free and transparent* elections today throughout the Muslim world, be they for political or professional bodies. Hallaq explains that "there is no doubt that Islamic law is today a significant cornerstone in the reaffirmation of Islamic identity, not only as a matter of positive law but also, most importantly, as the foundation of cultural uniqueness."[243] This is to be expected not only because of the sacred nature of Islamic law, but as Hallaq also explains, because "the intersection of the legal with the communal was a marker of the law's populism and communitarianism. . . . Enmeshed with local customs, moral values and social practices, it was a way of life."[244] Schacht notes that "the postulate that law, as well as other human relationships, must be ruled by religion has become an essential part of the outlook of Muslims in the Arab countries of the Near East."[245] Whether it is applied in its traditional or modernized form, or even replaced with secular laws, Schacht concludes that,

> the interest and importance of traditional Islamic law, which has existed for more than a thousand years and is eagerly studied all over the Islamic world, is not affected by these changes. It still casts its spell over the laws of contemporary Islamic states: in the states of traditional orientation, such as Saudi Arabia, as the law of the land; and in the states of modernist orientation as an ideal influencing and even inspiring secular legislation.[246]

Conclusion

The implication for this overview is twofold. First, and as stated in the previous chapter, although increasingly out of touch with modern life, Islamic law

241. Hallaq, *Impossible State*, x.
242. Hallaq, *Origins and Evolution*, 1. See also Kamali, *Shariʿah Law*, 249.
243. Hallaq, *Origins and Evolution*, 1.
244. Hallaq, *Sharīʿa*, 544.
245. Schacht, *Introduction to Islamic*, 106.
246. Schacht, 111.

still maintains its "relevance and centrality . . . to the individual Muslim."[247] It is alive and well, and continues to be the revered sacred law in the hearts of Muslims and thus their most trusted guide to evaluate evidence. Second, this study will refer to *traditional* Islamic law as developed during the formative period and forged in the fourth Hijri century rather than to its reformed hybrid forms in modernity. Conservative Muslims consider the earliest litigation in Islam, i.e. during the lifetime of Mohammad, to be the purist form of litigation in Islam and the most faithful to the Qur'ān and *Sunna*, and the cornerstone for subsequent developments.[248] They accept it as it stood at the closing of the gate of *ijtihād* at the end of the formative period. This study will therefore avoid the easier task of referring to the *Mejelle*, the only "Islamic" code, despite its continuing wide reference in scholarly works and despite its forming part of the civil laws of several Arab countries, including Jordan.[249] Referring to the unadulterated traditional Islamic law form is more acceptable to Muslims as a trustworthy arbiter of Christian evidence.

Introductory Overview of Court Procedure and Evidence

This overview aims at giving a general picture of the court system and the main principles governing the process of admitting and evaluating evidence. The rules governing evidence are associated more with criminal rather than civil procedure due to the higher standard of required proof. Criminal procedure in Islamic law is not as developed as in Western legal systems, and so the two are not equitably comparable.[250]

Court System

A typical Islamic court consists of a single judge, assisted by his clerical staff.[251] He must be a Muslim adult male who is known to be "wise, patient, honest,

247. Hallaq, *Sharīʿa*, 446.

248. Baʿyoun, *Nithām al-qaḍāʾ*, 213.

249. Schacht, *Introduction to Islamic*, 93.

250. Sherif, "Generalities on Criminal Procedure," 3.

251. Schacht, *Introduction to Islamic Law*, 188–89.

humble, learned and inquisitive."[252] Although the duty of the judge is to act impartially, his verdict is final even if the judgment is unjust, with no recourse to appeal.[253] He cannot revoke or revise his judgment except when he subsequently discovers that it contradicts the Qur'ān or *Sunna*; in that case another judge can also annul his judgment on the same grounds.[254] It is therefore exceedingly important that the judge not pronounce a verdict hastily or based on insufficient evidence. When he is uncertain, Islamic legal doctrine encourages him to consult with one or more jurisconsults if needed, given that the Qur'ān urged Muhammad himself to "consult them in the matter" (Qur'ān 3:159).[255] The jurisconsults used to sit beside the judge to provide immediate consultation though the final decision remained with the judge.[256] The necessity for such consultation was first addressed by the renowned *Ḥanafī* jurist al-Khassāf (d. 261 AH/874 CE).[257] It was not because the judges as a class were less conversant than the jurisconsults but rather "the role of extrajudicial authority in consultation reflected an early awareness of the limits of law as text and method."[258] The ultimate aim of seeking advice is to arrive at the truth.[259] This facility of consultation may be resorted to in this study in the form of consulting the writings of Islamic jurisconsults rather than stumble at the ambiguity, rigidity, or limitation in a given rule or procedure.

The Islamic court is less formal and tends to carry out its proceedings with simplicity and expeditiousness. It follows an inquisitorial rather than an adversarial system; the judge himself investigates rather than the prosecutor or the defense.[260] To assist him in investigating and achieving justice, the judge may appoint witnesses to verify alleged facts and events.[261] He may also appoint investigators tasked with preparing a shortlist of qualified witnesses

252. Masud, Peters, and Powers, "Qadis and their Courts," 20. *Ḥanafīs* allow a woman to be a judge, yet only in civil cases.

253. Schacht, *Introduction to Islamic Law*, 189.

254. Sherif, "Generalities on Criminal Procedure," 10.

255. Samour, "Critique of Adjudication," 48–49.

256. Samour, 55.

257. Samour, 54.

258. Samour, 53.

259. Samour, 49.

260. Sherif, "Generalities on Criminal Procedure," 4.

261. Hallaq, *Origins and Evolution*, 85.

after they examine and assess their integrity.[262] A judge must follow the rules of his school lest his judgment be challenged.[263] At times, however, judges "did cross [their schools' doctrinal] boundaries in the search for justice."[264]

The significance of the Islamic court and its high esteem in the eyes of Muslims is evident in the analogy drawn between the heavenly court and the earthly court by Muslim exegetes between the second and sixth Hijri centuries.[265] This metaphysical perspective gave judges additional prestige and authority as partners with God to the extent that, at times, the judge thought of himself as enjoying divine unaccountability with "absolute liberty to punish or forgive."[266] Muslim exegetes thus had to refer to this analogy to explain its intended meaning and rein in unaccountable power. Furthermore, "the analogy between the Judge and the judge made it possible that judges were on occasion thought to preenact God's justice on the day of judgment,"[267] with *Shāfiʿīs* counting *ḥadd* punishments as expiation. This analogy ultimately illustrates both the exceptional moral and religious responsibility of the Islamic judge as well as his esteemed authority and prestige.

Notwithstanding this authority, a distinctive feature of the Islamic court, especially in early Islam, was its informal nature and mediatorial role aimed at maintaining social harmony. The judge was more than a judge in the narrow sense as he presided over public welfare and, more importantly, was the guardian of the weak and the oppressed. The court was thus an integral part of the social fabric with which the judge had to be intimately familiar.[268] Whereas the modern court tends to be aloof and highly formalistic, the Islamic court was a down-to-earth part of the social fabric, allowing the litigants themselves rather than professional lawyers to directly plead their case.[269] Lawyers were unknown to Islamic law.[270] Litigants appeared and spoke before the judge

262. Masud, Peters, and Powers, "Qadis and their Courts," 21.
263. Schacht, *Introduction to Islamic Law*, 196.
264. Masud, Peters, and Powers, "Qadis and their Courts," 30.
265. Lange, "Judge and the judge," 91.
266. Lange, 91, 106.
267. Lange, 108.
268. Hallaq, *Sharīʿa*, 166.
269. Hallaq, *Introduction to Islamic Law*, 61.
270. Hallaq, 63.

informally and freely, expressing their concerns and innermost feelings.[271] The modus operandi of the court "demanded a moral logic of social equity rather than a logic of winner-takes-all resolutions."[272] The aim was to seek, whenever possible, a compromise whereby both parties claim some gain and restore their social roles and dignity in the closely-knit social fabric of honor and shame. Even when a party loses its case, the informal nature of the court would at least afford it, including its relatives and friends, the unrestrained opportunity to defend personal reputation and air its views.[273]

Important to this study, Islamic scholars stress that although non-Muslim minorities living in the Islamic world are not part of the Islamic nation or *ummah*, "the protective covenant of the *Shari'a*" guarantees that they enjoy all privileges without discrimination, including equal justice.[274] More specifically, they insist that, historically, Islamic courts did afford equal space and opportunity to all social classes: "The Muslim court succeeded precisely where the modern court fails, namely, in being a sanctified refuge within whose domain the weak and poor could win against the mighty and affluent."[275] This included the Jewish and Christian minorities, even their women, who could win cases against powerful Muslims, even the governor himself.[276] Surviving court records show many cases that support the claim that "Muslim courts were guided by a leveling practice of Shari'a law that disregarded the social status, place of residence, gender, and religious affiliation of its clients."[277] There may be different criteria applied to non-Muslims, yet "these have no bearing on the fundamentals of the integrity of the [judicial] process in its pursuit of truth."[278] Muslims insist that "in the Qur'an, the theme of justice is all embracing, free from any restrictions, and universal . . . because it does not discriminate on the grounds of race, rank, colour, nationality, status or religion."[279]

---

271. Hallaq, 63.
272. Hallaq, *Sharī'a*, 166.
273. Hallaq, 166.
274. Bassiouni, "Sources of Islamic Law," 21.
275. Hallaq, *Introduction to Islamic Law*, 61.
276. Hallaq, *Sharī'a*, 167.
277. Al-Qattan, "Dhimmis in the Muslim," 436.
278. Bassiouni, "Sources of Islamic Law," 23.
279. Surty, "Ethical Code," 163.

This study assumes that "in its pursuit of truth," a hypothetical Islamic court should afford a Christian similar opportunity and unrestricted freedom to provide evidence when he or she pleads the case for the crucifixion and resurrection of Christ. Such pleading also assumes a virtuous judge who is "wise, patient, honest, humble, learned and inquisitive."[280] It is predicated upon the ideal Islamic court described by Islamic law scholars and historians, marked by the decorous behavior of the judge and the high ethics of treating the litigants:

> Equity was of the essence, beginning with the litigants' physical approach to the *majlis al-hukm* (the court as it sits in session). Queues were to be maintained, and when claimants and disputants would arrive at the court simultaneously, or when the queue was lost, lots were to be drawn. The qadi [judge] was commanded to maintain respectful treatment of the litigants, to greet them, to invite them to sit in his *majlis*, to be serious yet polite, economic in speech and firm yet gentle, giving them his undivided attention.[281]

Admissibility of a Lawsuit

Under Islamic law, a case is admissible in the first place before a court, i.e. even before proffered evidence is considered, if several conditions are satisfied.[282] Both the plaintiff and defendant must be competent, i.e. adults and of sound mind. The plaintiff must have an interest in the case, and the defendant would shoulder a concrete obligation if convicted. A genuine dispute should exist, the defendant must be identifiable, and the crime and its causes must be known. The object of the case must be capable of proof and must be logically and customarily possible. Finally, the plaintiff must present his or her claims consistently and describe them confidently in clear and certain language and specific terms.[283] Our hypothetical case satisfies these conditions: Christians have a clear interest in defending their faith, and the consequences for the Muslim are not only concrete, but eternal. The dispute is real, and the object,

280. Masud, Peters, and Powers, "Qadis and their Courts," 20.

281. Hallaq, *Sharīʿa*, 343.

282. Daoud, *Al-qaḍāʾ wa al-daʿwa*, 1:9–10.

283. Hallaq, *Sharīʿa*, 344.

the historical events of the crucifixion and resurrection of Christ, is capable of proof.

Penal Law

Islamic law differs from the Western concept of crime and responsibility.[284] Penalties in Islamic law distinguish between offences against God and offences against others. Thus, offenses addressed in the Qur'ān and *Sunna* are committed against God and include adultery, wrongful accusation of adultery, alcohol drinking, theft, and highway robbery. Their penalties, called *ḥudūd* (sing. *ḥadd*), are more severe.[285] Thus, unlawful intercourse is punished by stoning to death; false accusation of unlawful intercourse is punished by eighty lashes; drinking wine is punished by eighty lashes; theft is punished by cutting off the right hand, and the left foot for a second theft; and highway robbery is punished similar to theft if no homicide is involved, and by crucifixion or decapitation otherwise.[286] Since these punishments are based on direct statements in revealed texts and so are the right of God, they must be executed according to the letter with no possibility for pardon or amicable settlement.[287] Indeed, "not even the Prophet . . . had the discretion to diverge even slightly from the letter of the *ḥudūd* laws."[288] Moreover, Muslims must not err in their application, noting that "worse than inadvertently failing to apply God's clear law was to . . . enforce *ḥudūd* laws wrongfully against individuals whose culpability was not certain.[289]

Offences against humans, including homicide or bodily harm, fall under the punishment of *qiṣāṣ*/retaliation, a *lex talionis* private right of vengeance

284. Schacht, *Introduction to Islamic Law*, 187.

285. Hallaq, *Sharīʿa*, 310–11. Apostacy is a *ḥadd* only in the *Maliki* school, yet the punishment is almost the same, death, in all schools (*Ḥanafīs* replace death with life imprisonment for apostate women). Hallaq, *Sharīʿa*, 318–20.

286. Schacht, *Introduction to Islamic Law*, 175–81.

287. Schacht, 176.

288. Rabb, *Doubt in Islamic Law*, 29.

289. Rabb, 37. Rabb notes that capital punishment for apostacy and blasphemy is never specified in the Qur'an but was added by post-prophetic jurists, an addition that *Ḥanafīs* and *Shafi'is* do not recognize. She explains that the Qur'an indeed commands Muslim armies to fight enemy apostates during war, and Muhammad authorized killing enemy apostates who are actively engaged in war against Muslims. Post-prophetic jurists who added apostacy and blasphemy to the list of *ḥudūd* capital punishment extended those qur'anic/prophetic commands from war law to criminal law. Rabb, *Doubt in Islamic Law*, 33.

exercised at the demand of the victim or next of kin. Thus, while the offended party may demand an eye-for-eye retaliation against the offender, it may also waive retaliation for financial compensation (blood-money), or even gratis.[290] Though not specified in the foundational texts of Qur'ān and *Sunna* like *ḥudūd* laws, *qiṣāṣ* laws are nonetheless inferred from revealed texts.[291] Offences that fall neither under *ḥudūd* nor under *qiṣāṣ* are subject to a discretionary punishment of the judge, called *ta'zīr* (literally "reprimand" in Arabic) and are the most common.[292] *Ta'zīr* penalties are not addressed in revealed texts nor inferable from them.[293] The judge can only select the punishment discretionally from a list of punishments sanctioned by law, though his discretion does not extend to defining the act as offence, which has to be based on a legal text.[294] Understanding the penal law in Islam is important for understanding the standard of proof to be adopted in this study.

Standard of Proof

Convicting the defendant must be based on certainty and not mere probability.[295] What one finds in Islamic law texts is the simple term "certainty," yet it is akin to the common law term "certainty beyond reasonable doubt."[296] Judging with certainty beyond reasonable doubt is paramount, and uncertainty was met with high criticism and sensitivity.[297] The ideal way to arrive at certainty regarding a past event is through eyewitness testimony or else through "successive evidence or the reports of a group of people for whom it would be impossible to collude in telling a lie."[298] Where this is not easy to investigate, however, the court may base its decision on likely or presumed proof.[299]

Due to the severity and irrevocability of *ḥudūd* punishment and the difficulty in achieving the high degree of certainty, coupled with the fear of

290. Schacht, *Introduction to Islamic Law*, 177, 181.

291. Rabb, *Doubt in Islamic Law*, 31.

292. Hallaq, *Sharī'a*, 322–23.

293. Rabb, *Doubt in Islamic Law*, 31.

294. Kamali, *Shari'ah Law: An Introduction*, 189.

295. Al-Saleh, "Right of the Individual," 67.

296. Kamali, *Shari'ah Law: An Introduction*, 182. See also Sherif, "Generalities on Criminal Procedure," 8.

297. Samour, "Critique of Adjudication," 66.

298. Ibrahim, "Basic Principles," 23.

299. Ibrahim, 23.

erring and offending God's command, Islamic jurists sought ways of avoiding *ḥudūd*.[300] The Qur'ān demands the highest degree of certainty and imposes difficult conditions and strict procedures to accept proffered evidence and convict a defendant.[301] The demanded certainty should cover the factual, the legal, and the moral, a difficult task for early Muslim jurists who "obsessed over devising an 'economy of certainty'" that was epistemological rather than just institutional.[302] Jurists thus devised a "doubt canon" in which doubt carries a wider meaning than the concept of reasonable doubt in common law: "Rather than representing a principally fact-based standard of proof, the Islamic doctrine covered factual uncertainties, legal ambiguities, and even extralegal considerations [or] 'moral doubt.'"[303] This doctrine encompasses at once the equivalents of such American mitigating doctrines as the principle of legality,[304] the presumption of innocence, rule of lenity, *mens rea* requirements,[305] mistake, ignorance, and impossibility, and allows room for mercy.[306] *Ḥudūd* punishments were thus to be "averted at the existence of the slightest doubt."[307] In the second Hijri century Abū Ḥanīfa forged the principle in its famous form: *idra'ul-ḥudūd bil-shubuhāt*, or "avoid *ḥudūd* by resorting to doubt."[308] This being firmly established over the years of applying it, "Muslim jurists asserted that it must have issued from the Prophet himself."[309] Thus, evidence of confession could be retracted only in *ḥudūd* cases, and only in *ḥudūd* secondhand testimony and written communication between judges were inadmissible as evidence.[310] Moreover, in case of adultery, a larger number of witnesses, four men, must appear simultaneously in

300. Rabb, *Doubt in Islamic Law*, 37–38.

301. Schacht, *Introduction to Islamic Law*, 198.

302. Rabb, *Doubt in Islamic Law*, 5.

303. Rabb, 4–5.

304. The principle of legality (*nullum crimen sine lege*) states that "conduct does not constitute crime unless it has previously been declared to be so by the law." *Oxford Dictionary of Law*, 7th ed., s.v. "nullum crimen sine lege."

305. The *mens rea* (guilty mind) is "the state of mind that the prosecution must prove a defendant to have had at the time of committing a crime to secure a conviction." *Oxford Dictionary of Law*, 7th ed., s.v. "mens rea."

306. Rabb, *Doubt in Islamic Law*, 4–5.

307. Hallaq, *Sharīʿa*, 311.

308. Rabb, *Doubt in Islamic Law*, 49.

309. Rabb, 56.

310. Hallaq, *Sharīʿa*, 311.

court and give identical descriptions of the act in minute details, rendering the *ḥudūd* capital punishment "nearly impossible to establish."[311] As a result, such punishment can "very seldom properly be imposed, on account of the almost impossible standard of proof required."[312]

Most Christian apologists in the West do not claim absolute certainty, possible only in deductive logic and mathematics. They insist that in factual and historical matters the standard cannot exceed a degree of probability, whether the highest standard of "certainty beyond reasonable doubt" required in criminal cases,[313] or the lower standard of "preponderance of evidence" followed in civil cases.[314] To the average Muslim, however, the term "probability" denotes doubt, and the slightest doubt in *ḥudūd* cases can annul a verdict. Therefore, a Christian apologist working with Muslims would do better to replace the term "high probability" with the synonymous term "certainty beyond reasonable doubt." Moreover, in evaluating evidence, this study will not be bound by the unreasonable doubt-obsessive standard of *ḥudūd*, noting that its most stringent requirement, that of proving adultery, exceeds the standard of "certainty beyond reasonable-doubt" to the uncalled-for standard of "certainty beyond *unreasonable* doubt."

Burden of Proof

The burden of proof falls on the plaintiff, and the requirement of an oath on the party that denies.[315] This is based on the well-known *Ḥadīth* that "the burden of proof is on him who makes the claim, whereas the oath is on him who denies."[316] The plaintiff starts by presenting his or her case before the judge, who then asks the defendant if he or she acknowledges the claim. If the defendant does, the judge will give his judgment, and if he orshe denies, the plaintiff will be asked to present his or her evidence and the witnesses. If the plaintiff fails to do so, the judge will ask the defendant to take the oath

311. Hallaq, 311–12.

312. Anderson, *Islamic Law*, 85–86.

313. Montgomery, *Tractatus Logico-Theologicus*, 106.

314. Craig, *Reasonable Faith*, 55, 360.

315. Schacht, *Introduction to Islamic Law*, 191. The English law places the legal burden of proof in criminal cases upon the prosecution for both positive and negative allegations and throughout the entire trial, and in civil cases upon the party that asserts the claim. Keane and McKeown, *Modern Law of Evidence*, 91, 106.

316. Kamali, *Shariʿah Law: An Introduction*, 182.

of innocence, though in most cases it is the plaintiff who decides whether the defendant is to take oath.[317] Taking the oath is decisive: the judge will dismiss the case if the oath is taken, and will judge in favor of the plaintiff if the defendant declines to take the oath.[318] Deciding who is plaintiff and who is defendant is therefore decisive as the presumption of innocence goes in favor of the defendant's denial if the plaintiff fails to produce evidence or meet the restricting rules of evidence.[319] Indeed, the judge decides who is the plaintiff and who is the defendant only after he hears the case, and the roles may change during the hearing such as when the defendant denies a claim and makes a counterclaim.[320] Both litigants take the oath in cases where a distinction between plaintiff and defendant cannot be easily made.[321] Oath is demanded from the litigants, not from the witnesses.[322] If both parties give equal evidence, preference will be given to the party that does not enjoy the presumption of truth, i.e. the party that shoulders the burden of proof.[323]

The Gospels were written in the first century CE and describe the crucifixion and resurrection of Christ. Muhammad denied them through the Qur'ān some six centuries later, thus acting as a plaintiff who should shoulder the burden of proving his claim. Notwithstanding this basic rule, this study will assume that the Christian is the plaintiff who claims the crucifixion and resurrection events, and so carries the primary burden of proof. The burden passes to the other side whenever it gives an alternative account rather than simply denies a Gospel account.

Categories of Evidence

Evidence in Islamic law includes documentary evidence, eyewitness testimony, confession, expert witness testimony, circumstantial evidence, oath (for the denying party), and personal knowledge of the judge.[324] The degrees

317. Hallaq, *Sharīʿa*, 173.

318. Schacht, *Introduction to Islamic Law*, 190.

319. Schacht, 190–91.

320. Masud, Peters, and Powers, "Qadis and their Courts," 22–23.

321. Schacht, *Introduction to Islamic Law*, 191.

322. Schacht, 190.

323. Schacht, 195.

324. Daoud, *Al-qaḍā' wa al-daʿwa*, 2:5–9. See also the title page in al-Ḥossari, *ʿIlm al- qaḍā'*. Judicial evidence in the English law includes the three forms of oral evidence, documentary evidence, and real evidence or things. These cover such labels as testimony, hearsay evidence,

and conditions of the various types of evidence, however, vary across the four Sunnī schools. For example, all recognize witness testimony and confession as prime evidence. The *Ḥanafī*, *Mālikī*, and *Ḥanbalī* schools do not recognize the judge's personal knowledge while the *Shāfi ʿī* school accepts it.[325] The *Ḥanafī*, *Mālikī*, and late *Ḥanbalī* schools accept circumstantial evidence to varying degrees, whereas the *Shāfi ʿī* school rejects it.[326]

Types of evidence relevant to this study are documentary evidence, eyewitness testimony, confession, expert witness testimony, and circumstantial evidence. These will be expounded in their appropriate contexts in the following chapters.

---

confession, documentary evidence, real evidence, circumstantial evidence, expert opinion, and conclusive evidence. Adrian and McKeown, *Modern Law of Evidence*, 11, 402, 579.

325. Masud, Peters, and Powers, "Qadis and their Courts," 30.

326. Modarressi, "Circumstantial Evidence," 19. See also Jaradat, *Al-niḍhām* 212.

CHAPTER 3

Authenticity of the New Testament Documents

The two most important types of evidence under the Islamic law are eyewitness testimony and confession given before a court by living eyewitnesses and confessors. Christian testimonies and confessions, however, are available to us only in documentary form (the New Testament books), since the apostles and Evangelists are long deceased. Therefore, the first step towards the admission of these written testimonies and confessions as valid evidence is to demonstrate their authenticity, i.e. that they pertain to their purported witnesses and confessors. This authentication is especially important when addressing Muslims who staunchly believe that the extant Bible is largely corrupted.[1]

This chapter will first explore the admissibility status of the New Testament documents vis-à-vis the rules and principles of admissible evidence under the Islamic law, i.e. *de jure*. Given the undeveloped status of documentary evidence in Islamic law, however, the chapter will then examine the admissibility status of the New Testament documents *de facto*, i.e. vis-à-vis the historiographical principles used to defend the authenticity of the primary sources of Islamic law, the Qur'ān and *Sunna*. Like the New Testament documents, they themselves come in a documentary form that needs authentication before the Islamic law that is derived from them can be used to validate Christian evidence.

1. Qur'an 2:75, 3:78, 4:46, 5:13, 5:41. See also Crook, *New Testament*, 3, 13.

De Jure Admissibility of Documentary Evidence

Oral testimony and confession by living witnesses remain the foremost types of evidence in Islamic law. Jurists, especially in early Islam, viewed documents with suspicion and so rejected them as standalone evidence.[2] Ironically, the Qur'ān, the first source of Islamic law, itself underlines the significance of documentary evidence in an explicit injunction: "O, you who believe! When you contract a debt with one another for a term appointed, write it down. And let a scribe write between you justly and let not any scribe refuse to write as God taught him" (Qur'ān 2:282). Yet this injunction seems to have fallen short of convincing early jurists. Many of them understood it as mere recommendation, with a minority regarding it as mandatory.[3] Moreover, they noted that this injunction does not mean that documents replace oral testimony but merely aid memory.[4] Schacht argues that this is an important example of "several cases in which the early doctrine of Islamic law diverged from the clear and explicit wording of the Koran."[5]

The reason may be attributed to the lingering influence of the pre-Islamic primitive Arabian culture that largely relied on oral transactions, itself implicitly evidenced by the very qur'anic injunction to document. Evidentiary documentation was hardly the norm in the mostly illiterate seventh-century Arabian society, which was predominantly characterized by the primitive pastoral and nomadic lifestyle.[6] The first to establish an official *diwan* (registry) was the second caliph, Omar I (d. 23 AH/644 CE).[7] Yet judicial rulings and verdicts continued to be oral and were not documented until the second half of the first Hijri century when Islamic territory expanded from garrisons to large cities during the Umayyad dynasty.[8]

---

2. Schacht, *Introduction to Islamic Law*, 82. See also Ergene, "Evidence in Ottoman Courts," 487.

3. Shammouṭ, *Al-ithbāt al-qaḍā'ī*, 183. See also Daoud, *Al-ṣukouk*, 23–24.

4. Nasr, *Study Quran*, 122–23.

5. Schacht, *Introduction to Islamic Law*, 18–19.

6. Robinson, *Islamic Historiography*, 8.

7. Daoud, *Al-qaḍā' wa al-da'wa*, 2:183.

8. Al-Naif, *Al-bayyina al-qaḍā'iyya*, 280. See also Daoud, *Al-ṣukouk*, 36–37.

Documents between Theory and Practice

With time, however, Islamic jurists increasingly acknowledged the importance of documentation in protecting personal property, resolving disputes, guarding against invalid contracts, and removing doubt.[9] Jurists would point to the qur'anic injunction to document transactions and put forth prerequisites for the eligibility of a writer such as his skill, knowledge, integrity, and virtue.[10] To serve as evidence, a document must be handwritten and signed by its author, written in clear and unambiguous language, and be free from signs of forgery.[11] Jurists and rulers gradually came to realize that documents were indispensable in practice and so used them extensively, yet without the audacity to depart completely from the explicit rules of Islamic law. In practice, however, they resorted to such devices as the doctrines of *ḍarūra* (necessity) and *maṣlaḥa* (public interest) to validate the admission of documentary evidence where strict law did not otherwise help.[12] This is more so in modern times when documents are quite indispensable. For example, modern jurists sometimes provide printed forms that facilitate and address most practical needs: "these had only to be 'witnessed' in order to become legally valid."[13] Schacht notes that "theory continued to reason as if there were no documents but only the oral testimony of witnesses, possibly helped by private records of their own; practice continued to act as if documents were almost essential and the 'witnessing' only a formality to make them fully valid."[14]

In all these provisions, documents are viewed with suspicion even in the presence of evidence. The shape of handwriting, for example, is not decisive because the handwritings of two persons can be too similar to differentiate or can be imitated.[15] The general rule, therefore, is that a document can only aid memory; it cannot be admitted as evidence on its own except upon living witnesses testifying in person that the handwriting is indeed that of its purported writer.[16]

9. Daoud, *Al-qaḍā' wa al-da'wa*, 2:377.
10. Daoud, 2:379.
11. Daoud, 2:383–284.
12. Layish, "Shahādat Naql," 496–97.
13. Layish, 497.
14. Schacht, *Introduction to Islamic Law*, 82.
15. Al-Naif, *Al-bayyina al-qaḍā'iyya*, 273.
16. Schacht, *Introduction to Islamic Law*, 82, 193.

Rules for Admissibility of Documents

Documents addressed by Islamic law are broadly classified into official and non-official documents. Official documents issued by a sovereign are admissible if free from forgery, which is to be assumed if stamped and kept in safe repository.[17] Likewise, judicial documents issued by the judge and safely kept in court archives are admissible if free from signs of forgery, with no need for further evidence.[18] Correspondences between judges on cases common to both jurisdictions are also admissible as evidence,[19] except for criminal cases involving *ḥudūd*.[20] Admissibility is conditioned, though, upon the presence of opposing litigant and witnesses testifying that the sending judge is the writer of the letter.[21] Although a judge's seal was first acceptable, attestation by two witnesses became necessary later due to cases of seal forgery.[22] Moreover, such letter becomes invalid upon the death of the judge unless stated otherwise.[23]

An unofficial document written by the public is admissible if the writer attests that the handwriting is his or hers and arguably gives evidence of remembering that he or she wrote the document.[24] A document written by a deceased or absentee is not admissible due to the absence of eyewitnesses.[25] Nevertheless, the heir is bound by a document written by the deceased acknowledging a personal debt if the handwriting can be attributed to the deceased.[26] A confessional document is admissible if the writer testifies that the handwriting is his or hers.[27] A document written by a merchant acknowledging a debt is admissible if the merchant testifies that the handwriting is his or hers.[28] Letters exchanged between absent individuals are admissible as evidence against the writer once the writer's handwriting is attested, except

17. Daoud, *Al-qaḍā'wa al-da'wa*, 2:183, 188. See also al-Naif, *Al-bayyina al-qaḍā'iyya*, 278–79.

18. Daoud, 2:188. See also al-Naif, 308–9.

19. Al-Naif, *Al-bayyina al-qaḍāiyya*, 279–81.

20. Al-Nasafī, *Kanz al-daqā'iq*, 462.

21. Al-Nasafī, *Kanz al-daqā'iq*, 462. See also al-Kulaibouli, *Majma' al-anhur fī*, 230–32.

22. Aḥmad al-Ḥossari, *'Ilm al- qaḍā'*, 1:48.

23. Al-Nasafī, *kanz al-daqā'iq*, 463.

24. Daoud, *Al-qaḍā' wa al-da'wa*, 2:190, 192–93. See also al-Hossari, *'Ilm al-qaḍā'*, 47.

25. Daoud, 2:196–97. See also al-Naif, *Al-bayyina al-qaḍāiyya*, 285–86.

26. Daoud, *Al-ṣukouk*, 51.

27. Al-Naif, *Al-bayyina al-qaḍā'iyya*, 287–88.

28. Daoud, *Al-ṣukouk*, 48. See also al-Naif, 279–81.

in criminal cases involving *ḥudūd* and *qiṣāṣ*.[29] To be admissible, written contracts must be free from signs of forgery.[30] The general principle in Islamic law therefore is that documentary evidence is inadmissible unless attested by living witnesses.[31] The main reason is that such documents are subject to indistinguishable forgery of both handwriting and seal.[32]

The above shows that, in requiring the live testimony of writers to validate their documents, Islamic law addresses *contemporaneous* handwritten documents, be they official and judicial records, civil status records, commercial transactions, or personal letters. The legal debate revolves around ways of authenticating them, mainly through live testimony that they were handwritten by their writers. But the New Testament consists of *ancient* documents whose authors are long deceased, with no handwriting to recognize. The main difficulty is that, unlike the common law,[33] Islamic law rules are silent on the admissibility status of ancient documents. This renders its rules inapplicable to New Testament documents.

Broad Principles vs. New Testament Documents

Nevertheless, and for the purposes of this study, a *de jure* admissibility of the New Testament documents may be attempted through showing that they satisfy relevant *broad principles* that can be reasonably inferred from the above rules. This still excludes rules for recognizing the handwriting of unofficial documents, whether by the writer or others; biblical writers are deceased, and a document written by a deceased or absentee is generally not admissible, and thus no relevant principle seems derivable. Judicial documents may be more

---

29. Daoud, *Al-qaḍāʿ wa al-daʿwa*, 2:204–6. See also al-Naif, 292.

30. Al-Naif, *Al-bayyina al-qadaʾiyya*, 293–94.

31. Shammouṭ, *Al-ithbāt al-qaḍāʾī*, 186.

32. Shammouṭ, 187.

33. As in Islamic law, the primary evidence under the Anglo-American common law remains the testimony of living first-hand witnesses present in court. The difficulty of establishing admissibility of ancient documents whose writers are unavailable is solved in the US by the Ancient Documents Rule: a document is admissible if it is older than twenty years and its authenticity is established. This can be achieved through such means as showing that it lacks signs of forgery on its face and is of proper provenance. Broun, *McCormick on Evidence*, 509–10. The old common law rule of requiring a party relying on an admissible written statement to produce the original document is now replaced in the English law by accepting the production of a copy authenticated by the court as it deems sufficient. This especially applies when it can be proven that the original has been destroyed, lost, or is physically or legally impossible to produce. Keane and McKeown, *Modern Law of Evidence*, 280, 284.

relevant in that no attestation is required if they have no apparent signs of forgery and are kept in court repository. This corresponds to the American common law rule that "a writing [is] sufficiently authenticated if the party who offered it produced sufficient evidence that the writing . . . was unsuspicious in appearance, and further proved that the writing was produced from a place of custody *natural* for such a document [italics mine]."[34]

One can therefore argue that the New Testament documents satisfy this principle. The two most complete and accurate manuscripts of the New Testament, the mid-fourth century Codex Vaticanus and Codex Sinaiticus, were found in their natural places of custody, i.e. churches, the Vatican and the monastery of St. Catherine at Mount Sinai in Egypt respectively.[35] A Muslim would rightly object, however, that the Islamic law principle of custody differs substantially from the common law one in that the Islamic law principle is predicated on safe and *neutral* custody rather than *natural* custody and that the court is a safe and neutral place where forgery cannot possibly take place.[36] A church, however, is not neutral; it is the very suspect. It follows that both rules and principles related to documentary evidence in Islamic law are silent on the admissibility status of ancient documents, hence are inapplicable to the New Testament documents.

The Evidence of *Istiṣḥāb*

One secondary source of Islamic law is *istiṣḥāb*, the presumption of continuity of the existence or non-existence of something (a state of affairs, an attribute, or a rule of law) proven to have existed so in the past unless and until proven otherwise. It is a means of proof that may be used only when no other indications are available.[37] Continuity has several types. First, continuity of original absence whereby a fact or legal rule that did not exist in the past is presumed to continue so unless proven otherwise. Second, continuity of original presence, such as presuming that a debt proven to have existed in the past continues until repayment is proven. Third, continuity of a legal rule or principle. Fourth, continuity of attributes that existed in the past,

34. Broun, *McCormick on Evidence*, 509–10.

35. Bruce, *New Testament Documents*, 10.

36. Daoud, *Al-qaḍāʿ wa al-daʿwa*, 2:189.

37. Kamali, *Principles of Islamic Jurisprudence*, 384, 387–88.

such as purity of water, until the contrary is proven.[38] Both the *Shāfi'ī* and *Ḥanbalī* schools accept *istiṣḥāb* without qualification as a source of law. The *Ḥanafī* and *Mālikī* schools, however, accept only the fourth type of *istiṣḥāb*, the continuity of attributes.[39] Moreover, they accept it only "as a means of defense, that is, to defend the continued existence of an attribute, but not as a means of proving new rights and new attributes."[40]

According to the Qur'ān, God revealed the *Injīl*, or New Testament,[41] and sent it down to Jesus:

> We sent Jesus, son of Mary, in their footsteps, to confirm the Torah that had been sent before him: We gave him the Gospel with guidance, light, and confirmation of the Torah already revealed – a guide and lesson for those who take heed of God. So let the followers of the Gospel judge according to what God has sent down in it. Those who do not judge according to what God has revealed are lawbreakers (Qur'ān 5:46–47).

Under the *Ḥanafī* principle of *istiṣḥāb*, the attributes of the New Testament are supposed to continue unless proven otherwise. Indeed, the above example of purity of water drawn by Islamic scholar Muhammad Hashim Kamali corresponds neatly to our purpose: purity of the text of the New Testament. Moreover, in applying it to the textual purity of the New Testament, *istiṣḥāb* is used here within the *Ḥanafī* confines of defending the continued existence of an attribute, that of original textual purity rather than acquiring new attributes. Though this *de jure* validation of New Testament documents is valid, it is based on one secondary source. A stronger validation is *de facto*.

De Facto Admissibility of Documentary Evidence

As aforesaid, the Qur'ān and *Sunna* are the fundamental revealed sources of Islamic law. All other sources gain their legitimacy and authority from being derived or reasoned from these two sources. The Islamic law that is

38. Kamali, 387–88.

39. Kamali, 388.

40. Kamali, *Principles of Islamic Jurisprudence*, 388–89.

41. The Arabic term *Injīl* is a transliteration of the Greek word εὐαγγέλιον (gospel), but Muslims use it to refer to the New Testament.

contained in and derived or reasoned from the Qur'ān and *Sunna* views documents with suspicion and does not recognize them as evidence on their own without authentication by their authors in live testimony. It does not address the status of ancient documents. Yet the Qur'ān and *Sunna* are themselves ancient documents. Their authenticity cannot be evaluated by Islamic law per se. First, Islamic law does not address the evaluation of the authenticity of ancient documents. Second, even if the Islamic law addresses such authentication and they pass the authentication test, this would be circular reasoning.

The authenticity of the Qur'ān and *Sunna* should therefore be examined by instruments external to them and to the law contained in them or derived from them. They can therefore be examined *de facto*, based on the history and historiography of their compilation. This also provides the means to evaluate the authenticity of the New Testament on a par with the Qur'ān and *Sunna* vis-à-vis the same principles used to authenticate them. This provides the surest possible basis for establishing the authenticity of the New Testament, not by the law contained in the Qur'ān and *Sunna* or derived from them, but by the very principles that recognize their authenticity. The history, historiography, and authentication principles of the compilation of the Qur'ān and *Sunna* will be addressed separately, first for the Qur'ān, and then for the *Sunna*.[42]

Compilation and Authentication of the Qur'ān

The Qur'ān is the prime foundation of Islam and its supreme authority. Muslims believe that it is God's words dictated to Muhammad verbatim. They also believe that it is uncreated, i.e. that it existed with God eternally, beyond time, but was revealed to Muhammad in time.[43] While the traditional Islamic story of its compilation and authenticity tends to be neatly compatible with its absolute sanctity to Muslims, the views of Western scholarship range between extreme skepticism to a general approval.

Traditional Islamic story

Muslims believe that God revealed the entire text of the Qur'ān to Muhammad gradually, over a period of twenty-three years. His Companions memorized

42. Figure 2 on page 155 provides a roadmap that can help the reader keep track of the main argument of this chapter.

43. Nasr, *Study Quran*, xxiv.

various extensive parts of the Qur'ān by heart, and some of them wrote fragments of it on parchments, camel bones, and stone. When Muhammad died in 11 AH, however, no complete compilation of the Qur'ān authorized by him existed.[44]

The first caliph, Abū Bakr, started *ridda* (apostacy) wars against rebellious Arab tribes. With many Companions who memorized the Qur'ān killed during the *ridda* wars and the expectation that more would be killed, Abū Bakr ordered Zayd Ibn Thābet, a former scribe of the Prophet, to compile the entire corpus of the Qur'ān in writing before it was lost irretrievably. After Abū Bakr died in 13 AH, the qur'anic sheets were given to his successor, caliph ʿUmar I, who deposited them before his death in 23 AH with his daughter Ḥafṣa, one of the Prophet's widows.[45]

The third caliph, ʿUthmān (23–35 AH), however, received reports that Muslim armies who converged from various regions of the Muslim world on a battlefront had serious dissensions over differences in reciting the Qur'ān. Keen on containing the dispute, he ordered Zayd ibn Thābet, assisted by three Companions from the Prophet's tribe Quraysh, to compile an official collection of the Qur'ān based on the Ḥafṣa copy. In addition to the Ḥafṣa copy, he relied on memorized texts and texts written on parchments, bones, and stones. One main difference from the Ḥafṣa copy was that this second collection adopted the Quraysh dialect and recitation to the exclusion of all other variants. ʿUthmān then destroyed all other versions and dispatched four copies to the main centers of Islamic territory and kept one for himself. This collection, known as the ʿUthmanic codex, became the *textus receptus* for all Muslims. Although the variants were destroyed, scholars can still have some idea about their nature. This is because the ʿUthmanic codex still provides for the possibility of various citations due to its ancient Arabic script. Unlike modern Arabic, it consisted of homographs that lacked vowels and diacritics, thus accepting various pronunciations, inflections, passive or active tense, and differences in meaning. These, however, were of minor significance.[46]

44. Mattson, *Story of the Qur'an*, 94–96. Mattson is a Muslim convert.

45. Mattson, 94–96. Wael Hallaq believes that Abū Bakr's attempt to collect the Qur'an seems to have failed. Hallaq, *Origins and Evolution*, 33.

46. Mattson, *Story of the Qur'an*, 94–96.

A Shiite version

Shiite scholars challenge the traditional story of the collection of the Qur'ān in the sense that a master copy with a final approved reading, arrangement, and sequence was collected during the Prophet's lifetime and entrusted to ʿAlī Ibn Abī Ṭālib, who would become the fourth caliph. It was this master copy that formed the basis of the ʿUthmanic codex, which was but a reproduction of it. Shiites claim that recent philological, epigraphical, and textual critical studies support their argument.[47] They challenge the traditional view that the Qur'ān was not compiled in one definitive volume, a *textus receptus ne variteur*, during the Prophet's lifetime as amounting to an impossible negligence on his part to safeguard the integrity of the Qur'ān. They reject that the Qur'ān was revealed in seven modes or dialects though they acknowledge that the Companions may have written some copies in such dialects. They also reject the view that the five ʿUthmanic copies differed from each other.[48] Rather, they attribute any divergence in the ʿUthmanic codex to the absence of spelling conventions, minor differences in pronunciation and orthography, poor transcription due to the rough writing materials that rendered some words ambiguous, and the difficulties associated with oral dictation.[49]

Indeed, some Sunnī scholars subscribe to the view that qur'anic text and *Ḥadīth* indicate that Muhammad did compile a complete codex of the Qur'ān during his lifetime, but they stop short of recognizing ʿAlī Ibn Abī Ṭālib as its custodian. They attribute the variant readings to other compilations made by Companions and successors.[50] Others simply gloss over the ʿUthmanic controversial episode and present a neat, seamless story of Muhammad committing the entire Qur'ān to writing before his death, yet uncollated. They then picture caliph ʿUthmān's role as carrying out the merely mechanical task of compiling the uncollated segments into one corpus, with no mention of destroying variant copies, or even their existence.[51]

47. El-Wakil, "New Light," 409–10.
48. El-Wakil, 410–11.
49. El-Wakil, 418.
50. Rabb, "Non-canonical Readings," 86.
51. Abdel Haleem, "Qur'an and Hadith,", 21–22.

Arguments against authenticity

Western scholarship began to cast doubt on the traditional Islamic story towards the end of the nineteenth century. Prominent German scholar Ignaz Goldziher argued that the *Sunna*, which relates the history of the Prophet and his Companions, is quite inauthentic as a historical source. Goldhizer believes that it was fabricated with good intentions, what he calls "the pious fraud of the inventors of ḥadīth."[52] Friedrich Schwally reflected this on the history of the Qur'ān as told by *Sunna* and argued that the first collection by Abū Bakr never took place but was invented during ʿUthmān's caliphate to give authority to the ʿUthmanic codex and quell objections.[53] In defense of his thesis, he argued that the list of those killed in the Yamama battle included very few memorizers, and, at any rate, the Qur'ān is supposed to have been already written down by then. He also questioned the appointment of Zayd Ibn Thābet to head the ʿUthmanic collection committee when he had already done the job during Abū Bakr's caliphate. Moreover, he argued that the dissension concerning the variant readings of the Qur'ān is incompatible with the existence of an official copy authorized by Abū Bakr. Finally, he questioned the rationale of caliph ʿUmar entrusting Abū Bakr's caliphal copy to his daughter Ḥafṣa rather than formally to his successor.[54]

Following Schwally, Paul Casanova went further and claimed that the Qur'ān was not officially collected until the reign of the fifth caliph ʿAbd al-Malik (d. 86 AH).[55] His thesis was advanced by Alphonse Mingana who argued that the earliest *Ḥadīth* reports on collecting the Qur'ān came two hundred years after Muhammad, made no mention of Abū Bakr or ʿUthmān, and were full of contradictions. Mingana thus based his research on contemporary Syrian-Christian sources, such as records of a dispute between the Islamic leader ʿAmr Ibn al-Āṣ and the Patriarch of Antioch, a description of Muslims by an anonymous Christian in 60 AH, and chronicles by John Bar Penkaye in 70 AH. Mingana noted that neither these nor the writings of historians in the early second Hijri century made any mention of the Qur'ān

52. Goldziher, *Introduction to Islamic Theology*, 44.

53. Motzki, "Collection of the Qur'an," 6, 8.

54. Motzki, "Collection of the Qur'an," 7–8. Possession by Ḥafṣa prompted some to argue that she took part in editing the Qur'an. See Khan, "Did a Woman Edit," 174–216. For an opposing view see Anthony and Bronson, "Did Ḥafṣah bint ʿUmar," 93–125.

55. Motzki, "Collection of the Qur'an," 8.

or any sacred Islamic book. He concluded that an official collection of the Qur'ān did not exist before the first quarter of the second Hijri century.[56]

While most Western scholars rejected such radical skepticism,[57] Joseph Schacht's 1950 notable work, *Origins of Muhammadan Jurisprudence*, underpinned and revived Goldziher's skepticism in the historical reliability of *Ḥadīth* and influenced Western scholarship thenceforth.[58] Relying on Schacht, John Wansbrough took a radical stand in dating the collection of the Qur'ān from oral pericopes to the end of the second Hijri century. He concluded that the history of the Qur'ān's collection can no more be trusted, nor can the Qur'ān itself be trusted as reflecting Muhammad's utterances. He even questioned the Qur'ān's provenance in Hijaz during Muhammad's lifetime. Rather, it was invented at a later stage far north in the Fertile Crescent with the aim of retaking the Holy Land in Palestine.[59] Following suit, Michael Cook and Patricia Crone claimed that the entire edifice of early Islamic history is a fabrication. John Burton rejected the stories of both Abū Bakr and ʿUthmān's collections as fictitious attempts by Islamic legal scholars to justify legal doctrines that were not based on the Qur'ān. Burton, however, concluded that there was always one copy, the one compiled by Muhammad himself and is in use today.[60]

Other revisionist theories were built on linguistic considerations. Christopher Luxenberg, for instance, has concluded from the presence of Syriac loan words in the Qur'ān's supposedly pure Arabic text that the Qur'ān is a collection of translations and paraphrases of Syriac liturgies that were used in church services.[61]

In a most recent study on corrections in early qur'anic manuscripts, qur'anic scholar Daniel Brubaker notes that, though he started his research with eight hundred corrections, thousands more came up, with "no end in

56. Motzki, 8–10.

57. Motzki, 4.

58. Schacht, *Origins of Muhammadan Jurisprudence*.

59. Neuwirth, "Qur'an and History," 4–6.

60. Motzki, "Collection of the Qur'an," 11–12. See also John Burton's article in the *Encyclopedia of the Qur'ān*, s.v. "Collection of the Qur'ān."

61. Neuwirth, "Qur'an and History," 7, 10.

sight."[62] Such corrections include inserting, erasing, and replacing, whether by erasure overwriting, tape overwriting, or overwriting without erasing.[63] He excluded corrections made due to innocent scribal mistakes and focused on corrections that carry some agenda.[64] After analyzing thousands of corrections, he concluded that the variations in the consonantal text (*rasm*) cannot be explained away by the traditional story of being variant readings (*qirā'āt*) sanctioned by Muhammad to accommodate various tribal dialects. Rather, the *rasm* and the *qirā'āt* are independent phenomena where "in most cases the one is not affected in the least by the other."[65]

Brubaker suggests that these corrections denote greater flexibility in the qur'anic text than the traditional story admits.[66] They also show a gradual movement towards conformity with the text/*rasm* of the now-standard 1924 Cairo edition.[67] The fact that so many manuscripts were still undergoing corrections long after ʿUthmān's death casts doubt over the traditional claim that the ʿUthmanic codex produced perfect uniformity to the letter. This is coupled with the fact that we do not have an authentic ʿUthmanic manuscript, with the present ones dating long after.[68] Brubaker concludes that textual instability and differences over the ʿUthmanic standardized text persisted for several centuries after Muhammad's death. They exceeded the flexibility attributed to Muhammad to cater for variations in tribal and regional dialects though they were not substantive in terms of affecting meaning. Brubaker argues that such changes are consistent with Robinson's view that the qur'anic text, though substantially recognized before 40 AH, underwent further revisions until the reign of the Umayyad caliph ʿAbd al-Malik Ibn Marwān, i.e. around 80 AH, and even continued past that date.[69]

62. Brubaker, *Corrections in Early Qur'ān's*, xxiv. This book was published in July 2019 while work on this chapter was well underway.

63. Brubaker, 10.

64. Brubaker, 19–20.

65. Brubaker, 8–9. Readers interested in the Arabic script in the Qur'ān can refer to *Encyclopedia of the Qur'ān*, s.v. "Arabic Script."

66. Brubaker, 9.

67. Brubaker, 10.

68. Brubaker, 19.

69. Brubaker, 95–96.

Arguments in defense of authenticity

Leading Dutch scholar Harald Motzki argues that the above views tend to underestimate the historical value of Muslim traditions and promote instead other sources and personal theories on the provenance of the Qur'ān.[70] They differed widely in dating the canonical collection of the Qur'ān, from the time of Muhammad to the beginning of the third Hijri century, and their assumptions, conclusions, and methods are questionable.[71] Thus, Wansbrough bases his view "not on an investigation of the relevant traditions themselves," but on the strength of Schacht's views and his own form-analytical study.[72] Schwally makes assumptions based on universal recognitions by scholars when "unanimity on a scholarly issue is a temporary phenomenon," makes choices between alternatives arbitrarily, and fails to historically analyze the historical reports that he gathered.[73] Mingana makes questionable assumptions such as the unreliability of the orally transmitted *Ḥadīth*, and relies heavily on the *argumenta e silentio* as in concluding from the silence of contemporary Christian sources that there was no official collection of the Qur'ān.[74] Burton juxtaposes historical reports based on personal views that lack any historical analysis.[75]

Motzki then provides his own analysis using recent methodological developments. He dates the traditions that narrate the collection of the Qur'ān on the basis of both *matn* (content) and *isnād* (transmission bundles) and finds that *matn* changes with each *isnād* bundle. Identifying a common link in *isnād* bundles for Abū Bakr's collection, he concludes that what is deemed by Western scholars to be the earliest source on the collection of the Qur'ān is not al-Bukhārī (d. 256 AH). Rather, al-Bukhārī draws upon an earlier source, Ibn Shihāb al-Zuhrī, whose death in 124 AH means that the tradition was known by then.[76] In his analysis, he posits two possibilities that explain the common link: either the *isnād* bundles are real, or they are the result of systematic forgery. He rejects the latter as improbable, first, for lack of evidence

70. Motzki, "Collection of the Qur'an," 12.
71. Motzki, 12, 15.
72. Motzki, 11, 14–15.
73. Motzki, 13–14.
74. Motzki, 14.
75. Motzki, 15.
76. Motzki, 28–29.

that *isnāds* developed in this systematic manner. Second, the *isnād* bundle means that a great number of transmitters and collectors "must have used exactly the same procedure of forgery." Third, for the forgery scheme to work, forgers must have also changed the texts "very systematically" in addition to *isnāds*.[77] Motzki then reasons that, as al-Zuhrī must have received the tradition from earlier sources, reports on Abū Bakr's collection were in circulation towards the end of the first Hijri century rather than early third Hijri century as per Wansbrough and Burton.[78] Motzki concludes:

> We cannot be able to prove that the accounts on the history of the Qur'ān go back to eyewitnesses of the events which are alleged to have occurred. We cannot be sure that things really happened as is reported in the traditions. However, Muslim accounts are much earlier and thus much nearer to the time of the alleged events than hitherto assumed in Western scholarship.[79]

German scholar and Oxford professor of Islamic studies Nicolai Sinai tends to agree. He acknowledges that "the most serious rival of the traditional dating of the standard *rasm* [ancient qur'anic bare consonantal Arabic text] would at present seem to be the hypothesis that the Quranic text, in spite of having achieved a recognizable form by 660, continued to be reworked and revised until c. 700."[80] His analysis reveals, however, that "neither the epigraphic nor the literary evidence examined is incompatible with the conventional dating of the Quranic text."[81] He notes in his historical-critical study of the Qur'ān that "a very considerable portion of the qur'anic text was around, albeit not without variants, by the 650's [30's AH]." This is within some two decades of Muhammad's death. He bases his statement on radiocarbon tests of some early manuscripts of parts of the Qur'ān. Thus, a palimpsest discovered in a Yemeni mosque gives 95 percent probability that it is older than 660 CE (40 AH). A fragment kept at Tübingen University Library gives 95 percent probability that it dates between 649 and 675 CE (28 and 55 AH). Another manuscript kept at Berlin State Library is dated between 606 and 652 CE

77. Motzki, 27–28.

78. Motzki, 31.

79. Motzki, 31.

80. Sinai, "When Did the Consonantal ," 276.

81. Sinai, 273.

(-17 and 31 AH). Finally, a fragment in Birmingham dates between 568 and 645 CE (-54 and 24 AH).[82]

Another evidence on which Sinai draws is the early consensus among Muslims that relates the standard version of the Qur'ān to caliph ʿUthmān. Such consensus cannot be dismissed as occasioned after the late first Hijri century when Islamic territory had expanded and suffered divisions. Sinai notes that Muslim scholars do acknowledge the controversy surrounding ʿUthmān's version and the accusation that he burned God's book, which would suggest that the act is not a legend, but actually took place. Moreover, differences have to do with the legitimacy of the ʿUthmanic standardization rather than with whether the event of standardization took place or not.[83]

Internal evidence also supports an early finalization of qur'anic text. The Qur'ān is silent on epochal developments that took place between 10 and 70 AH, such the Islamic northward expansion to the Fertile Crescent and the ensuing civil wars. Moreover, rather than calculated late redaction, the Qur'ān shows signs of hurried stabilization of its text as seen in several anomalies vs. classical Arabic.[84] A study of the qur'anic text, Sinai notes, reveals that

> it seems unlikely that the Qur'an's plentiful contextual references could merely be a fallout of calculated literary staging by authors who were posthumous to Muhammad: it is precisely because these references are so allusive and reliant on prior acquaintance with the events that are talked about that the scriptural passages in question are best placed in the midst of these events, wherever they unfolded, rather than as a later attempt at reimagining them from a historical distance. For in the latter case, we would have expected the Qur'anic texts to make at least some effort to provide a structured narrative of Muhammad's career.[85]

Internal evidence also shows signs of coherence. In determining whether a *sūra* (qur'anic chapter) is coherent or else built up from former disparate parts, Sinai shows with an illustration from *sūra* 37 that "it is replete with internal echoes and cross-references, it displays a transparent macrostructure, and

82. Sinai, *Qur'an: A Historical-Critical Introduction*, 46.

83. Sinai, 46–47.

84. Sinai, 47.

85. Sinai, 51.

its concatenation of ideas is generally organic and logical."[86] This is despite it lacking a unified literary form and jumping from one topic to another. He concludes that, with such evidence, the burden of proof falls on the one who denies its coherence.[87] Nevertheless, he notes that showing coherence in longer *sūras* is more complicated and leaves probable the possibility of secondary expansion.[88] Though he does not exclude the possibility that the qur'anic text may have undergone "a limited degree of expansion, reshaping, and updating," he stresses that such changes must have happened early, within a few years of Muhammad's death.[89]

Canadian Islamic scholar and Muslim convert Ingrid Mattson admits that the dating of the earliest writing of the Qur'ān is controversial due to the scarcity of manuscripts from the first Hijri century. Yet some information can be gleaned from Islamic traditions, though only after ascertaining their authenticity through sound historiographical examination.[90] She also acknowledges that many believe the variants were not only a matter of pronunciation of letters and recitations, but also synonymous terms of the different tribal dialects. She notes, however, that these variants "yield mostly insignificant differences in meaning, although sometimes their differences allow a more nuanced understanding of certain passages."[91] She draws attention to the Muslim belief that "it was the Prophet himself who validated this diversity – a diversity that did not lead to significant divergent meanings, but affirmed the distinct linguistic patterns of various tribes and peoples."[92] She also admits that the ʿUthmanic codex did not eliminate all these variants since, in addition to the limited variants caused by the homographs, "the consonantal script allowed for significant ambiguity with respect to the short vowels and inflections, among other things."[93] Nevertheless, she notes that the high degree of textual consistency demonstrated by extensive scholarly analysis points in the direction of an accurate oral and written preservation

86. Sinai, 92.
87. Sinai, 92.
88. Sinai, 97.
89. Sinai, 51.
90. Mattson, *Story of the Qur'an*, 29.
91. Mattson, 96.
92. Mattson, 100.
93. Mattson, 96.

of the Qur'ān. She also notes that believing Muslims deny the existence of even the smallest mistake in the text and admits that this cannot be proven scientifically but accepted upon the authority of God's promise: "Truly it is We Who have sent down the Reminder [i.e. the Qur'ān] and surely We are its Preservers" (Qur'ān 15:9).[94]

Mattson rejects the theories of Wansbrough for four reasons. The first is that Wansbrough "must assume the existence of a widespread conspiracy among second and third Hijri century Muslims to conceal the truth. That such a conspiracy could be perfectly concealed from the gaze of history and achieved among Muslims who, by the second century, were deeply divided by sectarian identities and partisan politics is untenable." Second, Mattson refers to Motzki, who has shown (as discussed above) that Wansbrough was wrong in dating the earliest traditions on collecting the Qur'ān to the late second Hijri century. Rather, the fact that they were formally taught before the end of the first century means that they were in circulation before then and that "substantially incorrect statements about the Qur'an could not have withstood public scrutiny at such an early period." Third, she refers to the discovery of more early manuscripts and numismatic evidence in favor of the Qur'ān. Fourth, she refers to scholarly work on the variant recitations and slight graphic differences in early Arabic text of the Qur'ān, which shows that their consistency is evidence of an "early and accurate simultaneous oral and written preservation of the Qur'an." The combined oral-written transmission avoids oral transmission errors, such as wrong hearing and forgetfulness, and copyists' errors in written transmission.[95]

Another defense comes from Angelika Neuwirth, prominent German scholar of qur'anic studies. She invites scholars to analyze the text of the Qur'ān itself rather than the circumstances of its formation because its history "does not start with canonization but is inherent in the text itself where not only contents but also form and structure can be read as traces of a historical or a canonical process.[96] She notes that

> the Qur'anic text as we have it, the *textus receptus*, betrays a peculiar composition. The sequence of the single text units does

94. Mattson, 98–99.

95. Mattson, 98.

96. Neuwirth, "Qur'an and History," 16.

> not follow any logical let alone theological principle, yet the division into suras, most of them evidently genuine literary units, is maintained. This is at once a conservative and a theologically disinterested arrangement of the text which suggests that the redaction was carried out without elaborate planning, perhaps in a hurry, anyway before prophetological conceptions like that underlying the *sīra* had emerged.[97]

She concludes that the text must have been finalized before the early conquests and that "the traditional scenario of the ʿUthmanic redaction, the hypothesis that the remnants of the Prophet's recitations were collected soon after his death to form the corpus we have before us, is thus plausible though not possible to prove."[98]

In a similar vein, Islamic scholar Fazlur Rahman responds to Wansbrough's assertion that the Qur'ān was composed of several traditions after the time of Muhammad and notes that "there is a distinct lack of historical data on the origin, character, evaluation, and personalities involved in these 'traditions.'" He also notes that the best response to Wansbrough is the Qur'ān itself.[99]

More recently, Islamic scholar Raymond Farrin argues that the authenticity of the Qur'ān is attested by the structural continuity between each *sūra* and the next, as well as the overall consistency of the important doctrine of *jihād* throughout the Qur'ān, which suggest a single author.[100] He also argues convincingly that the Qur'ān must have been written down during the life of the Prophet; if the Qur'ān urges Muslims to write down debts in order to ensure full repayment, "could it be that something so important as the Qurʾān was not written also?"[101] Finally, Farrin appeals to Occam's razor in defending a simple Islamic story of assembling the Qur'ān "from a complete text left at the Prophet's death, to a proliferation of copies in the years after, to a recognition of the existence of variants and a correction of them during the caliphate of ʿUthmān, to a destruction of the original during the early

97. Neuwirth, 10–11.

98. Neuwirth, 11.

99. Rahman, *Major Themes of the Qur'an*, xvii–xviii.

100. Farrin, "Composition and Writing," n.p.

101. Farrin, n.p.

Umayyad period." He concludes that "using Ockham's razor, one cuts away more involved explanations of how the Qur'ān came to us."[102]

New Testament Authenticity vs. Qur'ān Authenticity

This section will draw on the above arguments that Muslim and sympathetic Western scholars employ to defend the authenticity of the Qur'ān and will apply them to the evaluation of the relative authenticity of the New Testament. It will ignore the aforesaid liberal Western critiques against the reliability of the Qur'ān yet will highlight and address liberal Western critiques against the New Testament, usually quoted by Muslim scholars in their polemics. Unreasoned dogmatic defenses on both sides will also be ignored.[103]

Objective historical analysis

Pro-Muslim scholars argue that any scholarly evaluation should be based on objective historical analysis of the traditions themselves rather than on theories advanced by others even if they are widespread, or on personal views and presuppositions, or on arbitrary choices between alternatives.[104] Scholars cannot insist on underestimating the value of long-held Muslim historical traditions.[105] They cannot ignore available evidence, such as consensus among Muslim scholars in early Islam.[106]

Christians would first respond that, when it comes to the New Testament, Muslim scholars hardly follow this principle consistently. First, their insistence that the Bible has been changed is based a priori on the Qur'ān,[107] that is, on authority rather than on scientific grounds, and on the failure of the New Testament to predict the coming of Muhammad and its sharp theological and factual differences with the Quran.[108] Second, they largely base their polemic on the arguments of liberal Western New Testament scholarship

---

102. Farrin, n.p. For more on the history of the authenticity of the Qur'ān see *Encyclopedia of the Qur'ān*, s.v. "Ḥadīth and the Qur'ān."

103. For each category, the first paragraph will briefly state the Islamic principle, followed in the succeeding paragraphs by application to the New Testament.

104. Motzki, "Collection of the Qur'an," 13–15.

105. Motzki, 12.

106. Sinai, *Qur'ān*, 46–47.

107. Qur'an 2:75, 3:78, 4:46, 5:13, 5:41.

108. Greifenhagen, "Scripture Wars," 31.

as undisputable evidence. In both cases, they hardly base their conclusions on their own analyses employing sound historiographical scholarship and objective evidence.

For example, Islamic scholar and Muslim convert Jay R. Crook refers in his polemic against the New Testament exclusively to liberal Western scholars,[109] particularly Bart Ehrman, as if their scholarship is all there is: "Modern scholarship is virtually unanimous in the opinion that none of the authors of the gospels were actual observers of any part of the life of Jesus."[110] He then confidently asserts that "textual criticism has done its work, and content criticism has done its work. There is no going back. It is increasingly difficult to point to a passage in the gospels and say with confidence that this is what Jesus actually said, even in translation."[111] He never interacts with conservative Western scholars vis-à-vis his liberal sources or even acknowledges that such scholarship exists. His target is clearly not the scientific quest for true history but rather "to get behind the New Testament and to observe . . . a Jesus who would, Muslims confidently feel, be in harmony with the Jesus found in the Quran."[112] This runs against calls on anti-Islamic scholarship by Muslim scholars and sympathetic Western scholars to deal with matters of history in a scholarly manner that is based on historiographical analysis.

In appealing to liberal Western scholars in their common attack against the reliability of the New Testament, Muslim scholars prove to be inconsistent in yet another aspect.[113] Starting with Julius Wellhausen,[114] many of these liberal Western scholars who attack the New Testament also attack the authenticity of the Qur'ān and *Sunna*, mostly employing the same presuppositions, principles, and methodologies. This study is aware, however, that Christian scholars can easily fall into the same trap of inconsistency. Therefore, while

109. Such as Rudolf Bultmann, Bart Ehrman, Robert J. Miller, Robin Griffith-Jones, Hyam Maccoby, Burton L. Mack, etc.

110. Crook, *New Testament*, 117.

111. Crook, 118.

112. Crook, 118.

113. One scholar notes that "some Muslims have taken [Western liberal] historical-critical scholarship as confirmation of the doubts the tradition has long harboured about the integrity of the Bible, and this seems to have provided the warrant for the further assumption that the Qur'ān itself need not be subjected to the purgative fires of historical criticism. This [is a] manifest double standard." Howard, "'Who Do You Say,'" 305.

114. Humphreys, *Islamic History*, 82.

mentioning some of the liberal Western anti-Islamic views, this study will adopt the views of notable pro-Muslim scholars yet exclude dogmatic writers who merely base their unreasoned argument on authority rather than on historiographical evidence. Indeed, the Christian faith has nothing to lose in recognizing the authenticity of the Qur'ān and *Sunna*. Understandably, this cannot be reciprocated by Islam. A recognition of the authenticity of the New Testament, which the Qur'ān recognizes as God's revealed Word before its alleged corruption, would necessarily amount to an implicit recognition of the truthfulness of the Christian claims about the deity of Christ, his crucifixion, and his resurrection.

The onslaught of liberal scholarship on the reliability of the New Testament, ever since modernity, reached its zenith with the Jesus Seminar that considered a scant 18 percent of the sayings of Jesus and 16 percent of his deeds recorded in the Gospels as reasonably authentic.[115] Yet such extreme liberal scholarship is hardly scholarly. New Testament scholar Gary Habermas notes that the Jesus Seminar seldom gives reasons for their assertions, which also suffer from many informal logical fallacies such as "a priori preaching," question-begging arguments, and genetic fallacies.[116] Nevertheless, conservative Christian scholarship took the liberal challenge seriously. Never content to offer general answers, it made every effort to follow a scientific approach to vindicate Scripture based on historiographical analysis. For example, the Gospels were written within a few decades after Christ, with two of the authors being direct eyewitnesses and two indirect witnesses. While one can rightly claim that this period is too short for legend to creep into the records, leading New Testament scholar Craig Blomberg makes the conditioned acknowledgment that this is a "sufficient scenario for errors and distortions to creep into their accounts, if other factors conducive to such changes were present."[117]

Conservative scholars have thus examined all kinds of criticisms initiated by liberal scholarship, whether form, source, textual, redaction, or literary, to ensure that no such "other factors" exist. Indeed, almost all conclude that such examination has enriched their understanding of the New Testament

115. Blomberg, *Historical Reliability*, 17.

116. Habermas, *Historical Jesus*, 138.

117. Blomberg, *Historical Reliability*, 20.

and provided surer grounds for trusting its authenticity. Originally devised to discredit the historical reliability of the Gospels, these new criticisms have provided new methods that proved to be great tools to corroborate such reliability.[118]

Christianity is based on God's acting in history and so sees history as necessarily vindicating its claims. It encourages seekers to examine the historical evidence, confident that such evidence and rational arguments produce a rational faith founded on factual grounds rather than an irrational leap in the dark.[119] In carrying out their scholarship, therefore, Christian scholars confidently strive to be scientific. Blomberg states at the outset of his major work, *The Historical Reliability of the Gospels*: "I wear my historian's hat, not my Christian believer's hat in this project. If readers wish to reject my conclusions, let them show how my arguments fail on historical grounds rather than simply accusing me of presupposing my conclusions."[120] He confidently feels that the determined sceptics' views are "novel and aberrant in comparison with the vast majority of people who have carefully examined the issues throughout church history."[121] Another noted scholar, Birger Gerhardsson, makes a similar statement: "I shall approach the problem as one would in secular historiography."[122] New Testament scholar John Wenham, in his attempt to redate the Synoptic Gospels, acknowledges that some readers may be looking for more specific dates and so responds that "the best scholarship knows that our nearest approach to truth comes when we try to go as far as the evidence leads, but no further."[123]

This approach is in stark contrast with liberal scholarship, mostly represented by the Jesus Seminar scholars, that is gladly quoted by Muslim scholarship. Few as they are, Gerhardsson notes that they "eagerly foist their views upon the public as representative of true scholarship applied to the Gospels, while failing to pay any attention to the vast majority of mainstream critical scholars who disagree with them – indeed, not even hinting that such scholars

118. Blomberg, 49.

119. Blomberg, 36.

120. Blomberg, 23.

121. Blomberg, 23.

122. Gerhardsson, *Reliability of the Gospel*, 2–3.

123. Wenham, *Redating Matthew, Mark*, 244.

exist."[124] In similar vein, Blomberg laments the "unfortunate tendency in modern scholarship to prefer an ancient testimony to that of the Gospels when it seems to conflict with them while "refusing potential corroboration from extra-biblical sources unless they pass the most stringent tests of historicity."[125]

The landscape is gradually yet undeniably changing, however, though unacknowledged by the Jesus Seminar scholars or, for this matter, Muslim scholars who continue to quote them uncritically. Blomberg notes that "with each passing decade since the 1950s, when a group of mostly German scholars, discontented with the wholesale historical scepticism of a previous era, embarked on 'the new quest for the historical Jesus,' more and more of the Gospel tradition has been acknowledged as genuine."[126] In what is known as the third quest of the historical Jesus, "a large number of scholars, and by no means just conservative Christian ones, have been growing in their confidence in how much we can know about the Jesus of history and in how reliable the New Testament Gospels are."[127]

Textual purity

Muslims pride themselves that the Qur'ān, God's eternal word, was mechanically revealed to Muhammad, word by word, with Muhammad acting no more than its "passive recipient" who then faithfully transmitted it verbatim.[128] They admit that, due to the appearance of variant recitations of the Qur'ān, caliph ʿUthmān (23–35 AH) destroyed all variant copies and canonized what he believed was the authentic text. Many also admit that the variants were not limited to pronunciation of letters and recitations, but also synonymous terms that varied with the different tribal dialects. Yet they note that these differences have insignificant effect on meaning, though sometimes they can have nuances in understanding certain passages.[129] Moreover, this diversity was sanctioned by the Prophet himself in recognition of the distinct dialects of the various tribes.[130] While the ʿUthmanic codex precluded some of these

124. Gerhardsson, *Reliability of the Gospel*, ix.
125. Blomberg, *Historical Reliability*, 247.
126. Blomberg, 310.
127. Blomberg, 17.
128. Abdel Haleem, "Qur'an and Hadith," 20–21.
129. Mattson, *Story of the Qur'an*, 96.
130. Mattson, 100.

variants, its homographs and consonantal script did not eliminate all possible variances.[131] Despite these variances, extensive scholarly analysis has demonstrated a high degree of textual consistency, which points towards an accurate oral and written preservation of the Qur'ān.[132] These scholars admit that absolute authenticity and inerrancy of the extant Qur'ān, so basic to Muslim dogma, cannot be proven scientifically but rather accepted on the authority of qur'anic assurance that God preserves the text (Qur'ān 15:9).[133]

The Christian concept of textual purity is different. The New Testament is the inerrant Word of God who, rather than mechanically dictating it, inspired it through human agency.[134] In this he utilized the writers' conventions such that what they wrote is what God himself wanted to be included in his Scripture.[135] Geisler and Nix thus define inspiration as "that mysterious process by which the divine causality worked through the human prophets without destroying their individual personalities and styles to produce divinely authoritative and inerrant writings."[136] In this process, God may express the same truth in various wordings under the direction and guidance of his Holy Spirit, as evident in the parallels of the Synoptics. Rather than mechanical dictation, Wenham notes that "it is better to imagine careful instruction (with particular attention paid to Jesus's words), given in an atmosphere of spontaneity – the freedom of the Spirit accompanying fidelity of witnesses."[137] In other words, such freedom was sanctioned by God himself.

Moreover, God gives no promise of an inerrant process of copying and translating; copyists and translators do err.[138] As noted by Daniel Wallace, the explanation of C. S. Lewis is illuminating here: "The moment [the miracle] enters [nature's] realm it obeys all her laws. Miraculous wine will intoxicate, miraculous conception will lead to pregnancy, inspired books will suffer all the ordinary processes of textual corruption, miraculous bread will be

131. Mattson, 96.

132. Mattson, 98.

133. Mattson, 99.

134. Geisler and Nix, *General Introduction*, 36.

135. Geisler and Nix, 37–39.

136. Geisler and Nix, 39.

137. Wenham, *Redating Matthew, Mark*, 200.

138. Wallace, "Lost in Transmission," 39–40.

digested."[139] Nonetheless, variances are limited in number and marginal in significance so that they do not affect any major doctrine. Thus, "even when the accuracy of a reading in the original *text* cannot be known with 100 percent accuracy, it is possible to be 100 percent certain of the *truth* preserved in the texts that survive."[140]

If Muslims see the ʿUthmanic codex as securing textual purity and preventing forgery, it must be noted that the New Testament, with its many early translations and the multitude of manuscripts that were circulated throughout the Roman Empire, made any attempt at changing it much more difficult to succeed. Wallace refers to B. F. Westcott's words: "A classical text which rests finally on a single archetype is that which is open to the most serious suspicions."[141] Foremost liberal scholar Bart Ehrman throws back the charge at the New Testament: a dominant party in the patristic era conquered all other views and affixed its version of the New Testament as orthodoxy.[142] In response, Wallace notes that Ehrman is applying to Christianity an alien Muslim phenomenon, i.e. ʿUthmān's burning of all variants of the Qur'ān to impose his own version. In contrast, no evidence shows that any church authority destroyed inaccurate copies of the New Testament.[143] To the contrary, evidence shows that defective copies and heretical scriptures were stored in jars or buried near a cemetery and never destroyed because they bear the name of God.[144] In another creative yet unsupported claim, Muslim scholar Jay Crook argues that Roman authorities regularly destroyed Christian writings during the first three persecution centuries, yet because there were many copies, "the more popular heterodox works survived this period largely intact."[145]

Ehrman uses as evidence of the scale of corruption the number of variants in New Testament manuscripts which ranges between three and four hundred thousand, more than any Greek or Latin work. Yet this is misleading. The reason for the great number of variants is that the number of manuscripts of the New Testament is exceedingly greater than that of any other work.

139. Lewis, *Miracles*, 95.

140. Geisler and Nix, *General Introduction*, 44.

141. Wallace, "Lost in Transmission," 37–38.

142. Wallace, 34.

143. Wallace, 34–35.

144. Wallace, 35.

145. Crook, *New Testament*, 84.

The more the manuscripts, the more the variants; if we have just one manuscript, there would be no variants.[146] Moreover, an increase in the number of manuscripts also means a proportional increase in sources for correcting the errors.[147] Considering this fact, the real number of errors remains minimal, with textual accuracy of the New Testament exceeding 99 percent, more than any other great classical work of antiquity.[148]

The main debate between conservative and liberal scholars, however, is not so much about the nature of the variant texts as about the interpretation of their origins and significance.[149] In addition to the small number of variants, their significance is so small that it has very little effect on historical facts or matters of doctrine and practice.[150] Variants fall into four categories, "spelling differences and nonsense errors," which are obviously solved; "minor differences that do not affect translation or that involve synonyms," which are easily detectable; "differences that affect the meaning of the text but are not viable," where the error can be readily dismissed; and, by far the smallest, "differences that both affect the meaning of the text [to a limited degree] and are viable," yet without affecting any tenet of faith.[151]

During a dialogue between Wallace and Ehrman, whom Wallace describes as the leader of scornful attacks by liberal scholars,[152] a student asked Ehrman: "Dr. Ehrman, at this point in scholarship, does the earliest reconstructible form of the text portray an orthodox understanding of the resurrection and the deity of Christ?" Ehrman interestingly responded: "I don't think that the texts affect those views one way or another. My own view is that the biblical authors thought Jesus was physically resurrected from the dead but that most of the biblical authors did not think Jesus was God. . . . But I don't think in most cases that is affected by textual variations."[153]

146. Wallace, "Lost in Transmission," 28.

147. Bruce, *New Testament Documents*, 14.

148. Geisler and Nix, *General Introduction*, 405, 408.

149. Wallace, "Lost in Transmission," 21.

150. Bruce, *New Testament Documents*, 14–15.

151. Wallace, "Lost in Transmission," 40–43.

152. Wallace, 19. The dialogue took place in 2008 at the New Orleans Baptist Seminary.

153. Stewart, *Reliability*, 56.

Wallace notes that Ehrman gives the misleading impression that transmission of the New Testament text resembles the telephone parlor game.[154] The New Testament text, however, unlike the game, is passed on through manuscripts rather than orally, with multiple lines of transmission. Moreover, rather than the last person in the parlor row determining the result, several sources closer to the first century are available for verification, let alone the patristic writers who were continually checking the text. Indeed, one fourth-century manuscript is more accurate than all second-century manuscripts.[155] Despite his severe attacks, however, Ehrman seems to contradict himself when he admits the possibility of reconstructing the original text "with reasonable accuracy."[156] The variations between parallels in the Synoptics are too limited to justify the liberals' claim that the process of transmission was fluid. They "are not of the nature they would have been had originally elastic material been formulated in different ways."[157] To illustrate, two of the most accurate manuscripts, P^{75} and Codex Vaticanus (referred to as B), have "incredibly strong agreement," though P^{75} is 100 to 150 years older yet is not the ancestor of B. Both have a common ancestor. Any text taken from the combination of these two manuscripts is thus traced back to the early second century.[158]

Another fact worth mentioning is that paraphrasing was the norm in the ancient world such that the historian was within his rights to use whatever words he wanted if they convey the same meaning, i.e. *ipsissima vox* (actual voice) rather than *ipsissima verba* (actual words).[159] Blomberg notes that "there is every reason to believe that many of the sayings and actions of Jesus would have been very carefully safeguarded in the first decades of the church's history, not so lavishly as to hamper freedom to paraphrase, explain, abbreviate and rearrange, but faithfully enough to produce reliable accounts."[160] Yet one should consider that not all variations between apparent parallels

---

154. In a round of some ten or twenty children, the first child whispers in the ear of the second a short story or statement. The second whispers it to the third, and so on until the last child who then says it aloud, with laughter bursting at how much multiple transmission changed it from the original story.

155. Wallace, "Lost in Transmission," 31–33.

156. Wallace, 23–24.

157. Gerhardsson, *Reliability of the Gospel*, 54.

158. Wallace, "Lost in Transmission," 33.

159. Blomberg, *Historical Reliability*, 157.

160. Blomberg, 62.

denote free paraphrasing or a later redaction. Rather, many are attributable to the fact that Jesus repeated the same saying in different wordings in more than one setting. Other variants are attributable to instances of translating to Greek from Aramaic, the language spoken by Jesus.[161] Moreover, the Evangelists or their direct sources were inspired apostles who had their own observations, experiences, and memories, and so each had the authority to include his unique contribution. The Holy Spirit was at work in them, reminding and selecting the words that he wanted to be include in his Word (John 14:26).[162]

A recent intensive technical analysis carried out by experts on the early text of the New Testament reveals that, regarding Matthew, the text was "transmitted across 100 or more years without any change in meaning" despite limited fluidity in transmission. Moreover, it represents "a pure line of transmission from the earliest time, in contrast to some scholars, who think it represents an attempt to establish a controlled text at the end of the second century after the text had developed freely."[163] On Mark, examination of papyri from the fourth century shows that "a good case can be made that our fourth-century witnesses represent copies of a well preserved early text of Mark."[164] On Luke, examination of second-century papyri shows that the early papyri "reflect a good, even excellent transmission," with the textual variations not indicating textual chaos.[165] Regarding John, examination of early manuscripts, all originating in Egypt, concludes that, as a general rule, surviving papyri are "based on a text that is close to the original as it is presented hypothetically in NA [Nestle-Aland Greek NT]." The examination also concludes that "there is no evidence as to a deliberate, conscious, [*sic*] attempt to interpret or alter it. Most variants arise through negligence due to the speed the copy was produced and lapses of attention. The differences between the texts, if they were ever perceived by the scribes or hearers, were insignificant."[166] The examiner further notes that "the role the texts played in the liturgy makes one think the communities knew these texts well, accepted them, copied them, respected

161. Gerhardsson, *Memory and Manuscript*, 334–35. See also Blomberg, 69.

162. Blomberg, 73.

163. Wasserman, "Early Text of Matthew," 104.

164. Head, "Early Text of Mark," 120.

165. Hernández, "Early Text of Luke," 138.

166. Chapa, "Early Text of John," 154–55.

them, and had no desire to alter them. The Gospel of John belongs, without a doubt, to this group of texts."[167]

Dating evidence

Muslim scholars acknowledge that the dating of the earliest writing of the Qur'ān is challenging due to the dearth of manuscripts from the first Hijri century. Nevertheless, they point to reports from Islamic tradition which, after subjecting them to sound historiographical examination, can shed some light.[168] Positive evidence (apart from manuscripts, which will be addressed separately) and the absence of evidence to the contrary provide undeniable clues to the dating of the Qur'ān. For example, the fact that traditions about the Qur'ān were formally taught throughout the Islamic territories before the end of the first Hijri century means that they were in circulation well before then.[169] Moreover, the silence of the Qur'ān on epochal events and developments that took place between 10 and 70 AH such as the conquest of the Fertile Crescent and consequent civil wars places the finalization of the Qur'ān before then, i.e. during the life of Muhammad.[170]

The New Testament enjoys similar and wider evidentiary sources that substantiate the authorship, provenance, and dating of its various components, with information dating to the early second century. Thus, according to the earliest sources, Papias (70–163 CE), probably writing before 110 CE,[171] mentioned that Matthew authored the first Gospel, at first recording the sayings of Jesus as draft Logia in a Hebrew dialect, probably Aramaic. Irenaeus (130–202 CE) affirmed that Matthew wrote the first Gospel while Paul and Peter were ministering in Rome, i.e. in the early sixties, which also means that his draft mentioned by Papias goes back to the fifties.[172] Papias also wrote that Mark, who was Peter's interpreter, wrote the second Gospel in which he accurately recorded all that Peter remembered of what Jesus said and did, though not in chronological order. This is affirmed by Irenaeus and by Clement of Alexandria (150–215 CE) who added that Mark wrote while

167. Chapa, "Early Text of John," 156.

168. Mattson, *Story of the Qur'an*, 29

169. Mattson, 98.

170. Sinai, *Qur'an*, 47.

171. Bauckham, *Jesus and the Eyewitnesses*, 14.

172. Blomberg, *Historical Reliability*, 25–26.

Peter was still alive. With Peter martyred in the mid-sixties, Mark must have written his Gospel before then, which also agrees with a report by Jerome (347–420 CE) that Mark died in Egypt in 62 CE.[173] The abrupt ending of Luke's second volume, Acts, which does not mention the result of Paul's appeal to Caesar, suggests a writing date of Acts before 62 CE and the Gospel even earlier.[174] According to Irenaeus, John wrote his Gospel by the nineties having lived in Ephesus until the reign of Trajan in 98 CE.[175] The earliest sources thus show that the Gospels were written within one or two generations from the recorded events, i.e. within living memory of eyewitnesses.[176]

Modern dating of the New Testament, however, has "expanded and contracted with fashion" over the past two centuries.[177] Thus, by the year 1800, the span was some fifty years, from the year 50 to 100 CE. By the year 1850, the Tübingen liberal influence more than doubled the span, from the year 50 to 160 CE. By 1900, the Tübingen influence continued to stretch the span to over one hundred years, from around 50 to 160–175 CE, with conservative estimates as narrow as the period from 50 to 95 CE. By 1950, the span narrowed to range from the year 50 to 100+ CE except for 2 Peter (125–150 CE). By 1975, the span widened again to between 50 and 140 CE.[178] Conservative voices continued to be heard, however. Writing in 1846, for example, apologist and common law authority Simon Greenleaf argued that Matthew, the first Gospel, was written as early as 37 CE, reasoning from the "improbability that the Christians would be left for several years without a general and authentic history of our Savior's ministry."[179]

Relative dating of the Gospels is also influenced by the several theories of dependence that tend to explain the similarities between the Synoptics. One common theory places Mark as the earliest due to internal evidence that it must have been a common source to Matthew and Luke. These two, nevertheless, had another earlier common source dubbed Q, with the possibility that each also had his own unique source in addition to Q. This Markan

173. Blomberg, 25.

174. Blomberg, 26.

175. Blomberg, *Historical Reliability of John's*, 42.

176. Blomberg, *Historical Reliability*, 26.

177. Robinson, *Redating the New Testament*, 3.

178. Robinson, 3–7.

179. Greenleaf, *Testimony of the Evangelists*, 19.

hypothesis, however, has been challenged by reputable scholars. Evidence suggests that the material common to Matthew and Luke was translated from an Aramaic document. Papias says that "Matthew compiled the Logia in Hebrew [a reference to Aramaic], and every one translated them as best as he could." The Logia most probably refers to the sayings of Jesus since the beginning of his ministry. This places Matthew's earlier writing, the Logia, as the probable Q, with the belief that it was used to educate the new converts and must have been in circulation by 50 CE.[180] Thus, Matthew is earliest, with Mark giving a summary of Matthew in Greek and Luke tapping on both. Another theory has Luke depending on Matthew, and Mark depending on both, and another has Mark as the earliest with Matthew depending on Mark, and Luke on both. Yet another posits that Luke depended on Mark, and Matthew on both Mark and Luke.[181] Blomberg notes that "it seems as if the arguments cancel each other out or at least reveal how tenuous it is to assert direct dependence by either Gospel on the other."[182] He concludes that the Q hypothesis is speculative, with no external evidence that it ever existed, hence garnering little confidence.[183]

Indeed, the Fathers believed that the Gospels were written in the same order in which they were arranged rather than a Markan priority.[184] Blomberg notes that one cannot ignore their view that Matthew was first written in Aramaic, making it the real Q source. He reasons that "it is hard to imagine an apostle and eyewitness of most of Jesus' ministry so indebted to a non-apostolic writer like Mark, who at best caught firsthand only glimpses of isolated events in Jesus' life."[185]

Regarding Paul's letters, noted scholar F. F. Bruce believed that they were written between 48 and 65, with Galatians in 48; 1 and 2 Thessalonians in 50; 1 and 2 Corinthians in 54–55; Romans in 57; Philippians, Colossians, Philemon, and Ephesians in 60; and the pastoral letters in 63–65 CE.[186] Blomberg be-

180. Bruce, *New Testament Documents*, 34–37.

181. Blomberg, *Historical Reliability*, 38–43.

182. Blomberg, 43.

183. Blomberg, 45.

184. For a defense of the reliability of the writings of the Fathers as sources of information on the Synoptics see Smith, "Defense of Using Patristic," 63–83.

185. Blomberg, *Historical Reliability*, 45.

186. Bruce, *New Testament Documents*, 8.

lieves that James most likely was written in the forties, making it the earliest New Testament writing and providing early evidence to the Gospel tradition within some fifteen years from Christ's ascension.[187]

Anglican scholar John A. T. Robinson, despite his liberal theology, renewed in 1975 the argument for an earlier dating and much narrower span for the composition of the New Testament. He based his argument on the silence of all New Testament books on the fall of Jerusalem and the destruction of its temple in 70 CE.[188] Thus, after a thorough analysis he dated James to the years 47–48, Pauline letters to 50–58, Mark to 45–60, Matthew to 40–60+, Luke to 57–60+, John to 40–65+, Jude and 2 Peter to 61–62, Acts to 57–62, the Johannine letters to 60–65, 1 Peter to 65, Hebrews to 67, and Revelation to 68 CE.[189] In brief, he dates the Gospels to the period from 40 to 65+ CE, and the entire process of the formation of the New Testament to the forty years from 30 to before 70 CE.[190] This is less than forty years after the resurrection, when most eyewitnesses were still alive. Blomberg, however, believes that Robinson's *argumentum ex silentio* is weak evidence as John is silent on other major issues and events. He also notes that the late date of the nineties vis-à-vis 70 CE explains the silence, being far removed from the event.[191] Bruce notes that he "should not go all the way with some of [Robinson's] early dating." He dates the Synoptics between 64 and shortly after 70 CE.[192] Nevertheless, he concludes that "Dr. Robinson's case is so well researched and closely reasoned that no one from now on should deal with this question of dating without paying the most serious attention to his arguments."[193]

Robert Newman argues that internal evidence shows that the *content* of Mark is prior to Matthew, while external evidence (the Fathers) shows that the *writing* of Matthew is prior to Mark. Newman suggests a reconciliation. Mark's content, derived from Peter, is the oral testimony that the apostles, led by Peter, selected from the life and sayings of Jesus, hence the agreements between the Synoptics. Matthew used this oral material in writing

187. Blomberg, *Historical Reliability*, 293.

188. Robinson, *Redating the New Testament*, 13.

189. Robinson, 352.

190. Robinson, 311.

191. Blomberg, *Historical Reliability of John's*, 42–43.

192. Bruce, *New Testament Documents*, 6–7.

193. Bruce, 15.

his Gospel before Mark while supplementing it from his own memory and sources. Newman therefore suggests that Aramaic Matthew was written in the forties or fifties, followed by Luke in the late fifties or early sixties, then Greek Matthew, and lastly Mark in the mid-sixties.[194]

A subsequent study by New Testament scholar John Wenham advocates another early dating of the Synoptic Gospels, even earlier than Robinson's dating, though totally independent of it. He attributes the Gospels to their traditional authors and rejects the common assumption of literary dependence as the explanation of similarities between the Synoptics, though he allows for a degree of structural dependence (genre and order). He insists that "what they write is fundamentally what they themselves are accustomed to teach."[195] He also notes that "verbal synoptic likeness and differences are best explained by independent use of the primitive form of oral instruction."[196]

Like Robinson, Wenham's starting point is scriptural silence, not on the fall of Jerusalem like Robinson, but on the long-awaited trial of Paul in Rome in Acts 28. Luke's silence is inexplicable after having traced the developments that led to the trial in detail since Paul's Caesarean imprisonment and their long sea journey to Rome. Wenham thus starts from 62 CE as the latest dating of Acts and moves backward. He argues that Luke knew about Mark's Gospel and may have been guided by Mark's structure and order yet without literary dependence.[197] Fifty-two pericopes show common origin with Mark and follow a similar sense, while fourteen others that address the same topics have no commonality.[198] Luke also came long after Matthew yet did not borrow from him as evidenced by their "differences in sense" despite cases of similar wording that can be due to independent transmission of the same discourse.[199] Finally, tradition says that Luke is the one whom Paul describes as the "brother whose fame in the things of the gospel has spread through all the churches" (2 Cor 8:18), the emissary who carried Paul's second letter

194. Newman, "Synoptic Problem," 149–51.

195. Wenham, *Redating Matthew, Mark*, xxii–xxiii.

196. Wenham, 243.

197. Wenham, 87.

198. Wenham, 11–12.

199. Wenham, 40.

to the Corinthians in 56 CE, and so his Gospel must have been well known by the mid-fifties.[200]

Mark was Peter's interpreter, not in the sense of translating from Peter's Aramaic into Greek but of expounding his teaching.[201] Wenham notes that the church of Rome has long held that Peter left Palestine after his escape from prison in 42 CE and founded the church there. This fits well with the tradition that the apostles fled Palestine in 42 CE and the fact that there was a well-established church in Rome by 57 CE when Paul wrote his letter.[202] Indications suggest that Mark wrote his Gospel shortly after Peter left Rome in 44 CE upon Herod's death and before Mark joined Paul.[203]

Finally, Wenham argues that Matthew's Gospel departed from Mark considerably and looks to be of early Palestinian origin, particularly with its focus on the clash between Jesus and the Jewish authorities. As a tax-collector, Matthew may well have taken down notes in Aramaic from the days of Jesus's ministry.[204] This is compatible with the uncontradicted testimony for a Matthean authorship, priority, and Aramaic origin that comes unanimously from the Fathers such as Papias (60–130 CE), Irenaeus (130–200 CE), Pantaenus (d. 190 CE), Origen (185–254 CE), and several others.[205]

Wenham thus concludes that Luke wrote his Gospel before writing Acts in 62 and was well known by the mid-fifties, hence around 54 CE. Peter taught in Rome between 42 and 44 CE, and Mark wrote up his teachings after Peter left, thus around 45 CE. Matthew, according to unanimous tradition, wrote his Gospel first, hence around 40 CE.[206] In his entire method, Wenham places heavy emphasis on the unanimity of the early church tradition:

> In the search for literary relationships the most decisive question in this debate is likely to be the weight to be attached to patristic tradition. If it is considered worthless, the purely literary debate is likely to remain indecisive, insufficient to create a

---

200. Wenham, 230.
201. Wenham, 136.
202. Wenham, 142.
203. Wenham, 182, 238.
204. Wenham, 88–89.
205. Wenham, 116–17.
206. Wenham, xxv, 243.

> new consensus. If it is thought to be of weight, it is likely to tip the scale in favour of Matthean priority.[207]

Other external evidence also corroborates a first-century range of dates. For example, a letter to the Philippians in 120 CE by John's disciple Polycarp (69–155 CE) quoted from the Synoptics, Acts, nine Pauline letters, Hebrews, 1 Peter, and 1 John. This means that the quoted writings came from considerably earlier dates.[208] Both the Fathers and several scholars today agree that most of the New Testament was written before 70 CE, with the Johannine writings by the nineties. More generally, it is largely agreed that the entire New Testament was written during the first century, with most of its contents already in circulation much earlier. Compared with the great works of antiquity, which are separated from the reported events by centuries, the New Testament is exceedingly more trustworthy.[209] Even with the liberal late dating, many of the eyewitnesses of Jesus's ministry and resurrection were still alive, even as late as the time of John's writing his Gospel, himself being an eyewitness.[210]

Finally, the observation of Bruce is worth noting. The late dating by liberal scholarship was the result "not so much of historical evidence but out of philosophical presuppositions." Secular writings, "the authenticity of which no one dreams of questioning," do not enjoy a small fraction of New Testament evidence.[211]

Manuscript evidence

Discoveries of early manuscripts and numismatic evidence from the first Hijri century, limited as they are, support an early compilation of the Qur'ān.[212] Radiocarbon tests of available early manuscripts of parts of the Qur'ān date them to the first Hijri century. These tests gave results with very high probabilities and so provide today scientific evidence that a very substantial

207. Wenham, 196–97.

208. Bruce, *New Testament Documents*, 13.

209. Blomberg, *Historical Reliability*, 26.

210. Bruce, *New Testament Documents*, 7.

211. Bruce, 9–10.

212. Mattson, *Story of the* Qur'an, 98.

portion of the qur'anic text was already in circulation, though not without some variants, by the 650s.[213]

Christians would respond that New Testament authenticity is supported by an unparalleled wealth of manuscript evidence. More than five thousand six hundred manuscripts of the New Testament in Greek alone exist, totaling more than 2.6 million pages. With manuscripts in other languages translated from Greek, the total number of New Testament manuscripts is about twenty thousand. Even if all these manuscripts vanish, the New Testament can still be reconstructed from the more than one million quotations by the church fathers.[214]

Twelve New Testament manuscripts exist today from the second century, sixty-four from the third, and forty-eight from the fourth, totaling 124 manuscripts within three centuries of the finalization of the New Testament. Collectively, they comprise the whole New Testament text multiple times.[215] Manuscripts dating to within 150 years from the writing of the New Testament comprise 40 percent of all New Testament text.[216] Moreover, all great classical works of antiquity are incomparable with New Testament evidence, both in number and time span. For example, the *Gallic Wars* by Julius Caesar (100–44 BCE) has only 10 good extant manuscripts, the oldest dating to 900 CE, with a gap of one thousand years after Caesar. The *Annals*, written by the great Roman historian Tacitus (56–120 CE), has twenty extant manuscripts, the oldest dating from 1100 CE, with a gap of one thousand years. The *History of Thucydides* (460–400 BCE) has eight extant manuscripts, the earliest dating to c. 900 CE, with a gap of one thousand three hundred years.[217]

The average number of total manuscripts for any classical author, regardless of the time of writing, is around a dozen.[218] Wallace notes that, comparing this with the New Testament manuscripts, "the NT textual critic is confronted with an embarrassment of riches." He adds that "if we have doubts about what the autographic NT said, those doubts would have to be multiplied a

213. Sinai, *Qur'an*, 46.

214. Wallace, "Lost in Transmission," 28.

215. Wallace, 28–29.

216. Wallace, 30.

217. Geisler and Nix, *General Introduction*, 408.

218. Wallace, "Lost in Transmission," 29.

hundredfold for the average classical author."[219] He concludes that the New Testament is "by far the best-attested work of Greek or Latin literature from the ancient world."[220]

The most complete and accurate manuscripts of the New Testament are Codex Vaticanus and Codex Sinaiticus, both of which date to around 350 CE or a bit earlier.[221] They are the oldest uncial manuscripts on parchment or vellum. Codex Sinaiticus (340 CE) is "the most important witness to text because of its antiquity, accuracy, and lack of omissions."[222] The Bodmer Papyri date between 175 and 225 CE and include most of Luke (this is the oldest discovered copy of Luke) and John "in clear and carefully printed uncials."[223] They also contain the letters of Peter and Jude.[224] The oldest discovered New Testament fragment is the John Rylands papyrus that contains portions of John 18:31–33, 37–38 and dates to the period between 117 and 130 CE, with some arguing that it is even earlier. Considering that it was discovered in Egypt, which, in ancient standards, is relatively far from its place of origin in Asia Minor, the Gospel of John must have been written before the end of the first century.[225] One evidence against the charge that it is a Greek document that could not have been written by a Palestinian Jew is the Dead Sea manuscripts of the non-biblical Jewish sect of the Essenes, which show a strong contrasting dualism between good and evil. John's Gospel, with its similar emphasis, shows that it is perhaps the most Jewish of the four Gospels.[226]

Finally, it is noteworthy that the church bound the Scripture in the form of codex as early as the early second century at a time when the scroll was the supreme form of documenting literary work in the Greco-Roman world.[227]

---

219. Wallace, 29.
220. Wallace, 30.
221. Bruce, *New Testament Documents*, 10.
222. Geisler and Nix, *General Introduction*, 392.
223. Geisler and Nix, 390.
224. Bruce, *New Testament Documents*, 13.
225. Geisler and Nix, *General Introduction*, 388–89.
226. Yamauchi, "Jesus outside," 211.
227. Gerhardsson, *Memory and Manuscript*, 201.

Internal evidence

The history of the Qur'ān precedes formal canonization and should be inferred from the internal evidence of its text in terms of both content and structure.[228] Thus, "a canon from below precedes a canon from above."[229] For example, a study of the arrangement of single textual units in the Qur'ān shows that it does not denote any theological pattern, which is incompatible with fabricated theologizing.[230] Nevertheless, a careful analysis of a *sūra* reveals an organic interconnection of ideas and "internal echoes" that cannot be a staged assembly of disparate parts.[231] Moreover, the many contextual references in the Qur'ān clearly presuppose natural contemporaneous interaction with the subject events and integral consistency that cannot possibly be the creative fabrication of authors of later times.[232]

The Christian would respond that the internal evidence of the authenticity of the New Testament is powerful and self-attesting vis-à-vis the various charges brought by both Western liberal and Muslim scholars. A particular target is its canonization in the fourth century, viewed as denoting a long controlled process of widescale changes and selective exclusions and inclusions.[233] Yet collections of early Christian writings provide evidence that the New Testament canonization process started early in the second century, i.e. shortly after the completion of its writing.[234] The dispute centered solely on the last few books such Hebrews, 2 Peter, 3 John, James, and Jude, until Athanasius (296–373 CE) listed the canonical twenty-seven books of the New Testament in 367.[235] The role of the church, however, was far from exerting tendentious control over what comprises Scripture. Rather, "the New Testament books did not become authoritative for the Church because they were formally included in her canon; on the contrary, the Church included them in her canon because she already regarded them as divinely inspired, recognizing their innate worth and generally apostolic authority, direct or

228. Neuwirth, "Qur'an and History," 16.

229. Neuwirth, 14.

230. Neuwirth, 10–11.

231. Sinai, *Qur'an*, 92.

232. Sinai, 51.

233. Crook, *New Testament*, 88.

234. Bruce, *New Testament Documents*, 18.

235. Bruce, 20–21.

indirect."[236] In other words, the church discovers and recognizes canonicity; it does not determine it.[237] If, as aforesaid, the canonization of the Qur'ān is described as a process from *below* rather than from above, the canonization of the New Testament can also be described as a process from *within* rather than without. It started from within the text, which attests itself and bears the marks of canonicity.

In examining the history of the Qur'ān, Neuwirth calls critics to refer to the text itself rather the external processes.[238] Bruce similarly stresses that available New Testament documents are more important than the unavailable putative source documents posited by source criticism, which remain largely speculative.[239] Credibility of the New Testament text is thus supported by the internal evidence of its very text. Its narratives are "vivid but uncluttered, full of incidental details, ordinary people and psychological realism, which sets it apart from most ancient fiction and tendentious history."[240] The literary style is "simple and alive." The Gospels are "full of proper names, dates, cultural details, historical events, and customs and opinions of that time."[241] Richard Bauckham has consulted Israeli scholar Tal Ilan's *Lexicon of Jewish Names in Late Antiquity* on Jewish names during the period from 330 BCE–200 CE and compared them with personal names mentioned in the Gospels. The conclusion of his extensive onomastic analysis is telling:

> The evidence [of the analysis] shows that the relative frequency of the various personal names in the Gospels corresponds well to the relative frequency in the full database of three thousand individual instances of names in the Palestinian Jewish sources of the period. This correspondence is very unlikely to have resulted from addition of names to the traditions, even within Palestinian Jewish community, and could not possibly have resulted from the addition of names to the traditions outside Jewish Palestine, since the pattern of Jewish name usage in the Diaspora was very

236. Bruce, 22.
237. Geisler and Nix, *General Introduction*, 211.
238. As mentioned above.
239. Bruce, *New Testament Documents*, 26–27.
240. Blomberg, *Historical Reliability*, 296.
241. Craig, *Reasonable Faith*, 334.

> different. . . . These features of the New Testament data would be difficult to explain as a result of random invention of names within Palestinian Jewish Christianity and impossible to explain as the result of such invention outside Jewish Palestine. All the evidence indicates the general authenticity of the personal names in the Gospels. . . . They indicate the eyewitness sources of the individual stories in which they occur.[242]

The incidental details in the New Testament "line up, even in largely independent accounts, in ways that would be almost impossible to fabricate."[243] For example, John mentions in chapter 6 of his Gospel that Jesus ordered his disciples to seat the crowd of five thousand on the ground, with the remark that "there was much grass in the place" (John 6:10). A few verses before John mentions that Jesus went up to the mountain to teach the crowd, with the incidental note that "the Passover, the feast of the Jews, was near" (John 6:4). The Passover falls on Nisan 15 in the spring. Residents of Palestine know that the area is almost arid with hardly any grass throughout the year, except in early spring after the rainy season when the green cover changes the whole scene. Another incidental agreement is when Paul exclaims: "Do we not have a right to take along a believing wife, even as . . . Cephas?" (1 Cor 9:5). The incidental agreement with the story of Jesus's entering the house of Peter (Cephas) and his wife and healing his mother-in-law (Mark 1:29–31) is evident.

New Testament translator J. B. Phillips concludes his personal testimony, addressed to the layperson, of the impression from his work in translating the New Testament text with these oft-quoted words: "It is my serious conclusion that we have here in the New Testament, words that bear the hall-mark of reality and the ring of truth."[244] Commenting on the Gospels he notes: "I have read, in Greek and Latin, scores of myths but I did not find the slightest flavor of myth here. There is no hysteria, no careful working for effect and no attempt at collusion. These are not embroidered tales: the material is cut to the bone."[245] The Evangelists dared mention the human weakness

---

242. Bauckham, *Jesus and the Eyewitnesses*, 84.
243. Blomberg, *Historical Reliability*, 296.
244. Phillips, *Ring of Truth*, 124.
245. Phillips, *Ring of Truth*, 79.

of the Son of God and did not hesitate to mention in detail their own moral weaknesses. Moreover, "it would have been impossible for forgers to put together so consistent a narrative as that which we find in the Gospels. The Gospels do not try to suppress apparent discrepancies, which indicates their originality. There is no attempt at harmonization between the Gospels, such as we might expect from forgers."[246] Regarding the historical worth of the letters of Paul and others, Phillips notes that "if the historian can lay his hands upon a packet of letters he has priceless evidence for the period of which he is writing. For letters, speaking generally, are not written with any political axe to grind nor are they usually written for posterity. They reflect accurately the times in which they are written."[247]

Memory and oral tradition

Preliterate societies, as in early Islam, have an extraordinary ability at memorizing.[248] One could memorize with astounding accuracy more than ten pages a day, and cumulatively tens of thousands of reports.[249] This is even true in modern societies where Muslims as young as twelve can memorize the entire Qur'ān.[250] The primary and privileged means by which the Qur'ān has been preserved and transmitted is oral recitation.[251] Still, the combined oral-written transmission avoids oral transmission errors such as wrong hearing and forgetfulness, and the copyists' errors of written transmission.[252]

Christians argue along similar lines and can provide detailed evidence of the viability of oral memorization by the apostles and early Christians. Birger Gerhardsson argues that the oral transmission in the first century should not be evaluated based on the present fluid process of transmitting folk tales but rather the rabbinic practice, which Jesus most likely followed. Rabbis could memorize the entire Old Testament and much of the Mishna, or oral Torah. Jesus thus may well have taught his disciples to memorize his significant

---

246. Craig, *Reasonable Faith*, 334.

247. Phillips, *Ring of Truth*, 44.

248. Robinson, *Islamic Historiography*, 173. See also Mattson, *Story of the Qur'an*, 91.

249. Robinson, 173.

250. Mattson, *Story of the Qur'an*, 80, 91.

251. Mattson, 87.

252. Mattson, 98.

sayings.[253] Likewise, the circle of the apostles saw to it that the tradition is preserved, as is evident in Paul's citation of church traditions and his stressing that he *received* them from such circle (1 Cor 11:23, 15:3).[254]

While preservation by memorization may sound strange today, it was the natural and only means prior to the advent of writing. The art of writing took a long time to establish itself, particularly in the religious circles, and a longer time to become common practice in all circles. Even more time was needed for writing to become a standalone vehicle for transmission rather than a mere aid to memory, and it was only recently that writing almost replaced memory.[255] Orality was so important in the rabbinic community that the Pharisees resisted attempts to write down the oral Torah, or Mishna.[256] Pupils with good memories were entrusted with memorizing.[257] Under the supervision of their teachers, they were the repository and reference of authorized tradition, "purely and simply living *books*: textbooks and concordances."[258] They were "traditionists *par excellence*," but were not the only memorizers as both teachers and pupils shared this task.[259]

Rabbinic teachers stressed here the principle of continuous repetition for learning, thus applying "to its fullest extent" Cicero's principle: *repetitio est mater studiorum*. Repetition was to be carried out in a catchy "sonorous and distinct voice" that facilitated memorization and prevented forgetfulness.[260] To further assist memorization, teachers were careful to express the tradition, especially important doctrinal statements, as concisely as possible: "Rabbis' terseness is legendary."[261] They also resorted to mnemonics, or the principle of association, such as using verses of Scripture, well-known doctrinal statements and proverbs, catchwords or memory-sentences that were otherwise meaningless, and images from nature to lead thoughts and prevent mistakes.[262]

253. Gerhardsson, *Memory and Manuscript*, 328–29.

254. Gerhardsson, 290, 300.

255. Gerhardsson, 123.

256. Gerhardsson, 23.

257. Gerhardsson, 95.

258. Gerhardsson, 99.

259. Gerhardsson, 106.

260. Gerhardsson, 164–65, 168.

261. Gerhardsson, 136, 142.

262. Gerhardsson, *Reliability of the Gospel*, 11.

Poetic sentences also aided memory since "it is easier to remember poetry than prose, rhythmic sentences than nonrhythmic, the picturesque than the pedestrian, the well-organized than the unorganized."[263]

Jesus, as a Jewish teacher, may well have used methods similar to those of the rabbis, making his disciples, especially the Twelve, learn his teachings by heart so that they were "stamped on their memories."[264] Translating the sayings of Jesus back into their original form, Aramaic, shows that Jesus uttered them in a poetical form full of parallelism that also typifies the manner Old Testament prophets uttered their oracles. Such manner of speech is to be expected if Jesus wanted his disciples to memorize his sayings. This is a further corroboration of the originality of the sayings of the Gospels.[265] As in rabbinic circles, the memorized sayings of Jesus were "repeated, expounded, and applied" by the apostles and the disciples. Indeed, knowing that Jesus was no mere teacher or rabbi but the Messiah himself, they considered his words even more sacred and authoritative than the disciples of the rabbis did for rabbinic sayings.[266]

Importantly, and as an aid to the expanding Mishna, both teachers and pupils also used to write private notes on tablets, scrolls and notebooks, and sometimes even on walls.[267] Bauckham notes that, in the oral culture of the rabbinic world and early Christianity, "writing and orality were not alternatives but complementary."[268] Notebooks were common and were most probably used by the disciples of Jesus to aid their memory as he spoke. This practice continued after his ascension as indicated by Paul's reference to his notebooks and parchments that he used in his travels (2 Tim 4:13).[269] One may object that the apostles were illiterate, being fishermen and artisans, yet clearly some of them were well-educated as evident, for example, in the high literary standard of the letter of James.[270] Indeed, Jewish boys had to learn reading and writing until the age of twelve, and the apostles were no

263. Gerhardsson, *Memory and Manuscript*, 148, 154–55.

264. Gerhardsson, 328–30.

265. Bruce, *New Testament Documents*, 36.

266. Gerhardsson, *Memory and Manuscript*, 332.

267. Gerhardsson, 160–61.

268. Bauckham, *Jesus and the Eyewitnesses*, 287.

269. Bauckham, 288.

270. Bauckham, 289.

exception; their description in Acts 4:13 does not mean utter illiteracy but rather lack of rabbinic higher education.[271] Bauckham notes that the "tradition language" in New Testament accounts "entails neither cross-generational distance nor even orality to the exclusion of written records."[272]

Some objected that Jesus may well have differed in his teaching style from the rabbis, and that the variations between parallels in the Synoptics do not support strict memorization.[273] In response, others proposed that Jesus, like Old Testament prophets, announced the Word of God authoritatively in a manner that prompted the hearers to treat it with awe and respect; he spoke as the very Messiah. Moreover, as a teacher of wisdom, he, like his contemporary teachers, wanted his disciples to perpetuate his teaching, which he also delivered in a form that is easy to memorize.[274]

Regarding variations in the Synoptic parallels, these are attributable to the fact that oral tradition, rather than being transmitted verbatim, was subject to controlled flexibility.[275] A study from the Middle East identifies three manners of oral tradition in illiterate or semiliterate cultures today: "formal, controlled transmission; informal, uncontrolled transmission; and informal, controlled transmission."[276] The third applies to the Synoptics and explains their limited variations.[277] Such flexible transmission does not contradict the doctrine of inerrancy: God inspired his Word through human agency and tradition such that human words convey the meaning and the exact words that God wanted to be included in his Scripture.[278] Indeed, inerrancy does not necessarily mean perfect compliance with grammar, modern-world precision, use of modern scientific language, recording the *ipsissima verba* of Jesus's Logia, or verbal exactness in citing Old Testament quotations.[279] Scripture is "the word of

271. Blomberg, *Historical Reliability*, 56–57.
272. Bauckham, *Jesus and the Eyewitnesses*, 38.
273. Blomberg, *Historical Reliability*, 56.
274. Blomberg, 56–57.
275. Blomberg, 57–58.
276. Blomberg, 59.
277. Blomberg, 59–60.
278. Blomberg, 60.
279. Feinberg, "Meaning of Inerrancy," 299–301.

God in the language of men."[280] Inerrancy is a concept of *truth*. It means that Scripture is "wholly true."[281]

While some criticize the Synoptics for variances in parallels, others center their criticism on similarity. They argue that verbal agreements among parallels in the Synoptics mean that the writers must have borrowed from a literary source which, apart from strict rabbinic practice, cannot happen in oral traditions. One study disagrees with this assumption. The author argues that verbal agreements do occur in oral traditions, which places the burden of proof on those making such assumption.[282] He supports his conclusion with an empirical study in Jordan and concludes that "it is reasonable to conclude that those levels of verbal agreement could have occurred among independent oral recitations of Jesus traditions as well."[283]

Finally, New Testament studies usually refer to the oral accounts behind the Gospel as *traditions*. Oral tradition authority Jan Vansina, however, defines oral traditions as "all messages [that] are transmitted beyond the generation that gave rise to them."[284] If they are delivered during the contemporary generation that gave rise to them, they are called oral *history* rather than *tradition*.[285] The verbal traditions comprising the Gospels were recorded in writing during the lifetime of their eyewitnesses, and so cannot be termed *oral tradition* but *oral history*.[286] Moreover, even if they count as *oral tradition*, the time span between Jesus and the Gospels is much smaller than that required for changes, even relatively small ones, to creep in as per Vansina's findings.[287] Vansina also distinguishes between historical *accounts* and historical *tales*. Tales change much more than accounts over time and they "never have a beginning, a composition, and never end, but rather disappear into later tales."[288] Bauckham builds on Vansina's distinction and stresses that the

280. Geisler and Nix, *General Introduction*, 39.

281. Feinberg, "Meaning of Inerrancy," 303–4.

282. Derico, *Oral Tradition*, 204. This book is based on a Ph.D. dissertation at Oxford.

283. Derico, 265.

284. Vansina, *Oral Tradition as History*, 13, 27.

285. Vansina, 28.

286. Bauckham, *Jesus and the Eyewitnesses*, 273.

287. Bauckham, 273.

288. Vansina, *Oral Tradition as History*, 26.

Gospels qualify as *accounts*, not tales as liberal scholars claim.[289] He drives the idea further home and calls the Gospel accounts *eyewitness testimony*:

> If . . . the period between the "historical" Jesus and the Gospels was actually spanned, not by anonymous community transmission, but by the continuing presence and testimony of the eyewitnesses, who remained the authoritative sources of their traditions until their deaths, then the usual ways of thinking of oral tradition are not appropriate at all. Gospel traditions did not, for the most part, circulate anonymously but in the name of the eyewitnesses to whom they were due. Throughout the lifetime of the eyewitnesses, Christians remained interested in and aware of the ways the eyewitnesses themselves told their stories. So, in imagining how the traditions reached the Gospel writers, not oral tradition but eyewitness testimony should be our principal model.[290]

Conspiracy and Occam's razor

Fabrications at an early period could not have escaped public scrutiny when eyewitnesses were still alive. Fabrications in the second and third Hijri centuries must assume a conspiracy project that is carefully devised to alter the truth and secure the consensus of all Muslims in the now wide and deeply divided territories of Islam, or secure perfect concealment from "the gaze of history."[291] Such conspiracies requires an extraordinary ability to fabricate in a very systematic and airtight manner.[292] Even the simple consensus on the ʿUthmanic codex as the *textus receptus* cannot have happened after the first century when divisions abounded in the expanded Islamic territory.[293] Finally, Occam's razor dictates that wherever an explanation suffices, adding further complications is unwarranted.[294]

---

289. Bauckham, *Jesus and the Eyewitnesses*, 272–73.
290. Bauckham, 8, 31.
291. Mattson, *Story of the Qur'an*, 98.
292. Motzki, "Collection of the Qur'an," 28–29.
293. Sinai, *Qur'an*, 46–47.
294. Farrin, "Composition and Writing," 14.

In response, claims of liberal form criticism that the Gospel writers invented the sayings and deeds of Jesus, or that stories about Jesus were distorted in the process of transmission from oral tradition to writing, collapse in view of the historical facts. Considering Matthew's first Aramaic draft that dates to no later than the fifties, the span between the rise of oral tradition after the resurrection and the earliest written record is barely more than twenty years.[295] John Wenham argues that it is only ten years.[296] Even if this is increased to thirty or forty years, it is still incomparable with the span between oral transmission and written records for the other works in antiquity that those same critics admire, which may well span entire centuries. Such a span is also too short for legend to creep into the accounts and take hold in the absence of extraordinary factors. Any distortion by the apostles would have been corrected by the many other disciples who were also eyewitnesses and remembered the actual events and sayings. Moreover, supposing the implausible possibility that all Christians staged a worldwide conspiracy in the rapidly expanding new faith to distort the real story, hostile eyewitnesses would have easily exposed the attempt and discredited Christians.[297] Indeed, the apostles appealed to the memories of those hostile eyewitnesses when they told them: "Jesus the Nazarene, a man attested to you by God with miracles and wonders and signs which God performed through Him in your midst, *just as you yourselves know* [italic mine]" (Acts 2:22).[298] One should also remember that matters so important as to make the multitude of believers risk their lives were not let loose, as "the authoritative control of the apostles would have kept legendary tendencies in check." They were "the guardians of the information of His life and teaching."[299]

Other factors also militate against such conspiracy. The sheer number of New Testament manuscripts, which evidently exceeds the number of qur'anic manuscripts or that of any classic work of antiquity, make it extremely difficult, if not impossible, to conspire to change all New Testament copies

---

295. Blomberg, *Historical Reliability*, 52–53.
296. Wenham, *Redating Matthew*, xxv, 243.
297. Blomberg, *Historical Reliability*, 52–53.
298. Bruce, *New Testament Documents*, 43.
299. Craig, *Son Rises*, 107.

scattered throughout the Roman Empire.[300] Indeed, Indian Muslim scholar Sir Sayyid Ahmad Khan mentioned this fact in his commentary on the Bible in 1862.[301] Moreover, attributing the first three Gospels to their respective writers despite their qualifications cannot be fabrication but rather inspires confidence in the Fathers who honestly followed evidence: Matthew with his background as a Jew who collaborated with the Roman enemy, Mark with his obscure non-apostolic identity and history of defection while in mission with Paul, and Luke with his obscure non-apostolic Greek background.[302] Furthermore, New Testament translator J. B. Phillips notes that "one thing is perfectly clear: these men were not in a conspiracy together or they would have been careful to avoid minor contradictions and discrepancies."[303] Most important, the gist of Christianity is the crucifixion and resurrection of Jesus Christ. That the apostles conspired to invent these accounts and then paid the ultimate price for boldly and persistently proclaiming what they well knew were inventions, would certainly defy explanation. Finally, the Christian story of writing the New Testament is simple and straightforward; Occam's razor eliminates all liberal theories of conspiracy.

Burden of proof

The authenticity of the Qur'ān is not mere assertion and is not an argument from authority. Rather, it rests on a multitude of internal and external evidences that cannot be ignored but await convincing arguments and answers to the contrary. Those who insist on denying the evidence must shoulder the burden of proof.[304]

The Christian can only hope that this principle is consistently applied to the New Testament in view of the plethora of available evidence, both internally and externally. Blomberg notes that

300. The recent Blockchain cryptographic technology is based on similar concept, decentralization and immutability: a transaction is instantly recorded on millions of computers all over the world, making it virtually impossible for forgers to change. With no transaction fees, it vies to control and organize all commercial transaction in the world, replacing middlemen like banks or e-marketplaces. See Hickey, "Using Blockchain," 143–47.

301. Guenther, "Christian Responses," 85.

302. Blomberg, *Historical Reliability*, 26–27.

303. Phillips, *Ring of Truth*, 80.

304. Sinai, *Qur'an*, 92.

> once one accepts that the Gospels reflect attempts to write reliable history or biography, however theological or stylized their presentations may be, then one must immediately recognize an important presupposition that guides most historians in their work. Unless there is good reason for believing otherwise, one will assume that a given detail in the work of a particular historian is factual. This method places the burden of proof squarely on the person who would doubt the reliability of a given portion of the text. The alternative is to presume the text unreliable unless convincing evidence can be brought forward in support of it. While many critical scholars of the Gospels adopt this latter method, it is wholly unjustified by the normal canons of historiography. Scholars who would consistently implement such a method when studying other ancient historical writings would find the corroborative data so insufficient that the vast majority of accepted history would have to be jettisoned.[305]

He adds that "a historian who has been found trustworthy where he or she can be tested should be given the benefit of the doubt in cases where no tests are available."[306]

In responding to liberal Western critics who accuse caliph ʿUthmān of destroying variant versions of the Qur'ān, Muslims struggle to support their claim that such variants are not significantly different from the ʿUthmanic *textus receptus*. Blomberg's argument above may provide them with a viable defense. But then Muslim scholars should accept it as equally legitimate defense for the New Testament against similar demands of proof where no evidence or tests are available.[307]

305. Blomberg, *Historical Reliability of the Gospels*, 304.

306. Blomberg, 63.

307. To the above eight categories one may add a ninth on external attestation to the historicity of Muhammad and then apply the principle to Jesus. Muhammad is referred to in non-Islamic sources, the earliest being the 634 CE (13 AH) Christian Greek work *Doctrina Iacobi*. It speaks of an anonymous "prophet coming with the Saracens" proclaiming the near coming of the Messiah and alleging to possess the keys to paradise, and leading campaigns to occupy Palestine (contrary to Muslim sources). A Syriac text written around 640 CE (20 AH) mentions a battle between the Romans and the "Arabs of Muhammad" on 4 February 634 CE (12 AH). Another Syriac text titled Chronicles of Khuzistan mentions Muhammad as leader of the Ishmaelite occupiers of Persian lands. Finally, an Armenian work titled *History of Psuedo-Sebeos* in the 660's CE (40's AH) mentions Muhammad as a merchant leading Arab

Compilation and Authentication of the Sunna

The Qur'ān is to Muslims God's very words, the ultimate authority in Islam. Yet the Qur'ān, unlike the Gospels, is not a historical account, but rather disparate messages that address events involving Muhammad as they arose, mostly without mentioning the very events that are addressed. It mentions names and places that seem contextless.[308] The *sūras* (chapters) and the verses within are arranged neither topically nor chronologically but rather in the order that is to be read by Muslims.[309] The Qur'ān thus cannot be properly understood or interpreted without an accompanying history that explains the events or circumstances behind a certain text and places the text in its historical context. This is one main function of *Sunna* (way of life) or its synonymous term, *Ḥadīth* (speech), defined as "attested reports of the sayings, actions, and tacit approvals and accounts of the Prophet Muhammad."[310] Thus, *Sunna* is revealed scripture that is second to the Qur'ān and the key to understanding and interpreting it in its context.[311] Indeed, its significance stems in the first instance from the qur'anic injunction to Muslims to obey the Prophet in whatever he instructs them: "He who obeys the Messenger [Muhammad] obeys God" (Qur'ān 4:80), and the direct instruction: "Whatsoever the Messenger ordains, you should accept, and whatsoever he forbids, you should abstain from" (Qur'ān 59:7).[312] Muslims therefore consider *Ḥadīth*, the main source of *Sunna*, as part of divinely revealed texts.[313]

Yet a marked difference exists between the degree of authenticity that the Qur'ān enjoys and that enjoyed by *Sunna*. Despite Western radical and revisionist criticisms of the provenance and timing of the Qur'ān, the prevailing view among both Western and Islamic scholars is that the traditional Islamic

---

armies and calling them to occupy Palestine as their legitimate land by virtue of their Abrahamic descent. Sinai notes that such sources negate claims that Muhammad, attested only on seventh Hijri century coins, is a late invention. Sinai, *Qur'an*, 43–44. Since Muslims do not deny the historicity of Jesus, this section will not address non-Christian sources supporting his historicity. Nevertheless, chapter 5 will refer to such sources insofar as they attest to his crucifixion and his followers' claim of his resurrection.

308. Mattson, *Story of the Qur'an*, 27–28.

309. Abdel Haleem, "Qur'an and Hadith," 21. See also Sinai, *Qur'an*, 11–12. For more details see *Encyclopedia of the Qur'ān*, s.v. "Chronology and the Qur'ān."

310. Abdel Haleem, 22.

311. Mattson, *Story of the Qur'an*, 27, 32. See also Abdel Haleem, 22.

312. Wael B. Hallaq, *Sharī'a: Theory, Practice, Transformations*, 41.

313. Kamali, *Shari'ah Law*, 23.

story is generally credible. Prominent Oxford historian and liberal scholar Chase F. Robinson admits that "it appears that the Qur'ān was set down in writing within a generation of the Prophet's death." Referring to the Islamic science of examining *Ḥadīth*, he observes that "the Qur'ān scored very high" in comparison.[314] He then notes that the *Sunna* was originally in oral form and started to be written down a century and a half later.[315] Reformist and outspoken Islamic scholar Khaled Abou El Fadl notes that he has made "the faith-based assumption that the Qur'ān is the immutable and uncorrupted Word of God." He then adds that "the Sunnah, and other historically relevant material, however, pose a very different challenge."[316]

The traditional Islamic story

Muhammad urged his followers to preserve his *Ḥadīth* in their memories and pass it to others. Caliph ʿUmar I (r. 13–23 AH) decided not to record *Ḥadīth* for fear it might replace the Qur'ān, a state that continued until the Umayyad caliph ʿUmar II (r. 99–101 AH).[317] Moreover, most of the Companions could not write.[318] Some Companions might have written down some *Ḥadīth*, but this is not certain and cannot be verified.[319] Due to this delay in recording the enormous corpus of *Ḥadīth* material, "the early Muslim scholars admitted the existence of a large number of forgeries and distortions, many of which echoed sectarian tensions."[320] This prompted a group of early Muslim scholars to develop a system of ensuring that only authentic *Ḥadīth* is recognized. Muḥammad Ibn Ismaʿīl al-Bukhārī (d. 256 AH), the foremost *Ḥadīth* scholar, recognized as sound only such parts of *Ḥadīth* that "have reached him from the Prophet on the authority of well-known Companion, by means of a continuous chain (*isnād*) of narrators who, according to his records, had been accepted unanimously by trustworthy scholars as men and women of integrity, retentive memories and firm faith."[321]

---

314. Robinson, *Islamic Historiography*, 87.
315. Robinson, 87.
316. Abou El Fadl, *Speaking in God's Name*, 87.
317. Abdel Haleem, "Qur'an and Hadith," 23.
318. Al-Qāsimī, *Qawāʿed al-taḥdīth*, 70.
319. Al-Azami, *On Schacht's Origins*, 111.
320. Abdel Haleem, "Qur'an and Hadith," 23.
321. Abdel Haleem, 24.

Arguments against authenticity

The authenticity of written records of the early history of Islam and the *Sunna* corpus is intrinsically linked with the process of transmission, or *isnād.* Written compilation, in general, emerged in the Islamic territories during the second half of the first Hijri century for state functions and took hold only by mid-second century, when *Ḥadīth* began to be widely recorded.[322] Robinson argues that the *Ḥadīth* attributed to Muhammad was modified and edited upon recording to "conform to values and conventions of subsequent periods."[323] Better controls that would improve authenticity were developed during the third century, but the stage was too late to rectify earlier records as reliable evidence was no more available to detect the "manifold sins of omission and commission."[324] Indeed, the *isnād* system was never put in place to actively control the documentation of oral transmission of text over time. Rather, it was assembled retrospectively by jurists who sought some authoritative support that went back to the Prophet to legitimize their already-established legal views.[325] Robinson notes that, "compared to the prestige form of the classical tradition of Greek and Roman historiography, which put the highest value on oral testimony for contemporary history, the choice made by early Muslim historians to rely on oral testimony for *non-contemporary* history is striking."[326]

Suspicion of the *isnād* system began in the West in the late nineteenth century with Julius Wellhausen. He argued that one can trust historians who merely refer to the authority of trustworthy earlier historians without citing *isnād* at all, while one cannot trust good *isnāds* drawn by bad historians. This was reinforced by his notable contemporary Ignaz Goldziher who demonstrated that a great number of *Ḥadīths*, even in the best Muslim collections, were outright forgeries from the late second and third Hijri centuries, together with their apparently solid supporting *isnāds.*[327] He argued, as evidence, that "every stream and counter-stream of thought in Islam has found its expression

322. Humphreys, *Islamic History*, 86.

323. Robinson, *Islamic Historiography*, 22.

324. Humphreys, *Islamic History*, 86. See also Robinson, 22.

325. Robinson, 88.

326. Robinson, 26.

327. Humphreys, *Islamic History*, 82–83.

in the form of a *ḥadīth*."[328] His views were revived and reinforced in 1950 by Joseph Schacht who noted that *isnāds* claiming to go back to the Prophet were widely known only in mid-second Hijri century. He argued that the more solid and formally correct an *isnād* seemed to be, the more likely it was a forgery. In general, Schacht concluded, *no* existing *Ḥadīth* could be reliably ascribed to the Prophet.[329] Historian R. Stephen Humphreys notes that "Schacht's conclusions were too well documented to be wished away."[330] Muslim scholars, notably M. Mustafa al-Azami, however, argued that Schacht did not properly understand the ancient texts he quoted and the process of *Ḥadīth* transmission in early Islam.[331] Others argued that Schacht was right but went too far. Humphreys concludes, "In the end, we may decide simply that Schacht is right."[332]

Humphreys laments the fact that the history of first-century Islam remains obscure to modern historians, even when compared with contemporaneous Western history written in the seventh century CE. Archaeological and manuscript sources offer fragmentary or limited information that cannot depict any convincing reconstruction of historical events, and Muslim Arabic literary sources cannot provide reliable answers to modern questions. Available narratives in Arabic are "late crystallization of a fluid oral tradition."[333] Their reliability cannot be established without knowing more about their true origins, the long process of oral transmission and accompanying alterations, the circumstances under which they were first put in writing, and changes made before they were forged into their final form in mid-third Hijri century.[334] All that have survived from the first century are quotations in works of later writers, some after a century, with extensive editing and sometimes signs of inauthenticity.[335] Robinson describes the loss of the tradition's earliest history as "nothing short of catastrophic."[336] He notes that, "aside from the

328. Goldziher, *Muslim Studies*, 2:126.
329. Schacht, *Origins of Muhammadan Jurisprudence*, 138–59.
330. Humphreys, *Islamic History*, 83.
331. Al-Azami, *On Schacht's Origins*, 3, 122.
332. Humphreys, *Islamic History*, 83–84.
333. Humphreys, 69.
334. Humphreys, 69–70.
335. Robinson, *Islamic Historiography*, 25.
336. Robinson, 50.

Qur'ān and a small handful of exceptions, modern historians are robbed of virtually any literary evidence composed within natural memory of the great moments of early Islam."[337]

Biographies about Muhammad were written in the second and early third Hijri centuries, among them Ibn Isḥāq's (d. 150 AH), al-Sinānī's (d. 212 AH), and Ibn Hishām's (d. 218 AH).[338] Most existing texts of early Islamic history were written in the third and early fourth Hijri centuries, the most important of which are the writings of al-Baladhūrī (d. 279 AH) and al-Ṭabarī (d. 310 AH). These writers ascribe the narrated events to *isnād* lists that claim to go back to contemporaries of the recorded events and sayings, yet the sources of such compilations are works of the late second Hijri century.[339] Humphreys notes that available evidence for the early period before 130 AH consists of "rather dubious citations in later compilations." He adds that, "deprived of direct evidence, scholars have had to compensate with bold surmises and moral certitude."[340] Humphreys concludes that "it is enough to say that no *isnād* should be accepted at face value."[341] He even adds that, even after we have works that are demonstrably forgeries, no scientific basis exists by which to judge that the rest is authentic. Rather, it is more a matter of intuition, hence the impossibility of reaching consensus.[342] Commenting on the *isnād* linear system, Vansina argues from his empirical studies that "a neat single line of transmission simply does not often exist. Rather, most oral tradition is told by many people to many people. . . . Hence the transmission really is communal and continuous."[343]

Western scholars are indeed not alone in their critiques. Shahab Ahmed, an outspoken Muslim scholar at Harvard, argues in his posthumously published work, *Before Orthodoxy: The Satanic Verses in Early Islam*, that historical evidence suggests that early Muslims did firmly believe that Muhammad had mistaken the Satanic verses for divine verses. In these verses Muhammad

337. Robinson, 50–51.

338. Sinai, *Qur'an*, 41–42.

339. Humphreys, *Islamic History*, 71–73.

340. Humphreys, 80.

341. Humphreys, 81.

342. Humphreys, 91.

343. Vansina, *Oral Tradition as History*, 30. One notes here that transmission of early church history was done communally, in the church.

praised pagan deities for their ability to intercede with the supreme God, thus contradicting the fundamental Islamic doctrine of God's absolute unicity.[344] Ahmed observes that this firm orthodox near-universal belief in the first two centuries of Islam gradually changed over time until the rejection of the historicity of the event became the unquestionable orthodox universal position of all Muslims in the last two centuries.[345]

Ahmed argues that this complete reversal from an unthinkable denial in early Islam to an unthinkable anathematized acceptance today needs explanation.[346] He attributes the present rejection of the event to rational epistemological reasons. Theologically, God protects his prophets from error: "It is We who have sent down upon you the [Qur'ān], and We are its Guardians" (Qur'ān 15: 9). Historiographically, an unbroken chain of trustworthy *isnād* of reports goes back to the event, and this is what concerns Ahmed.[347] He gets his clue from Schacht's argument that reports on early Muslim tradition were largely fabricated and so assumed authority by claiming chains of *isnād* that had "a tendency to grow backwards and to claim higher authority until they arrive at the Prophet."[348] Schacht concludes that the less complete *isnād* chains are, the older they are likely to be.[349]

To back his thesis, Ahmed notes that early Islamic history consists of *sīra-maghāzī*, the epics of the heroism and deeds of Muhammad; *Ḥadīth*, the authoritative and normative teachings and deeds of Muhammad; and *tafsir*, qur'anic exegesis that greatly depends on linking a qur'anic content with the historical events giving rise to it, largely derived from the *sīra-maghāzī*.[350] Authoritative *Ḥadīth* thus had to be supported by strictly conformant and unbroken chains of *isnād* given its prescriptive implications on the religious, legal, and creedal norms of Islam.[351] *Sīra-maghāzī* reports, on the other hand, aimed at invoking a spirit of heroism in hearers and encouraging virtuous deeds and morality, and so their historians did not deem it necessary to attach

344. Ahmed, *Before Orthodoxy*, 1–2.

345. Ahmed, *Before Orthodoxy*, 2–3, 6–7.

346. Ahmed, 3.

347. Ahmed, 8–9.

348. Schacht, *Origins of Muhammadan Jurisprudence*, 5.

349. Ahmed, *Before Orthodoxy*, 18–19.

350. Ahmed, 20–22.

351. Ahmed, 34.

strict *isnād* criteria as for *Ḥadīth*. Although their *isnāds* were mostly partial, they were tolerated by *Ḥadīth* scholars from the beginning as otherwise Islam would be bereft of the prophetic biography and Islam's early history,[352] so essential for establishing a historical ground of Islam and qur'anic exegesis.[353]

Ahmed concludes that much of the chains of *isnād* that underpinned *Ḥadīth* were fabricated, whereas the *isnād* chains of *sirah-maghazi* narratives, deemed non-conformant by *Ḥadīth* scholars, clearly did not undergo any fabrications by virtue of their very incompleteness. Their *isnāds* are, therefore, genuine transmission chains. The event of Satanic verses is narrated in the *sīra-maghāzī* reports.[354]

Reformist Muslim scholar Khaled Abou El Fadl argues that, while the Qur'ān commands Muslims to listen to Muhammad, yet in the long chain of transmission, his *Sunna* has undergone "multiple authorship, . . . fabrication, . . . creative selection and recollection" with the result that "each tradition attributed to the Prophet is the end-product of authorial enterprise."[355] Indeed, even in applying the science of *Ḥadīth*, "there is a considerable degree of creative subjectivity in the process of authenticating, documenting, organizing, and transmitting the reports attributed to the Prophet and the Companions."[356] The task then becomes distilling the prophetic kernel from the subjective husk. Abou El Fadl concludes that in most traditions such task is impossible to achieve because "the different forms of authorship are thoroughly intermingled with the Prophetic authorship, and it is practically impossible to differentiate between the various authorial voices."[357]

Arguments in defense of authenticity

Muslim scholars do not deny that extensive fabrication, both deliberate and unintentional, crept into the corpus of *Sunna*.[358] Muslim convert scholar Jonathan Brown admits that "a verse from the Qur'an was automatically considered 'certain in its attestation' because of the holy book's historical

352. Ahmed, 28–30.
353. Ahmed, 22.
354. Ahmed, *Before Orthodoxy*, 32–33.
355. Abou El Fadl, *Speaking in God's Name*, 87–88.
356. Abou El Fadl, 105.
357. Abou El Fadl, 109.
358. Kamali, *Textbook of Ḥadīth Studies*, 66–67.

intactness, while the vast majority even of *ṣaḥīḥ* [sound] Hadiths were only 'probable in their attestations.'"[359] They are quick to note, however, that the *isnād* system that early Muslims employed introduced well-studied methods for examining the alleged transmission, the quality of the transmitters, and conducting comparisons, all aimed at discovering forgery.[360] Thus, al-Bukhārī, whose compilation *Ṣaḥīḥ al-Bukhāri* is the most authoritative, interviewed one thousand *Ḥadīth* transmitters in five countries, and examined a corpus of six hundred thousand traditions (or *Ḥadīths*) and approved as authentic a mere 2,602 traditions (2,762 with repetitions).[361] Likewise, the authoritative *Ṣaḥīḥ Muslim* compiled 3,030 approved traditions (without repetition) from a corpus of three hundred thousand traditions.[362]

Muslim scholars advance other supporting arguments as well. Hallaq, who plainly admits that "much of the *ḥadīth* was inauthentic, representing accretions and significant additions,"[363] notes that the people of Medina continued to have memories of what the Prophet said and did, which was the arbiter in sifting sound tradition from the fabricated.[364] Mattson, after acknowledging the fabrication of *Ḥadīth* by individuals seeking to reinforce their political power, invites the reader to appreciate the concern early Muslims expressed over the authenticity of reports and their response in developing the science of *Ḥadīth/isnād* system.[365] Notable scholar Ahmed El Shamsy cautions that "indiscriminate rejection of the authenticity of the entire Hadith corpus is as misguided as its categorical acceptance."[366] He argues that the hypothesis that hundreds of Muslim scholars throughout the ages conspired against authentic *Ḥadīth* does not satisfy Occam's razor.[367] Similarly, al-Azami notes that

359. Brown, *Misquoting Muhammad*, 85.

360. Kamali, *Textbook of Ḥadīth Studies*, 80–81.

361. Kamali, 33–34.

362. Kamali, 36. This contradicts the dogmatic assertion of Muslim scholar M. Mustafa al-Azami that "scholars made every attempt to verify what was authentic and found the great majority of *ahadith* to be valid and traceable back to the Prophet." Al-Azami, *On Schacht's Origins*, 115.

363. Hallaq, *Sharīʿa*, 46.

364. Hallaq, 46–47.

365. Mattson, *Story of the Qur'an*, 29–30.

366. El Shamsy, *Canonization of Islamic Law*, 8.

367. El Shamsy, *Canonization of Islamic Law*, 8–9.

> Schacht asks us to believe that a massive confidence trick was perpetrated by scholars throughout the Muslim world in the second century A.H. . . . There is no way of proving to a cynic that scholars do not deliberately falsify records, but we may suggest that the political and geographical realities of the time militated against collusion on such a wide scale. Are we really to believe that without the benefit of the telephone, telegraph, or modern methods of transportation, scholars were able to communicate so well that the same *aḥadīth* [p. of *Ḥadīth*] grew up in such widely disparate areas?[368]

Scholar Mohammad Hashim Kamali enumerates several conditions that early Muslim scholars set as part of the science of *Ḥadīth* to identify forgery and ensure the best selection. First, the transmitter of a *Ḥadīth* must support his transmitted *Ḥadīth* by *isnād*, an unbreakable chain that purportedly goes back to the original eyewitnesses or hearers who saw and heard the Prophet say it.[369] Second, the transmitter must be a contemporary of his direct source, the teacher from whom he transmitted the tradition.[370] Third, every transmitter in the *isnād* chain must be *adl*, having upright and trustworthy character when reporting the *Ḥadīth*. As a minimum, positive evidence is required that the person has "not committed a major sin/crime and not persisted in committing minor ones, nor is [he] known for committing degrading profanities such as association with persons of ill repute and indulgence in humiliating jokes."[371] Companions of the Prophet, however, do not need such evidence as the Qur'ān already testifies that God is pleased with them.[372] Fourth, no transmitter in the chain should be involved in "sectarian, political and theological disputes," such as to favor advancing some doctrinal agenda.[373] Fifth, the transmitted *Ḥadīth* text must be consistent with the Qur'ān.[374] Sixth, the *Ḥadīth* text must not contradict historical evidence. Seventh, the *Ḥadīth*

368. Al-Azami, *On Schacht's Origins*, 122.
369. Kamali, *Textbook of Ḥadīth Studies*, 181.
370. Kamali, 192.
371. Kamali, 185–86.
372. Kamali, 187.
373. Kamali, 191–92.
374. Kamali, 195.

text must agree with reason, and not be illogical, self-contradictory, or superstitious. Eighth, the transmitter must ascertain that his direct source, or teacher, is knowledgeable and trustworthy.[375]

Abou El Fadl has compiled extensive lists of conditions that favor a tradition over others, some of which are not mentioned by Kamali.[376] For example, texts of a transmitter who was closer to the Prophet outweigh texts of transmitters who were not. A text that can be traced back to a Companion of the Prophet, i.e. a direct witness, outweighs a text traced back to a second-generation witness. A text whose transmitter had no personal interest in the text outweighs a text whose transmitter may have had such interest. Finally, a text whose circumstances are known outweighs a text whose context is unknown.[377]

New Testament Authenticity vs. Sunna Authenticity

This section will draw on the above principles employed by Muslim scholars to guarantee the authenticity of the *Sunna*. Part of the facts mentioned above to defend the New Testament reliability vis-à-vis the Qur'ān are similar to the facts that pertain to the above vis-à-vis the Qur'ān, and so they will be repeated here in shortened form wherever applicable.

Sound transmission chain

During the early period, the people of Medina, Muhammad's hometown, continued to have memories of what the Prophet said and did, which was the arbiter in sifting sound tradition from fabricated and safeguarding the authenticity of *Ḥadīth*.[378] During the later phases, Muslim scholars ensured that the transmitter of a *Ḥadīth* must support his transmission by *isnād*, an unbreakable chain that purportedly goes back to the original eyewitnesses.[379] One should appreciate the uniqueness of the Islamic tradition in the early

375. Kamali, 198–200.

376. Abou El Fadl gathered them from tens of original and secondary sources. See footnote 139, Abou El Fadl, *Speaking in God's Name*, 79.

377. Abou El Fadl, 40–42.

378. Hallaq, *Shar'ia*, 46–47.

379. Kamali, *Textbook of Ḥadīth Studies*, 181.

concern Muslims expressed over the authenticity of reports and their response in developing the science of *Ḥadīth* and requiring reporters to show their *isnād*.[380]

The Christian would respond that, in addition to the many Christian eyewitnesses who stayed in Jerusalem, the apostles in particular took upon themselves to preserve the tradition. They were not acting merely as individuals but rather as an authoritative collegium, with at least the triumvirate of Peter, James, and John staying in Jerusalem and ensuring that they protected the authentic Word.[381] Any distortion by the apostles would have been corrected by the many other disciples who were also eyewitnesses, as well as by hostile eyewitnesses who would have easily exposed the attempt and discredited Christians.[382]

Unlike *Sunna*, however, there were hardly "later phases" in the history of the New Testament traditions. The time span between Jesus and the earliest recording of the oral tradition ranges from ten to forty years. This period is too short for a long chain of transmitters, or *isnād*, to develop. Matthew and John were direct eyewitnesses; each needed one stage of transmitters, persons who were with them during the ministry of Jesus but who probably saw or heard things when they were not present on certain days. Luke and Mark, whatever their sources, obtained their information from the same generation. Paul passed on to his congregation in Corinth important authoritative gospel traditions, which he had received directly from the apostles, particularly Peter according to Galatians 1. In two of them, Paul quoted gospel tradition that circulated among early Christians and that he had received from the apostles. In the first he says: "I received from the Lord that which I also delivered to you" (1 Cor 11:23), which implies receipt through one or more of the apostles who attended the Last Supper.[383] In the second tradition Paul says: "For I delivered to you as of first importance what I also received (1 Cor 15:3)." This is a particularly significant one, for it summarizes the basic events that stand behind the Christian faith, i.e. the death and resurrection of Christ.[384]

380. Mattson, *Story of the Qur'an*, 29–30.

381. Gerhardsson, *Memory and Manuscript*, 328–330.

382. Blomberg, *Historical Reliability of the Gospels*, 52–53.

383. Gerhardsson, *Reliability of Gospel Tradition*, 21.

384. Gerhardsson, 24.

On the other hand, in transmitting the tradition of the history of the formation of the Gospels, church fathers were careful to preserve accuracy on a par with rabbinic traditions. Thus, Papias, who heard directly from the apostle John, said that "whenever someone came who had accompanied the elders [i.e. the apostles], I used to search for the words of the elders." Irenaeus used to give a chain of reliable transmitters that "he heard . . . from the elders who in turn had been disciples of the Apostles." This means that his transmission took place in just two stages. He also used to memorize the tradition accurately while taking notes to support his memory.[385]

In deciding upon the correct text among variants, scholars followed well-considered criteria. They gave priority to the more difficult reading, knowing that scribes tended to emend. They also gave priority to the shorter reading, knowing that scribes would be more ready to add and clarify than to delete. The more verbally dissonant reading is preferred as scribes tended to harmonize accounts. Finally, the less-refined grammatical expression is preferred as scribes tended to improve on the grammar.[386]

Eyewitness foundation

A text that can be traced back to a Companion of the Prophet, i.e. a direct witness, outweighs a text traced back to a later period.[387] Indeed, a text by a Companion who was closer to the Prophet outweighs a text of transmitters who were not as close.[388] Moreover, the transmitter had to be a contemporary of the teacher from whom he obtained the transmitted tradition.[389]

In response, if Muslim scholars required eyewitness foundations for their often centuries-long *isnāds*, New Testament writers were themselves the eyewitnesses or direct transmitters from the eyewitnesses. John's contemporary Papias, writing before 110 CE,[390] says that Matthew wrote the first Gospel after first recording Jesus's Logia in Hebrew or Aramaic. This is affirmed by Irenaeus. Papias also stated that Mark, who was Peter's interpreter, wrote the second Gospel in which he accurately recorded all that Peter remembered

---

385. Gerhardsson, *Memory and Manuscript*, 204–206.
386. Geisler and Nix, *General Introduction*, 477.
387. Abou El Fadl, *Speaking in God's Name*, 41.
388. Abou El Fadl, 41.
389. Kamali, *Textbook of Ḥadīth Studies*, 192.
390. Bauckham, *Jesus and the Eyewitnesses*, 14.

of what Jesus said and did.[391] Luke, Paul's companion, wrote at a time when he could interview the eyewitnesses. He must have received part of his material from the Palestinian disciples as evidenced by traces of oral Aramaic tradition, with other parts received from Hellenist disciples. Early church historian Eusebius noted that, according to Papias and others, Philip's four daughters were an important source of early history. Luke, therefore, must have interviewed them in their home in Caesarea when he visited Philip with Paul (Acts 21:8–9).[392] Evidence suggests that the written *sources* of the Synoptics date to no later than 60 CE, with parts based on notes taken by the disciples while Jesus was teaching. The entire oral (and partially written) tradition is traced back to the days of Jesus's earthly ministry. This takes us back to the eyewitnesses, the apostles who proclaimed before the authorities that "we are witnesses of these things" (Acts 5:32).[393]

The fourth Gospel expressly states that its author is a direct eyewitness: "This is the disciple who is testifying to these things and wrote these things, and we know that his testimony is true" (John 22:24). That the apostle John is its author is strongly confirmed by external evidence, notably Irenaeus: "John, the disciple of our Lord, who also had leaned upon his breast, did himself publish a Gospel during his residence at Ephesus in Asia."[394] John was the closest to Jesus. This should give his Gospel greater weight according to this criterion. Finally, in stressing Peter's words before the Sanhedrin, which carry a "distinctly legal sound," Luke pleads the case for the Evangelists: they spoke what they had "seen and heard." (Acts 4:20).[395] Bauckham notes that the Evangelists applied the historiographical principle that "the most authoritative eyewitness is one who was present at the events narrated from their beginning to their end and can therefore vouch for the overall shape of the story as well as for the specific events."[396]

391. Blomberg, *Historical Reliability*, 25.

392. Bruce, *New Testament Documents*, 39–40.

393. Bruce, 42–43.

394. Blomberg, *Historical Reliability of John's*, 24.

395. Gerhardsson, *Memory and Manuscript*, 221–222.

396. Bauckham, *Jesus and the Eyewitnesses*, 146.

Transmitters' integrity

One condition for recognizing a transmitted text is the integrity and uprightness of each transmitter in the *isnād* chain. He must be *adl*, having a trustworthy character, with positive evidence that he has "not committed a major sin/crime and not persisted in committing minor ones."[397] Companions of the Prophet, however, did not need such evidence as the Qur'ān already testifies that God is pleased with them.[398]

Neither did the apostles and Evangelists. Jesus himself testified to their character when he told them: "I chose you and appointed you that you would go and bear fruit" (John 15:16). Indeed, the Qur'ān itself testifies to them: "and when Jesus sensed disbelief in them, he said, 'Who are my helpers unto God?' The Apostles said, 'We are God's helpers. We believe in God; bear witness that we are submitters'" (Qur'ān 3:52). Resorting to such argument, however, is clearly circular and begs the question; the Muslim needs first evidence that those mentioned in the Gospels are indeed the true "Apostles" mentioned in the Qur'ān. The integrity of the apostles as faithful transmitters of what they saw and heard must therefore be established. This will be undertaken in chapter 4.

Transmitters' impartiality

Muslim scholars ensured that no transmitter in the chain is involved in "sectarian, political and theological disputes" that would suggest favoring or advancing some theological or legal agenda.[399] Moreover, the transmitter of a text should not have personal interest in its content.[400]

Likewise, church fathers gave priority to a reading if it showed no doctrinal bias.[401] They realized that the Gospels are isolated tradition in the sense that they deal entirely with the sayings and deeds of Jesus, "nothing else."[402] One finds no indication in the Gospels of any disputes, or of any attempts to advance sectarian doctrine. In writing the Gospels, the Evangelists "permit Jesus to speak for himself, as a rule in direct discourse. They report episodes

397. Kamali, *Textbook of Ḥadīth Studies*, 185–86.

398. Kamali, 187.

399. Kamali, 191–92.

400. Abou El Fadl, *Speaking in God's Name*, 42.

401. Geisler and Nix, *General Introduction*, 478.

402. Gerhardsson, *Reliability of Gospel Tradition*, 59.

involving Jesus tersely and to the point. They do not allow themselves to comment – except for occasional, concise, and scarcely noticeable remarks between pericopes."[403] Evidently, the apostles did not mix the sayings of Jesus with their own views and inferences, which was also evident in Paul's teaching.[404] For example, on occasions where Paul had to give guidance to his congregation, he was careful to distinguish between his own view and the Lord's authoritative teaching. Thus, "to the married *I give instructions, not I, but the Lord*, that the wife should not leave her husband . . . but to the rest *I say, not the Lord*, that if any brother has a wife who is an unbeliever, . . . he must not divorce her" (1 Cor 7:10, 12 emphasis mine).

Finally, the Evangelists and the apostles were not mere historians or transmitters. They had a divine commission to fulfill. The fact that they were ready to endure persecution and martyrdom for what they proclaimed, and the fact that they did, militates against accusations that they sought personal interest or gain in what they recorded. The claim by the Companion Ibn ʿAbbās that early Christians have distorted the Bible with their own hands to sell it "for a little gain" is untenable.[405]

Internal consistency

Muslim scholars ensured that the transmitted *Ḥadīth* text must be consistent with the Qur'ān. If it includes a conflict that cannot reasonably be reconciled with the Qur'ān, it must be rejected.[406]

Not only the New Testament, but the entire Bible centers around one theme, Christ. Augustine noted that the Old Testament is revealed and

403. Gerhardsson, 29.

404. Bruce, *New Testament Documents*, 43.

405. Islam, "Concept of the Injīl," 87.

406. Kamali, *Textbook of Ḥadīth Studies*, 195. Modern Muslim voices in the West point to internal contradictions in Islam such that there are "Islams" rather than Islam. Harvard scholar Shahab Ahmed even calls contradiction "a centrally constitutive [element] of Islam." Ahmed, *What Is Islam*, 329. In struggling with contradiction, Ahmed boldly attempts to devise special hermeneutical operatives to live with such contradiction and then creatively calls it "coherent contradiction." He notes: "To live with outright contradiction, as societies of Muslims historically have done, one must be able to conceive of contradiction in such a way that contradiction is coherent and meaningful in terms of one's paradigmatic values and truths. This is not possible unless a Muslim conceives of contradictory Truth as arising necessarily and directly from the structural and spatial dynamic of Revelation to Muḥammad as Pre-text, Text, and Context – that is, unless a Muslim conceives of contradictory Truth as coherent with and meaningful in terms of Revelation to Muḥammad." Ahmed, *What Is Islam*, 404.

explained in the New Testament and the New Testament is concealed in the Old.[407] New Testament scholar D. A. Carson draws a helpful analogy: The Bible is like a great jigsaw puzzle, with thousands of pieces "along with assurance that these pieces all belong to the same puzzle." This, he asserts, makes it possible to infer one systematic theology for the entire Bible.[408]

Historical accuracy and reference

Muslim scholars ensured that a *Ḥadīth* text must not contradict historical evidence.[409] Nonetheless, they preferred a *Ḥadīth* saying whose circumstances are known rather than one whose historical context is obscure or unknown.[410]

The Gospels, especially Luke, are full of historical details that confidently invite sceptics to examine the Gospels' historical accuracy. Luke mentions names of Roman emperors, provincial governors, kings, and historical events of the day and uses them as signposts to date key events in the Gospel. Bruce notes that "a writer who thus relates his story to the wider context of world history is courting trouble if he is not careful; he affords his critical readers so many opportunities for testing his accuracy." He then concludes that "Luke takes this risk, and stands the test admirably."[411] Blomberg argues that the standard of accuracy that Luke follows in supporting his account with eyewitness testimony, primary sources, and his close following of all things matches the standards for good historiography prescribed by the great historians of his time, such as Herodotus, Thucydides, and Josephus.[412] This historical accuracy is also evident in the other Gospels which, like Luke, quote the sayings of Jesus within their historical contexts, stating the occasion, the place, and sometimes the time.

---

407. Geisler and Nix, *General Introduction*, 22.
408. Carson, "Unity and Diversity," 81–82.
409. Kamali, *Textbook of Ḥadīth Studies*, 196.
410. Abou El Fadl, *Speaking in God's Name*, 42.
411. Bruce, *New Testament Documents*, 81–82.
412. Blomberg, *Historical Reliability*, 296–97.

Rationality

Muslim scholars ensured that the *Ḥadīth* text must agree with reason and the principles of logic. It cannot be self-contradictory, and it cannot be totally superstitious.[413]

Muslims believe in the supernatural. The Qur'ān mentions that Jesus performed miracles, such as speaking as an infant, giving life to clay birds, healing the blind and the leper, even raising the dead (Qur'ān 3:49). The Qur'ān, however, is quick to note that Jesus performed his miracles with God's permission, i.e. not because he was God (Qur'ān 5:110). Muslims thus question the historicity of the Gospel miracles not because they are supernatural but as part of their quest to discredit both the deity of Jesus and the reliability of the Gospels that narrate them. Quoting Western liberal scholars, Muslims dismiss the Gospel miracles as a Pauline invention borrowed from the alleged parallels of Greek and Jewish mythology.[414]

The differences, however, between the Gospel miracles and ancient Near Eastern mythology, or Jesus's extra-biblical qur'anic miracles, are striking. Unlike apocryphal writings, the Gospels narrate the miracles in simple language. Moreover, Gospel miracles do not portray a Jesus who performed miracles on demand to compel the crowds to believe.[415] They differ starkly from Greek myths of "humans talking with the animals and birds, and even transforming themselves into other creatures, charming rocks and trees with their music, appearing and disappearing, or appearing in two places at the same time, travelling the world without eating, or sending their souls on journeys while their bodies remained at home."[416] Jesus performed his miracles with divine dignity and for good reason: showing compassion for the people, or rewarding and encouraging their faith, and always authenticating his message and proclaiming the kingdom of God.[417] Regarding exorcisms, Jesus used "none of the elaborate spells and incantations, often involving the careful repetition of nonsense syllables, so prevalent in his day. He [did] not alter the tone of his voice, he [did] not appeal to any authority outside himself, . . .

---

413. Kamali, *Textbook of Ḥadīth Studies*, 197.
414. Crook, *New Testament*, 161, 171,
415. Blomberg, *Historical Reliability*, 113.
416. Blomberg, 116.
417. Blomberg, 113, 127, 128.

and he [did] not pray to God before commanding the demons to come out."[418] Unlike Greek or Jewish myths, the Evangelists narrated the miracles during the lives of those who experienced or witnessed them.[419] Peter's words suffice here: "For we did not follow cleverly devised tales [*myths* in the English Standard Version] when we made known to you the power and coming of our Lord Jesus Christ, but we were eyewitnesses of His majesty" (2 Pet 1:16).

Conspiracy and Occam's razor

The hypothesis that multitudes of Muslim scholars throughout the centuries converged on a well-knit conspiracy against authentic *Ḥadīth* does not pass Occam's razor.[420] Such conspiracy is even more difficult in the absence of the modern tools of communication.[421] The late emergence of *Ḥadīth* as a basic source of Islamic law in the second Hijri century is attributable to its late compilation and canonization rather than its invention.[422]

This issue has been covered in the previous section under a similar subheading. The additional argument raised above by al-Azami regarding the lack of telecommunications during early Islam (and early Christianity) equally applies to the unlikelihood of wide conspiracy by early Christians to change New Testament accounts.

---

418. Blomberg, 113.
419. Blomberg, 117.
420. El Shamsy, *Canonization of Islamic Law*, 8–9.
421. Al-Azami, *On Schacht's Origins*, 122.
422. El Shamsy, *Canonization of Islamic Law*, 8–9.

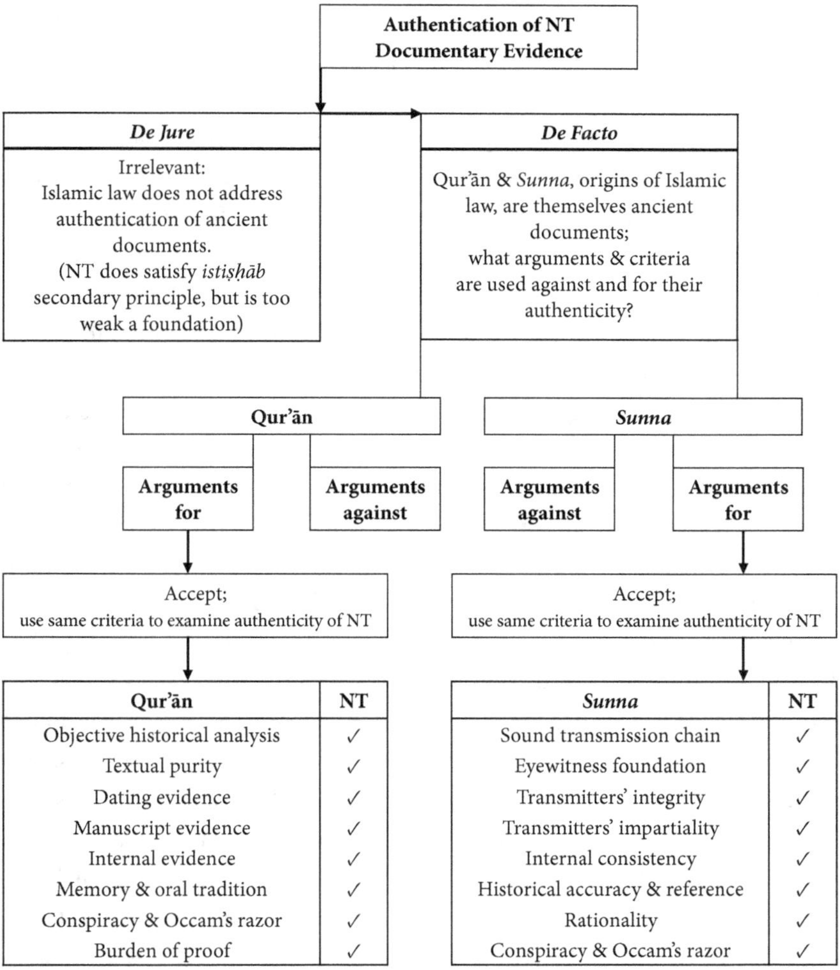

Figure 2. Authentication of NT documentary evidence

The Islamic Story of the Corruption of the New Testament

The Qur'ān does not say how the alleged corruption of the Bible took place, or when. It just asserts the corruption, which is then accepted by Muslims on mere authority. Indeed, the debate is considerable as to the real meaning of the qur'anic verses that most Muslims rely on for their belief that corruption has crept into the biblical texts. Most, Muslims and Christians alike, believe that these verses simply mean just how they sound, that is, corruption of the biblical text. A minority, however, with ecumenical leanings, argue that the subject qur'anic verses mean misinterpretation of an uncorrupted text.[423] Commenting on the oft-quoted qur'anic verse, "Among those who are Jews are those distorting the meaning of the word" (Qur'ān 4:46), leading Islamic studies scholar Gabriel Said Reynolds argues that "neither here nor elsewhere . . . does the Qur'ān argue that the Bible of the Jews and Christians is falsified. . . . Instead, the Qur'ān argues that the Jews (in particular) have hidden or misrepresented . . . their revelation."[424]

Some attribute the Muslim interpretation of textual corruption to a reaction to the refusal of Jews and Christians to recognize Islam.[425] Moreover, in view of the obvious disagreement between the Qur'ān and the New Testament on key issues, these scholars try to reconcile the main difference, the crucifixion. Reynolds argues that the qur'anic verse, "They did not kill him nor crucify him, but so it was made to appear to them" (Qur'ān 4:157), "does not deny that Jesus was crucified or that he died – it only denies that the Jews killed him. The reason for this denial is quite particular to the Qur'ān: the insistence that God is the one who gives life and death, . . . that God himself [caused] Jesus to die."[426] Others explain the difference away by arguing that Jesus died and was raised by God (hence the New Testament), yet in God's eyes he did not die but was taken up (hence the Qur'ān).[427] Some Christians also subscribe to the above explanations, often for apologetical and evangelistic purposes.[428]

Todd Lawson argues that the Islamic denial of the crucifixion is not based on the *ipsissima verba* of the Qur'ān alone but principally in exegesis.[429] He suggests that the Islamic denial to the crucifixion stems from the soteriological implications of the crucifixion of Jesus as God's vicarious atonement offered for man's salvation, which is at odds with the message of Islam. He refers to H. A. R. Gibb's view that the main difference between Islam and

423. Ahmed, "Bible and the Qur'an," 107.
424. Reynolds, *Qur'an and the Bible*, 161.
425. Ahmed, "Bible and the Qur'an," 107.
426. Reynolds, *Qur'an and the Bible*, 181.
427. Eshelbrenner, "Qur'an-Gospel Resurrection Resolution," 684–85.
428. See, for example, Anderson, *Qur'an in Context*, 253–54, 268.
429. Lawson, *Crucifixion and the Qur'an*, 26, Kindle.

Christianity is not so much the denial of the trinitarian nature of God as the soteriology of the cross.[430]

These attempts at reconciliation, however, fail to convince Muslims around the world who staunchly hold to the corruption of the Bible. Indeed, Lawson, after presenting several interpretations that tend to reconcile the Qur'ān and the New Testament on crucifixion, including the one he embraces (same as Reynolds' above), admits that "the first and by far the most frequent interpretation is that God rescued Jesus from the crucifixion in a miraculous manner and that someone else was substituted for Jesus on the cross."[431] What matters to this study is the general, almost unanimous belief of Muslims, regardless of exegesis or eisegesis to the contrary. Moreover, and in addition to the convoluted nature of attempts at reinterpreting the Qur'ān, such reinterpretations fail to withstand historical evidence, both in terms of Muslim belief throughout the centuries, and the tradition narrated in *Sunna/Ḥadīth*.[432]

According to a *Ḥadīth* tradition reported by one of the foremost Companions, Muhammad's cousin Ibn ʿAbbās, Muhammad narrated that a group of the disciples decided to alter the Gospel following the ascension of Jesus and to force the corrupted version on a smaller group who continued to read the authentic Gospel. With the help of authorities, they conquered and threatened the smaller group with death, yet the smaller group was later allowed to go into exile as hermits, thus starting the movement of monasticism.[433] In a separate comment, Ibn ʿAbbās claimed that Jews and Christians have distorted the Bible with their own hands to sell it "for a little gain."[434]

According to another *Ḥadīth* tradition reported by Companion ʿAbd Allah Ibn Masʿud, Muhammad said that, out of seventy-two groups of early Christians, only three resisted the enforcement of the corrupted Gospel by

430. Lawson, 22.

431. Lawson, 21.

432. Indeed, Christian apologists have tried from the early Hijri centuries to reinterpret qur'anic verses in support of Christian theological doctrine rejected by Muslims. For example, some tried to show that the verse, "The Messiah, Jesus, son of Mary, is only Allāh's Messenger and His Word, which He imparted to Mary, and is a spirit from Him" (Qur'an 4:171), affirms both the Trinity ("God, His Word, and a spirit from Him") and the incarnation ("His Word, which He imparted to Mary"). Griffith, *Church in the Shadow*, 167–68. Such attempts, however, are unsuccessful in convincing Muslims.

433. Islam, "Concept of the Injīl," 84–85.

434. Islam, 87.

the rulers. One group resisted the rulers but were slain, another continued to preach the authentic Gospel but were sawn into pieces, and the third fled into the mountains roaming as hermits.[435] These were excommunicated by the Christian authorities and their scriptures were condemned as apocryphal. While some of them later allowed heretical doctrine to creep in, a small minority persevered until Muhammad came, and believed in his message.[436]

This story in both *Ḥadīths* is in stark contradiction with obvious historical facts. The first Christians were not "rulers," but the ones persecuted by the rulers, whether Roman or Jewish. They wandered about in deserts and mountains, and some were "sawn into pieces." The author of the article that relates this *Ḥadīth*, embarrassed by this account, concludes with a correction: "It seems more likely to set the scene of the *ḥadīth* literature's account of the persecution in the fourth century C.E. when the Trinitarian Church started a vigorous campaign against its opponents after the conversion of Constantine I (r. 306–337 CE)."[437] But then this undermines the whole story.

Another problem with the Qur'ān's confident accusation of a corrupted Bible is the partial and often distorted knowledge of pre-Islam Arabs of the Bible. Prominent scholar Sydney Griffith notes that, although the Qur'ān relates several stories and names mentioned in the Bible, these are partial and often distorted, with an almost complete lack of direct quotations.[438] Moreover, no written texts of the Bible in Arabic exist from pre-Islamic times, not even in literature or poetry.[439] Griffith then makes the significant conclusion that historical and textual evidence shows that Arab Christians did not possess a written Bible or parts of it in Arabic in pre-Islamic times until the late second Hijri century.[440] Rather, "Christian clergy must have transmitted the biblical and homiletic literature orally in Arabic, perhaps even functioning within traditions of oral translation."[441] Indeed, this is agreed by Muslim scholars:

435. Islam, 85.
436. Islam, 86.
437. Islam, 95.
438. Griffith: *Bible in Arabic*, 52.
439. Griffith, 43.
440. Griffith, 52.
441. Griffith, 43. See also *Encyclopedia of the Qur'ān*, s.v. "Christians and Christianity."

> Some version or versions of this famous [crucifixion] story were doubtless known to the Arabs of Hijaz at the time of the Prophet. Though the transmission was oral (so far as we know) and the result of travelers' conversations when at leisure around the fire after a hard day's journey, taken together with contact with monks and priests during trading sojourns in Palestine and Syria, enough was known about the story to make it appear blasphemous to the Prophet."[442]

Clearly, neither Muhammad nor his advisers had access to a written Arabic New Testament (or the Old), let alone access to the "original" uncorrupted New Testament, which Muhammad thought was "sent down" from God per the Islamic sense of revelation. Muslims see that the similarities in the mode of revelation between the Qur'ān and the New Testament, both being sent down on a specific night during the month of Ramaḍān, "may imply that the original Injīl (Gospel) has been considered, in the *ḥadīth* literature, as verbatim word of God as are certain *sūrahs* of the Qur'ān and not as a posthumous historical or biographical record of Jesus' *logia* and deeds."[443] A New Testament that differs in so many tenets from the Qur'ān and posthumously narrates the life of Jesus, rather than descends from God, is, to them, inauthentic.[444] Israeli historian Hava Lazarus-Yafeh notes that

> this motif [of dismissing a rival scripture as inauthentic] was commonly used in pre-Islamic times by pagan, Samaritan, and Christian authors in order to discredit their opponents and their scriptures, especially the Hebrew Bible. In the Quran it becomes a central theme, used mainly to explain away contradictions between the Bible and the Quran and establish that the coming of Muhammad and the rise of Islam had indeed been predicted in the lost, uncorrupted, "true" Bible.[445]

---

442. Crook, *New Testament*, 296.
443. Islam, "Concept of the Injīl," 95.
444. Schlorff, "Theological and Apologetical Dimensions," 356.
445. Lazarus-Yafeh, "Some Neglected Aspects," 64.

Conclusion

The rules and principles of evidence under Islamic law do not address ancient documents but only contemporary handwritten documents, and so do not apply to the New Testament documents. Their authenticity can be validated *de facto* rather than *de jure*; the two revealed primary sources of Islamic law, the Qur'ān and *Sunna*, are themselves ancient documents and yet Muslims accept them as authentic. The very same principles that Muslim scholars employ to defend the authenticity of the Qur'ān vindicate the extant New Testament; it satisfies these principles and is at least as authentic as the extant Qur'ān. The New Testament, among other things, has the added benefit over the Qur'ān of not facing the charge of destroying unorthodox copies prior to its canonization. It is also attested by a larger number of manuscripts that are far more numerous and closer in time to the autographs than any other classical work of antiquity.

Applying the principles that Muslims use to defend the authenticity of the *Sunna* shows that the extant New Testament satisfies these principles and enjoys evidence of authenticity that is far stronger than the extant *Sunna*. The few thousand traditions that comprise the *Sunna* are extracted from hundreds of thousands of fake traditions backed by fabricated and lengthy *isnāds*, or chains of transmissions. The New Testament traditions were either written by the eyewitnesses themselves or transmitted from the eyewitnesses directly to their authors. Denying the authenticity of the New Testament means implicitly denying the authenticity of both the Qur'ān and *Sunna*.

Finally, the *Ḥadīth* story of the corruption of the New Testament is in stark contrast with obvious historical facts. One of the above-mentioned criteria, as laid down by early Muslim scholars, for distinguishing sound *Ḥadīth* is that it must not contradict historical evidence. Moreover, Muhammad was not in a position to pass judgment on a Bible he or his advisers never read or even saw.

CHAPTER 4

Eyewitness Testimony and Confession

Now that the New Testament documents are admissible as authentic, a court of law can treat its writers as witnesses standing before it to give oral testimony to the resurrection of Jesus Christ. The New Testament is their recorded testimony, and they are now examined as such before the court. It is a question of credibility of both the writers as persons and their testimonies. This chapter will consider as direct eyewitnesses Matthew, John, Paul, and Peter, with Mark and Luke as indirect witnesses. The testimony of Paul will also be considered as confession in addition to the confession of James. Moreover, Luke will also be considered in the next chapter as an expert witness.

Eyewitness Testimony

Live testimony by first-hand eyewitnesses is the primary evidence in Islamic law and "the most evincive" among all forms of evidence, so much so that the term for *testimony* in Arabic (*shehāda*) is almost interchangeable with the term for *evidence* (*bayyina*).[1] Some jurists argue that confession is stronger and more authoritative, but this does not relegate testimony to any secondary position as it remains the most common form,[2] particularly since confession is rare given the harshness of punishment in Islamic law. Indeed, confession in cases of *ḥudūd* is not encouraged, even by Muhammad.[3] To be admitted as sound evidence, eyewitness testimony must satisfy conditions related to

1. Hallaq, *Sharīʿa: Theory, Practice, Transformations*, 348.
2. El-Awa, "Confession and Other Methods," 112, 117.
3. Rabb, *Doubt in Islamic Law*, 25–26. See also Daoud, *Al-qaḍā' wa al-daʿwa*, 2:22.

the number and gender of witnesses, their qualifications, and the contents of their testimonies.

Number and Gender of Eyewitnesses

Islamic law, unlike the common law,[4] stipulates the specific numbers of eyewitnesses. For cases involving severe punishments, known as *ḥadd*, two male eyewitnesses are required, except for cases of adultery, which require four male witnesses.[5] According to Muhammad, women are mentally and morally deficient.[6] Two women thus equal one man and can testify only if accompanied by a man (to satisfy the equivalence of two males) and only in cases of money and trade, though they can testify without a male witness in private matters related to women.[7] Unlike the common law, Islamic law does not give more weight to a testimony if the number of witnesses exceeds the prescribed number, since it is prescribed by God in the Qur'ān. Thus, if two witnesses are prescribed, ten would not make their testimony more credible.[8]

Those who witnessed the crucifixion and saw the risen Jesus were both men and women. But those who testify in the New Testament, i.e. the apostles and Evangelists, are all men. The stipulated number of two witnesses is satisfied, even for the strictest *ḥadd* case of four witnesses: Matthew, John, Peter, and Paul are direct witnesses, and Mark and Luke are indirect witnesses.

4. The ancient Roman law held that one witness is not sufficient, and Europe's continental civil law follows the same principle. The papal ecclesiastical law also holds the same principle based on the biblical notion of two or three witnesses. Wigmore, "Required Numbers of Witnesses," 83–84. The common law, on the other hand, entirely rejected the numerical system by the mid-seventeenth century, although it kept a minimum of two witnesses in cases of high treason. Stephen, *Digest of the Law*, 116–17, 125. The common law, therefore, accepts as sufficient the testimony of a single credible and trustworthy witness since his or her testimony cannot be ignored: "that it is strong enough to produce actual belief, every man's experience will vouch." Nevertheless, "although the testimony of a single witness, whose credit is untainted, be sufficient to warrant a conviction, even in a criminal case, yet undoubtedly any additional and concurrent testimony adds greatly to the credibility of testimony, in all cases where it labors under doubt or suspicion." Starkie, *Practical Treatise*, 827–28.

5. Nyazee, *Outlines of Islamic Jurisprudence*, 468.

6. Daoud, *Al-qaḍā' wa al-da'wa*, 2:128.

7. Al-Ḥanafī, al-Ḥalabī, and al-'Alā' al-Ḥaṣkafī, *Majma' al-anhur fī sharḥ*, 3:262. See also Daoud, *Al-qaḍā' wa al-da'wa*, 2:127–128.

8. Schacht, *Introduction to Islamic Law*, 193.

Qualifications of Eyewitnesses

An eyewitness must satisfy two sets of conditions, one related to the time of witnessing the subject event in its location, and the other to the time of testifying in court.[9]

Qualifications at the time of witnessing

First, the witness must be able to reason and understand the particulars of the event that is being witnessed, so he or she cannot be mentally unfit or a minor.[10] The apostles and Evangelists were adult men who were able to understand and select the witnessed events. Nothing in the New Testament or tradition suggests that they were unable to reason or distinguish what they saw. Indeed, the Islamic law does not stipulate education or special abilities and skills but only the basic ability to reason. Yet these men, probably in their twenties or thirties at the time of the crucifixion and resurrection, possessed more than the basic ability of reasoning. Matthew was a former tax collector by profession and so had high discernment and the ability to reason and distinguish.[11] John, a Palestinian Jew, came from a business family and could write in Greek. Paul was a highly educated Pharisee trained under the respected Jewish law teacher Gamaliel. James, the younger brother of Jesus, was a learned man as evidenced by the high literary standard of his letter.[12] As to the two indirect witnesses, Mark was the interpreter of Peter and so had a good learning standing, and Luke was a physician by profession.

Second, the witness cannot be blind because, even if he can hear, he must also be able to see to distinguish the speaker's identity with certainty since

9. The common law had several restrictions on who is eligible to testify. Most exceptions, however, have been scrapped over centuries of judicial reform. This came out of a growing conviction that exclusions would deprive the judge of evidence necessary to find the facts. Appleton, *Rules of Evidence*, 13. According to the English law 1999 Act, anyone now is a competent witness and can give evidence in any proceedings and at every stage. The only exceptions are children, the mentally disabled, and the accused. Keane and McKeown, *Modern Law of Evidence*, 126–27. Under the US Federal Rules of Evidence, the witness's competency to testify "at most requires only a minimal ability to observe, recollect, and recount as well as an understanding to of the duty to tell the truth." Even the mentally disabled is allowed to testify, though the weight given to his or her testimony is reduced. Broun, *McCormick on Evidence*, 149–50.

10. Al-Ḥanafī, *Badā'i' al-ṣanā'i'*, 9:7. See also Daoud, *Al-qaḍā' wa al-da'wa*, 2:96. See also Jaradat, *Al-niḍhām al-qaḍā'i fī*, 109.

11. Greenleaf, *Testimony of the Evangelists*, 21.

12. Bauckham, *Jesus and the Eyewitnesses*, 289.

voices are sometimes similar.[13] None of the writers of the New Testament were blind. They proclaimed before the authorities: "We cannot stop speaking about what we have *seen* and heard" (Acts 4:20). Moreover, during their time with Jesus they witnessed the many cases in which he restored vision to the blind; if any of them were blind, he might well have been healed. To be sure, Paul became blind, but only for three days after he saw the risen Jesus on his way to Damascus: "I could not see because of the brightness of that light" (Acts 22:11). God sent Ananias, a disciple in Damascus, to restore his sight.

Islamic law does not stipulate conditions regarding the ability to see except that the witness not be blind. Yet given the wondrous and unique nature of a resurrection event, one may revive the old objection that David Strauss raised and popularized more than a century ago albeit now in the context of Islamic law: although the disciples were not blind, they did not satisfy the subject condition because they did not *see* a real figure, a risen Jesus. They only had a false perception of seeing a risen Jesus due to their strong affection for him, i.e. they were hallucinating. Indeed, psychologist Elizabeth Loftus warns in her respected research against indiscriminate reliance on witness testimony in criminal cases, where she refers to an older study that shows that "observation is peculiarly influenced by expectation, so that errors amounting to distinct illusions or hallucinations may arise from this source. . . . We tend to see and hear what we expect to see and hear."[14]

Several reasons, however, render the argument for hallucination untenable. First, hallucination is an individual rather than collective experience. A group of people, even with the same psychological state, cannot have the same false perception of the same thing at the same time.[15] Second, hallucination does not explain the empty tomb. Third, hallucination does not explain the conversion of Paul, the avid persecutor of the church, and of James, the brother of Jesus who did not believe in him before the resurrection. If affection and grief caused hallucination to the disciples, these two obviously had

13. Al-Ḥanafī, *Badā'i' al-ṣanā'i'*, 9:7–8. See also Daoud, *Al-qaḍā' wa al-da'wa*, 2:96. See also Jaradat, *Al-niḍhām al-qaḍā'i*, 109.

14. Loftus, *Eyewitness Testimony*, 27. Loftus quotes from an older study conducted in 1918.

15. Some argue that collective visions of religious figures do occur. But the figure in such alleged visions is reported as appearing in a glorious state. None of Jesus's appearances were glorious. O'Connell, "Jesus' Resurrection," 69.

no such affections. Fourth, Jesus appeared over forty days in different places, at different settings, and to persons of different states of mind.[16] He appeared to them both indoors and outdoors, early at dawn as by the Sea of Tiberius and late afternoon as on the way to Emmaus. He appeared to them while they were sitting down (the Eleven), walking (to Emmaus), running (the two Marys), and at work fishing (Sea of Tiberius). He appeared to individuals (Mary Magdalene, Peter, and James) and to duos (the Marys and the Emmaus disciples). He appeared to the Eleven and showed them his hands and feet and asked them to touch him, and to dispel any shred of doubt he ate with them (Luke 24:36–43). Indeed, what happened during this first large-group appearance provides a fifth evidence against the charge of hallucination and suggests that the case was the *opposite* of hallucination: "[Jesus] appeared to disciples who were *not* in a state of eager expectation and who did *not* quickly believe that it was he."[17] Rather than the disciples seeing something unreal and thinking they saw a real man, they saw a real person and thought they saw a ghost until they were assured by the risen Lord: "Why are you troubled, and why do doubts arise in your hearts? See my hands and my feet, that it is I myself. Touch me and see. For a spirit does not have flesh and bones as you see that I have" (Luke 24:38–39). The resurrection event is the last thing the disciples would expect. This lays to rest the hallucination hypothesis.

The third condition at the time of witnessing the event is that the witness must see the event personally and directly, i.e. be a direct eyewitness, except in special cases where indirect, hearsay witnessing is permitted (as will follow).[18] As shown in chapter 3, the writers of the New Testament were direct eyewitnesses who saw the crucified and then the resurrected Lord (Matthew, John, Paul, and Peter), or were indirect witnesses who obtained their reports directly from trusted eyewitnesses (Mark and Luke).

Thus, Matthew saw Jesus as he was arrested and led to trial, but then admitted in his account that "all the disciples left Him and fled" (Matt 26:56). Yet John and Peter soon returned to watch Jesus's trial, which suggests that others might also have returned, particularly the next day to see the public

16. Habermas and Licona, *Case for the Resurrection*, 105–9.

17. Wenham, *Easter Enigma*, 105.

18. Al-Ḥanafī, *Badā'iʿ al- ṣanā'iʿ*, 9:9. See also al-Nasafī, *Kanz al-daqā'iq fī al-fiqh*, 472. See also al-Ḥossari, *'Ilm al- qaḍā'*, 1:207–8. See also Daoud, *Al-qaḍā' wa al-daʿwa*, 2:97–98.

crucifixion. Indeed, Luke expressly says that "*all His acquaintances* and the women who accompanied Him from Galilee were standing at a distance, seeing these things" (Luke 23:49). These would primarily include the disciples, including Matthew. Matthew then testified that Jesus appeared to the Eleven in Galilee, including Matthew himself (Matt 28:16–17), and Luke and John testify that he appeared to the Eleven in Jerusalem and showed them his pierced hands and feet (Luke 24:36–43; John 20:19–23).

John expressly states in his testimony that he was standing so closely before the crucified Christ that Jesus spoke to him directly: "When Jesus saw his mother and the disciple whom he loved [John] standing nearby, he said to his mother, 'Woman, behold, your son!' Then he said to the disciple, 'Behold, your mother!'" (John 19:26–27). Though involving only one eyewitness, this direct testimony has a particular significance as it comes from the very person whom Jesus was speaking to from his cross, in the only Gospel that expressly states that its writer is a direct eyewitness: "This is the disciple who is bearing witness about these things, and who has written these things, and we know that his testimony is true" (John 21:24). This strongly militates against the Islamic claim in the Qur'ān that God sent someone who looked like Jesus to be crucified in his place so that the crucifiers mistook him for Jesus: "They did not kill him nor crucify him, but so it was made to appear to them" (Qur'ān 4:157). No one other than Jesus could speak thus to John, the closest disciple to him, and to his mother, Mary. Craig Blomberg notes that this is what was normally expected from Jesus in the first-century patriarchal Jewish culture. With Joseph, his adoptive father, dead, Jesus had to entrust his widowed mother to the care of the next head of his household. With his brothers not believing in him yet, who was better to entrust her to than his beloved disciple, who was also her nephew? Indeed, external corroboration comes from early church tradition to the effect that Mary accompanied John when he, in later years, moved to Asia Minor and lived under his care until her death.[19]

Paul, most likely, did not see the crucifixion, but he saw the risen Lord in his road-to-Damascus appearance (Acts 9). Much has been said since the Enlightenment about whether this event "was an 'objective' or 'subjective' experience; that is, whether Paul saw and heard something or someone who

19. Blomberg, *Historical Reliability of John's*, 252.

was 'really there' in the public domain, or whether what happened to him was an 'internal' experience without any correlate in external reality."[20] To liberal scholarship, the term *heavenly vision* means an inner experience. Leading New Testament and resurrection scholar N. T. Wright notes that the Jews, including Paul, understood the term *heaven* to mean a real external object "out there."[21] Paul was clearly not talking about a Berkeleyan or a religious experience devoid of any "objective correlate."[22] When Paul exclaimed, "Am I not an apostle? Have I not seen Jesus our Lord?" (1 Cor 9:1), he uses the Greek term *heoraka*, which means ordinary rather than subjective vision. Moreover, when he delivered to the Corinthian church the gospel which he received, he listed the appearances of the risen Christ: "He appeared to Cephas, then to the twelve. After that He appeared to more than five hundred brethren at one time, most of whom remain until now, but some have fallen asleep; then He appeared to James, then to all the apostles; and last of all, as to one untimely born, He appeared to me also" (1 Cor 15:5–8). Paul's use of the term *appeared* (*ophthe*) can mean both private vision and real physical appearance. Wright shows that Paul clearly means the latter sense for, first, the passage shortly follows his previous mention of the term *heoraka* (1 Cor 9:1). Second, he lists his appearance in the same sequence of the other appearances that preceded his and that were clearly physical. Third, the passage as a whole "speaks of a *public event* for which there is *evidence* in the form of *witnesses* who *saw something* and can be *interrogated*."[23] Finally, the rest of the chapter is about physical resurrection with a physical body; it does not speak of "that interesting oxymoron, a non-bodily 'resurrection.'"[24] Wright concludes,

> The very close connection between Paul's view of what happened and his view of what will happen to all Christians, and the robustly "bodily" account of the latter given throughout 1 Corinthians 15, presents an unanswerable case for the fact that when Paul spoke of Jesus "appearing" in verse 8 he did not

20. Wright, *Resurrection of the Son*, 377.
21. Wright, 377.
22. Wright, 378.
23. Wright, 383.
24. Wright, 383.

> mean that Jesus appeared in his (Paul's) heart or mind, but to his bodily eyes and sight, as a real human being, truly and bodily raised from the dead.[25]

Peter, the central figure among the apostles, was a leading disciple who accompanied Jesus during his earthly mission and even followed him as he was arrested. He courageously attended his trial, although later that night he denied Jesus and then repented in tears that very night as Jesus looked him right in his eyes (Luke 22:61–62). It is therefore inconceivable that he did not attend the crucifixion. The Gospels tell that the risen Jesus appeared to the disciples (Matt 28:16–17; Luke 24:36; John 20:19–20, 21:1–18), sent a personalized message to Peter (Mark 16:7), and then made a personal appearance to him (Luke 24:34). According to Luke, Peter himself testified on behalf of the disciples before the crowd on Pentecost day that the crucified Jesus is risen (Acts 2:23–24). One may object that these reports all are secondary testimonies about Peter made by others. But Peter himself makes a direct testimony that Jesus is risen: "He has caused us to be born again to a living hope through the resurrection of Jesus Christ from the dead" (1 Pet 1:3). Then shortly afterwards Peter refers to both Jesus's crucifixion and resurrection: "You were ransomed . . . with the precious blood of Christ, like that of a lamb without blemish or spot. . . . [T]hrough Him [you] are believers in God, who raised Him from the dead and gave Him glory" (1 Pet 1:18–21).

As aforesaid, Islamic law admits indirect, hearsay witnesses in special cases by way of *istiḥsān* (preference)[26] rather than *qiyās* (analogy).[27] These cases are marital status, kinship, and death, with some adding to them

---

25. Wright, 383.

26. As explained in chapter 2, this is a secondary source of law recognized by the Ḥanafī, Māilkī, and Ḥanbalī schools.

27. While hearsay evidence used to be admissible in the English law only exceptionally, it is normally admissible now with only a few exceptions. Keane and McKeown, *Modern Law of Evidence*, 12. Under the Criminal Justice Act 2003, hearsay is admissible if it can be admissible had the person testified personally in court; if the person is duly identified; and if the person is dead, unfit because of bodily or mentally conditions, is outside the UK and his attendance cannot be secured, cannot be found despite trying, or if he cannot testify in court due to fear. Keane and McKeown, *Modern Law of Evidence*, 322–23. Moreover, statements containing a public matter that is made by a public officer tasked with enquiring and recording his findings, and recorded in a public document or historical record, i.e. meant to inform the public and be retained for public reference or inspection, are presumed as true. Kean and McKeown, *Modern Law of Evidence*, 384–85.

consummation of marriage and the appointment of a judge.[28] In these cases the hearsay witness, having obtained his or her information from the community, is accepted as if he or she is a direct eyewitness.[29] The condition for accepting the hearsay witness is that the reported news has become a well-known recurrent tradition in the community (*tawātur*) such that it rules out the possibility of lying or colluding.[30] Such communal knowledge has the same evidentiary value as eyewitness knowledge.[31] Law does not set a minimum number of the persons through whom the news spread; some suggest two men, or a man and two women.[32] So powerful is such communal knowledge that even a blind person can testify as a hearsay witness. Indeed, Muslim jurists consider this communal *tawātur* in transmitting *Ḥadīth* surer than transmission by individuals such that anyone who denies its authenticity is considered an infidel.[33] In case of witnessing death, the testimony can be admitted even if the news came from only one man or one woman without communal knowledge as people usually hate to report such news which, nevertheless, will eventually spread in the community.[34]

The two indirect witnesses of the crucifixion and resurrection, Mark and Luke, do satisfy the said conditions for hearsay witnessing. Apart from the fact that Islamic law accepts hearsay witness from just one person in cases of death, the event was a public crucifixion that was open to all people to view, followed by a most unusual resurrection. News of both spread quickly in Jerusalem and beyond and became well-known recurrent tradition, or *tawātur*, in the community such that it rules out the possibility of lying or colluding.

---

28. Al-Ḥanafī, *Sharḥ fatḥ al-qadīr*, 7:362–363. See also al-Ḥanafī, *Badā'i' al-ṣanā'i'*, 9:9–11; al-Tomortāshī, *Tanwīr al-abṣār wa jāmi'*, 268; al-Nasafī, *Kanz al-daqā'iq*, 472; al-Ḥossari, *'Ilm al-qaḍā'*, 1:207–209; Daoud, *Al-qaḍā' wa al-da'wa*, 2:97–98.

29. Al-Ḥanafī, *Badā'i' al-ṣanā'i'*, 9:9. See also al-Ḥossari, *'Ilm al-qaḍā'*, 1:208.

30. Al-Ḥossari, *'Ilm al-qaḍā'*, 1:208–211.

31. Al-Ḥanafī, *Badā'i' al-ṣanā'i'*, 9:9.

32. Shammouṭ, *Al-ithbāt al-qaḍā'ī*, 99–100.

33. Al-Bouṭī, *Manhaj al-Ḥanafiyya fī naqd*, 102–103.

34. Al-Ḥanafī, *Sharḥ fatḥ al-qadīr*, 7:362–364. See also al-Ḥanafī, *Badā'i' al-ṣanā'i'*, 9:10; al-Ḥanafī, *Al-mabsūṭ fī al-fiqh al-Ḥanafī*, 8:184; al-Tomortāshī, *Tanwīr al-*abṣār, 268; Aḥmad al-Ḥossari, *'Ilm al-qaḍā'*, 1:209.

Mark was the interpreter of Peter. Papias (70–163 CE), writing before 110 CE,[35] related that the apostle John used to say that "Mark, in his capacity as Peter's interpreter, wrote down accurately as many things as Peter recalled from memory. . . . For he made it his one concern not to omit anything he had heard or to falsify anything."[36] Bauckham argues that internal evidence in Mark's Gospel gives credence to the Petrine influence in the Gospel, both in terms of its relying on Peter's preaching and its portrayal of his special character.[37] Thus, we have standing directly behind Mark no less an eyewitness than Peter, leader of the apostles. Moreover, Bauckham argues that it is quite possible that Mark is the anonymous young man who followed Jesus but fled naked as the soldiers tried to capture him.[38] It is also possible that Jesus might have held the Last Supper in Mark's house.[39] This can be reasonably inferred from the fact that the early church was meeting in Mark's house (Acts 12:12). If true, this qualifies him as a direct eyewitness. Luke, a companion of Paul, is an indirect eyewitness, but is also an expert witness, and so will be discussed under that title in the next chapter.

Indeed, non-Christian writers can also be included in this category of indirect witnesses to the crucifixion of Jesus, though perhaps at a lower tier, as they have come to us through third-hand transmission or beyond and were further separated from the generation of direct eyewitnesses. Yet they are an additional corroboration to the biblical accounts. The earliest source confirms the Gospel account of the supernatural darkness that befell the land during the crucifixion of Jesus as described in the three Synoptic Gospels: "Now from the sixth hour darkness fell upon all the land until the ninth hour" (Matt 27:45). Writing in 221 CE, early church scholar Julius Africanus (160–240 CE) describes what happened during the crucifixion: "On the whole world there pressed a most fearful darkness; and the rocks were rent by an earthquake, and many places in Judea and other districts were thrown down." He then refers disapprovingly to a description of the cause of the darkness in a writing dated to as early as 52 CE by the Greek-writing historian Thallus:

35. Bauckham, *Jesus and the Eyewitnesses*, 14.

36. Bauckham, 203.

37. Bauckham, 156, 172.

38. Bauckham, 198–99. Bauckham dedicates an entire chapter to exploring this possibility.

39. Bruce, *New Testament Documents*, 33. See also Isbouts, *Archaeology of the Bible*, 292.

"This darkness Thallus, in the third book of his History, calls, as appears to me without reason, an eclipse of the sun."[40] Africanus notes that the crucifixion happened during the Passover, and Passovers always fall in full moon; a solar eclipse never happens when the moon is full.[41] From his attributing this darkness to a natural rather than a supernatural event, it is evident that Thallus clearly accepted the happening of the darkness, though denying its supernatural causation. Indeed, Thallus may have seen it himself. Moreover, it shows that at least this part of the crucifixion tradition was already in circulation to a degree that Thallus felt the need to refute its causation. Thallus remains the only non-Christian to write about a Jesus tradition before the Gospels, and his writing, which we have access to in third-hand transmission, is the first known anti-Christian writing.[42]

The second source in chronological order that corroborates the crucifixion accounts comes from a letter written by the Syrian Stoic philosopher Mara Bar Serapion to his son in 73 CE, shortly after the fall of Jerusalem:

> What good did it do the Athenians to kill Socrates, for which deed they were punished with famine and pestilence? What did it avail the Samians to burn Pythagoras, since their country was entirely buried under sand in one moment? Or what did it avail the Jews to kill their wise king, since their kingdom was taken away from them from that time on? God justly avenged these three wise men.[43]

This might be the "earliest non-Christian philosophical reference to Christianity that we have."[44]

The third source comes from the prominent Jewish Roman historian Josephus (36–100 CE) in the early nineties.[45] In his work, *Antiquities* (18.63–64), we read:

> Now, there was about this time Jesus, a wise man, *if it be lawful to call him a man*, for he was a doer of wonderful works – a

40. Habermas, *Historical Jesus*, 196–97.

41. Van Voorst, *Jesus Outside the New*, 20.

42. Van Voorst, 23.

43. Bock, *Studying the Historical Jesus*, 52–53.

44. Van Voorst, *Jesus Outside the New*, 58.

45. Van Voorst, 82.

> teacher of such men as receive the truth with pleasure. He drew over to him both many of the Jews, and many of the Gentiles. *He was [the] Christ.* And when Pilate, at the suggestion of the principal men among us, had condemned him to the cross, those that loved him at the first did not forsake him: *for he appeared to them alive again the third day, as the divine prophets had foretold these and ten thousand other wonderful things concerning him*; and the tribe of Christians, so named for him, are not extinct at this day [all italics mine].[46]

Josephus was considered a traitor by the Jews, so they did not keep his records. Rather, it was Christians who recorded his works.[47] Many scholars since the sixteenth century have questioned parts of the text above (marked in italics) as being probably an addition from a Christian since it is unlikely to come from Josephus, a Jew. New Testament scholar Darrell Bock notes that, even without the italicized portions, of which he believes we cannot be certain, this testimony is of great importance. It corroborates the biblical accounts that Jesus was wise and taught wisdom, performed surprising works, had a large following, and started a movement that was still alive at the end of the century, and, most important to this study, that he was crucified.[48] Moreover, the undisputed text is evidently not Christian, since it refers to Jesus as a "wise man," miracles as "wonderful works," and Christians as "a tribe."[49] More to the point, experts in the works of Josephus note that this undisputed text matches the style of Josephus,[50] such as the phrase "those that loved him at the first did not forsake him."[51] The text, at least the non-italicized part, is authentic, with good corroborating manuscript evidence and no textual evidence to the contrary.[52] After thoroughly analyzing several reconstructions of the text that aimed at dealing with the suspected

46. Josephus, "Antiquities of the Jews," 18.3.3.

47. Van Voorst, *Jesus Outside the New*, 82–83.

48. Bock, *Studying the Historical Jesus*, 55–57.

49. Yamauchi, "Jesus Outside the New," 213. See also Van Voorst, *Jesus Outside the New*, 89–91.

50. Habermas, *Historical Jesus*, 193.

51. Yamauchi, "Jesus Outside the New," 213. See also Van Voorst, *Jesus Outside the New*, 90.

52. Habermas, *Historical Jesus*, 193.

Christianized insertions, New Testament scholar Robert Van Voorst agrees that the text is convincingly authentic once the above italicized parts are removed.[53] In all the reconstructions reviewed by Van Voorst, the part concerning the crucifixion is intact. Coming from an important and credible non-Christian historian like Josephus, this evidence carries significant weight. Darrell Bock believes that this is "the "most important extrabiblical evidence for Jesus."[54]

The fourth source comes from the Roman historian and senator Tacitus (56–120 CE). In describing the burning of Rome at the orders of Nero, who then threw the blame at Christians, Tacitus writes in his *Annals* around 116 CE:

> Therefore, to squelch the rumor, Nero created scapegoats and subjected to the most refined tortures those whom the common people called "Christians," [a group] hated for their abominable crimes. The author of this name, Christ, during the reign of Tiberius, had been executed by the procurator Pontius Pilate. Suppressed for the moment, the deadly superstition broke out again, not only in Judea, the land which originated this evil, but in the city of Rome.[55]

This is an important corroborative reference from a non-Christian and non-Jewish source to Pilate and the expansion of Christianity as far as Rome. More important, however, is its corroboration of the execution of Jesus. Habermas argues that, being a Roman senator, Tacitus must have obtained his information from official state records, perhaps from one of the reports that the Roman prefect Pontius Pilate had sent to the emperor.[56] Van Voorst, however, believes that Pilate is an unlikely source. There were two types of official Roman records, imperial and senatorial, and if Pilate had sent any report on Jesus's trial, it would be in imperial records, to which Tacitus had no access. Van Voorst also believes that Tacitus did not obtain it from the New Testament. Rather, he most probably obtained it during his membership

53. Van Voorst, *Jesus Outside the New*, 95–98.

54. Bock, *Studying the Historical Jesus*, 53.

55. Bock, 49.

56. Habermas, *Historical Jesus*, 189.

in a state priestly organization entrusted with dealing with foreign cults.[57] Van Voorst concludes that, "in his sparse but accurate detail, Tacitus gives the strongest evidence outside the New Testament for the death of Jesus."[58]

A fifth source comes in a book by the well-known Greek satirist Lucian of Samosata (115–200 CE), in which he mocks a group of Christians and refers to "that one whom they still worship today, the man in Palestine who was crucified because he brought this new form of initiation into the world."[59] Further references come from rabbinic sources, such as the Talmud in the period between 70 and 200 CE: "On the eve of the Passover Yeshu (the Nazarene) was hanged."[60] One can add other sources from Gnostics and the church fathers,[61] but the above are sufficient for the purpose of this study.

Qualifications at the time of testifying

Having satisfied the qualifications required at the time of witnessing the event, the said witnesses must now satisfy another set of conditions set by Islamic law to be eligible to testify to what they have witnessed.

First, the witness must be a Muslim, though a non-Muslim, or *kāfir* (infidel), can testify against a non-Muslim.[62] The apostles and Evangelists predated Islam by centuries, and so this condition is technically inapplicable. Nevertheless, one should bear in mind the rationale behind this rule: testifying effectively entails exercising a kind of power, and a Muslim cannot fall under the power of a non-Muslim.[63] The virtual case for the crucifixion and resurrection does not entail any jurisdiction or control over a Muslim. Indeed, the sought verdict does not aim at taking out rights to the Christian or inflicting loss or harm on the Muslim but rather comes out of the sincere wish that he or she "may have life and have it abundantly" (John 10:10). Moreover, Islam considers the good people who lived before Islam and are mentioned in the Qur'ān as being godly as if they were Muslims. This certainly includes

57. Van Voorst, *Jesus Outside the New*, 49–52.

58. Van Voorst, 52.

59. Van Voorst, 59

60. Habermas, *Historical Jesus*, 202–3.

61. Habermas, 208 ff., 229 ff.

62. al-Ḥanafī, *Badā'iʿ al-ṣanā'iʿ*, 9:47. See also Daoud, *Al-qaḍā' wa al-daʿwa*, 2:100.

63. El Shamsy, "Logic of Excluding Testimony," 12. See also Daoud, *Al-qaḍā' wa al-daʿwa*, 2:100.

the apostles, or *ḥawāriyyūn*, whom the Qur'ān mentions expressly and favorably: "And when Jesus sensed disbelief in them, he said, 'Who are my helpers unto God?' The Apostles said, 'We are God's helpers. We believe in God; bear witness that we are submitters [*muslimūn* in Arabic]'" (Qur'ān 3:52).

Second, the witness must be a freeman. A slave cannot testify because testimony is a sovereign act that implicitly authorizes the judge to pronounce judgment, and a slave cannot authorize.[64] The apostles and Evangelists were all freemen as indicated by their freedom to follow Jesus day and night, and then move around as witnesses to his resurrection.

Third, the witness must be an adult, having reached puberty. Nonetheless, his testimony will be admissible if he is still a minor at the time of witnessing the event but grows up to adulthood at the time of testifying.[65] All the apostles and Evangelists were clearly adults, at least in their twenties and thirties, both during witnessing the events and giving testimony.

Fourth, the witness cannot be blind during testifying even if he could see at the time of witnessing the event, neither can he be deaf or dumb, not the least because he cannot give oath.[66] No indication can be found in the New Testament or early church tradition that any of the apostles or Evangelists was blind, deaf, or dumb. As aforesaid, Paul became blind because of the bright light of the appearance of the risen Jesus after he saw him but was healed after a few days.

Fifth, the witness must be mentally sound with clear memory and understanding of the event, which also means that he cannot be drunk.[67] The Islamic law demands no more than ordinary mental abilities. The apostles and Evangelists were more than mentally sound. As discussed in the previous section, despite the lowly social status of some of them, they were bilingual or skilled in their respective callings. For example, Matthew was skilled in numbers as a tax collector, Mark was "useful to [Paul] for service" (2 Tim 4:11), Luke was a doctor, John spoke Greek, Paul was highly educated in Jewish law and Greek, and James had an admirable literary style.

---

64. Al-Ḥanafī, *Badā'i' al-ṣanā'i'*, 9:12. See also al-Ḥossari, *'Ilm al-qaḍā'*, 1:220.
65. Al-Ḥossari, 1:219.
66. Al-Kāsānī, *Badā'i' al-ṣanā'i'*, 9:13. See also Daoud, *Al-qaḍā' wa al-da'wa*, 2:112–113.
67. Daoud,2:103.

Moreover, and as discussed in chapter 3, the disciples' memorization skills were outstanding in comparison with modern generations as attested by the manner of their writings and the minute details and facts they contain. They had a long three-year close acquaintance with the extraordinary man Jesus and his unforgettable deeds. Loftus refers to studies that show that an eyewitness will recall an event better when it takes place and is observed over a longer duration.[68] This applies to the crucifixion event, which lasted some twenty-four hours, including six on the cross. She also notes that something that is experienced several times is remembered better than a one-time event.[69] This applies to the post-resurrection appearances of Jesus to his disciples, which happened at least ten times over a period of forty days. Another study referred to by Loftus shows that "the extraordinary, colorful, novel, unusual, and interesting scenes attract our attention and hold our interests, both attention and interest being important aids to memory. The opposite of this principle is true – routine, commonplace and insignificant circumstances are rarely remembered as specific incidents."[70] This applies to both the crucifixion and the post-resurrection appearances of Jesus, thus lending more support to the reliability of the disciples' memories.

Sixth, the witness must not be a beneficiary of his testimony, whether by way of gaining benefit or avoiding loss. This also means that the witness cannot be an enemy of the defendant or a direct family member of a litigant, or the defendant's slave, employee, or master.[71] None of the apostles and Evangelists benefited, or hoped to benefit, from his testimony. On the contrary, they proclaimed the good news

> with one voice, everywhere, . . . in the face of the most appalling terrors that can be presented to the mind of man. . . . The laws of every country were against [their] teachings. . . . The interests and passions of all the rulers and great men in the world were against them. The fashion of the world was against them. . . . They could expect nothing but contempt, opposition,

68. Loftus, *Eyewitness Testimony*, 23.

69. Loftus, 25. Loftus quotes this from an older study conducted in 1948.

70. Loftus, 27. Loftus quotes this from an older study conducted in 1933.

71. Al-Ḥanafī, *Badāʾiʿ al-ṣanāʾiʿ*, 9:24–26. See also al-Ḥanafī, *Sharḥ fatḥ al-qadīr*, 7:375–80; Jaradat, *Al-niḍhām al-qaḍāʾi*, 122–23; Daoud, *Al-qaḍāʾ wa al-daʿwa*, 2:115–17.

> revilings, bitter persecutions, stripes, imprisonments, torments, and cruel deaths.[72]

Tradition has it that all the apostles and Evangelists, except John, were martyred: Peter was crucified upside-down in Rome; Paul was beheaded in Rome; James son of Zebedee was beheaded in Jerusalem; James the brother of Jesus was stoned and clubbed to death in Jerusalem; Andrew was crucified on an X-shaped cross in Greece; Thomas was stabbed to death in India; Bartholomew was beaten to death in Turkey; Matthew was beheaded by the sword in Ethiopia; Jude was hit by arrows; Matthias was stoned then beheaded; Mark was dragged by horses through the streets of Alexandria, Egypt; and Luke was hanged in Greece.[73] More recently, Sean McDowell traced the historical evidence for martyrdom among the apostles (but not the Evangelists Mark and Luke), following strict rules of historiography to arrive at credible, academic conclusions. His research revealed that,

> in sum, there are three apostles [Peter, Paul, and James, son of Zebedee] in the category of *highest possible probability* [of being martyred], one [James, brother of Jesus] that is *very probably true*, two [Andrew and Thomas] that are *more probable than not*, two [Bartholomew and James, son of Alphaeus] that are *more possible than not*, five [Matthew, Philip, Thaddeus, Simon the Zealot, and Matthias] that are *possible*, and one [John] that is *improbable*. Thus, of the fourteen apostles, eight are at least *more possible than not*, five are *possible* and only one is *lower than possible*.[74]

Regardless of actual persecutions or martyrdom, however, what matters to this study is that the apostles not only had no interest or even dreams of making personal gains, but they "proclaimed the risen Jesus to skeptical and antagonistic audiences with full knowledge they would likely suffer and die for their beliefs."[75]

---

72. Greenleaf, *Testimony of the Evangelists*, 31.
73. Schmidt, *How Christianity Changed*, 19.
74. McDowell, "Historical Evaluation ," 428.
75. McDowell, 428.

Seventh, the witness must be of good character, or *adl*, one whose good deeds outnumber his evil acts and who did not commit a major crime nor persist in a minor one.[76] The *adl* person must also be known for reasonability and moderation.[77] This disqualifies a wide variety of people. In addition to murderers, thieves, liars, misers, deserters of public prayer, usurers, and transgenders, this disqualifies persons with criminal record, professional mourners because they pretend grief for money, singers and dancers because they entice people to commit indecency and so are worse than those who commit it, bird players[78] because they gaze at nudity from atop their roofs, chess players because they neglect prayer times, nude bathers because they break a prohibiting commandment, and homosexuals because they commit a major sin.[79] The uncircumcised are considered untrustworthy and cannot be witnesses except if poor health or old age render circumcision difficult. The eunuch and the illegitimate son, however, may testify.[80] If one commits a major crime and repents, he can be admitted as a witness, and if one commits a minor crime and does not repent, he cannot be a witness.[81] Interestingly, Islamic law is concerned with apparent integrity only rather than internal character.[82] As such, good character for a Muslim who shows no outer sign to the contrary should be presumed without seeking further evidence, except if his or her opponent raises an objection, or in cases involving *ḥadd*, where the judge has to investigate the honesty of the accused. In addition to the difficulty, if not utter impossibility, of ascertaining internal character and other practical considerations, the rationale behind this is that being a Muslim itself should imply integrity.[83]

The apostles and Evangelists will not be given this privileged presumption of innocence, which they do not need since their integrity and morality are

76. Al-Ḥanafī, *Badā'i' al-ṣanā'i'*, 9:13–14. See also Daoud, *Al-qaḍā' wa al-da'wa*, 2:104; al-Ḥossari, *'Ilm al-qaḍā'*, 1:227–28.

77. Al-Ḥanafī, *Al-mabsūṭ*, 8:132–33.

78. "Bird players" refers to men playing with pigeons on their rooftops.

79. Al-Ḥanafī, *Badā'i' al-ṣanā'i'*, 9:14–17. See also al-Ḥanafī, *Sharḥ fatḥ al-qadīr*, 7:381–88; al-Tomortāshī, *Tanwīr al-abṣār*, 268–69; al-Nasafī, *Kanz al-daqā'iq*, 473–474; al-Ḥossari, *'Ilm al-qaḍā'*, 1:229–34.

80. Al-Ḥanafī, *Badā'i' al-ṣanā'i'*, 9:16 –17. See also al-Ḥossari, *'Ilm al-qaḍā'*, 1:234–35.

81. Al-Ḥanafī, 9:18. See also al-Ḥossari, 1:239.

82. Al-Ḥanafī, 9:19. See also al-Ḥossari, 1:240.

83. Daoud, *Al-qaḍā' wa al-da'wa*, 2:105–7.

evident. They came from ordinary backgrounds, yet their lives were radically changed as their master called them and taught them by word and deed the highest standards of ethics and holy living that have changed the world.[84] Their integrity was unquestioned in their communities as they were "having favor with all the people" (Acts 2:47). This is also evidenced by the rapid acceptance of their testimonies. Indeed, the internal evidence of their testimony is self-attesting: "It is impossible to read their writings and not feel that we are conversing with men eminently holy and of tender consciences, with men acting under an abiding sense of the presence and omniscience of God, and of their accountability to him, living in his fear, and walking in his ways."[85]

Nineteenth century common law authority and Harvard professor Simon Greenleaf posits a dilemma. Supposing that the apostles and Evangelists were evil men, two possibilities exist. If they believed in a future judgment of reward or punishment, it is hard to believe that they would invent lies that were certainly jeopardizing all their gains and hopes in this world and secured them nothing but hell in the world to come. If, on the other hand, they did not believe in future judgment, it is equally hard to believe they had good reason to invent lies that would only bring forth the enmity of this world, destroy any prospect of good life, and then perish. In both cases, it is also inconceivable that such bad men, young as they were, would renounce every sin and live a life of self-denial to crucify the flesh and its strong desires.[86]

Greenleaf then provides from his hindsight as lawyer an insightful contrast between false and honest witnesses. False witnesses usually tend to be unnatural, profuse in pre-prepared statement related to the main matter, but beyond that they tend to be "reserved and meager, from fear of detection," resorting rather to the easy yet detestable *non mi-recordo* escape tactic.[87] In the testimony of truthful witnesses, on the other hand, "there is a visible and striking naturalness of manner, and an unaffected readiness and copiousness in the detail of circumstances, as well as in one part of the narrative as another, and evidently without the least regard to the facility or difficulty

84. Schmidt, *How Christianity Changed*, 9, 14.
85. Greenleaf, *Testimony of the Evangelists*, 32.
86. Greenleaf, 33.
87. Greenleaf, 39–40.

of verification or detection."[88] The testimony of the Evangelists evidently belongs to the latter:

> The writers allude, for example, to the existing manners and customs, and to the circumstances of the times and of their country, with the utmost minuteness of reference. And these references are never formally made, nor with preface and explanation, never multiplied and heaped on each other, nor brought together, as though introduced by design; but they are scattered broadcast and singly over every part of the story, and so connect themselves with every incident related as to render the detection of falsehood inevitable. . . . We therefore have it in our power to institute [a] cross-examination upon the writers of the New Testament; and the freedom and the frequency of their allusions to these circumstances supply us with ample material for it.[89]

Taking for example the crucifixion narrative alone, the Jews brought Jesus to Pontius Pilate to receive his verdict. Josephus and Tacitus, as well as archeology, tell us that Pilate was then the Roman governor over Judea, and we know that the Roman governor, not the Jews, had the power to sentence Jesus to death. The Gospels tell us that the soldiers derided Jesus, and history tells us that this was customary at the time. The Gospels also tell us that Pilate had Jesus whipped, and historical accounts tell us that the convicted was "stripped, whipped, and beheaded or executed." The Gospels tell us that the authorities nailed the charge to the top of the cross, and historians like Suetonius tell us that the Romans affixed a description of the crime to the punishment instrument. The Gospels further tell us that the charge was written in three languages, a fact Josephus confirms applied to all public announcements. Jesus had to carry his cross, and historical sources tell us that this was the usual practice. The body of Jesus was given to his friends at their request to bury it, and historical sources confirm the same practice applied except for notorious criminals.[90]

88. Greenleaf, 39–40.

89. Greenleaf, 42–43.

90. Greenleaf, 44.

Finally, and apart from the honest character of the Evangelists as evidenced by their historical accuracy, internal "marks of truth" abound in the very manner the Evangelists write, as exemplified in

> the nakedness of their narratives; the absence of all parade by the writers about their own integrity, of all anxiety to be believed, or to impress others with a good opinion of themselves or their cause, of all marks of wonder, or of desire to excite astonishment at the greatness of the events they record, and of all appearance of design to exalt their master. On the contrary, there is apparently the most perfect indifference on their part whether they are believed or not; or rather, the evident consciousness that they are recording events well known to all in their own country and times, and undoubtedly to be believed. . . . They have bestowed no epithets of harshness or even of just censure on the authors of all this wickedness, but have left the plain and unencumbered narrative to speak for itself; . . . like true witnesses, who have nothing to gain or to lose by the event of the cause, they state the fact, and leave them to their fate. Their simplicity and artlessness, also, should not pass unnoticed, in readily stating even those things most disparaging to themselves. Their want of faith in their master, their dullness of apprehension of his teachings, their strifes for preeminence, [and] their desertion of their Lord in his hour of extreme peril, . . . are nevertheless set down with all the directness and sincerity of truth.[91]

In the words of John Warwick Montgomery, "if anything, their simple literalness and directness is almost painful."[92]

Given the wondrous nature of the events witnessed by the disciples and the Evangelists during the life, death, resurrection, and appearances of Jesus, one would expect a journalist of today to write volumes. Strangely, this was not the case. John Wenham notes that "part of the greatness of all the evangelists lies in this ability to confine themselves to what serves their purpose and to omit a multitude of details and qualifications irrelevant to their purpose, no

91. Greenleaf, 45–46.

92. Montgomery, *History, Law and Christianity*, 77.

matter how important they may be in other connections."[93] John writes that "many other signs Jesus also performed in the presence of the disciples, which are not written in this book; but these have been written so that you may believe that Jesus is the Christ, the Son of God; and that believing you may have life in His name" (John 20:30–31).

The Gospels do not tell us much about the moral life and character of the disciples before Jesus called them. We know that Matthew was a despised tax collector, which implies both working for the enemy against his countrymen and making financial gains from both through dubious dealings. Regardless, when Jesus called the disciples, they repented and he changed their lives with his teaching and example, which they themselves recorded and conveyed to the world. After his departure, his indwelling Holy Spirit continued the sanctification work. The Islamic law provides that, if one commits a major crime and repents, he or she can be admitted as witness, and if one commits a minor crime and does not repent, he or she cannot be a witness.[94] Their repentance covered both.

Consistency of Testimonies

The Islamic law requires that testimonies by a specific number of witnesses be consistent in their details.[95] Abū Ḥanīfa stipulated that testimonies must agree both in meaning and words, though use of synonymous words is acceptable, while his two principal students, al-Shaybānī and Abū Yūsuf, accepted implicit rather than express, verbal agreement.[96] Thus, according to both Abū Ḥanīfa and his two disciples, if the plaintiff claims that he has given the defendant one thousand five hundred dollars and one witness testifies that the amount

93. Wenham, *Easter Enigma*, 52.

94. Al-Ḥanafī, *Badāʾiʿ al-ṣanāʾiʿ*, 9:41–43. See also al-Ḥanafī, *Sharḥ fatḥ al-qadīr*, 7:408–12; al-Sarkhasī al-Ḥanafī, *Al-mabsūṭ*, 8:204–8; Zaynuddīn Ibn Nujaym, *Al-ashbāh wa al-naẓāʾir*, 185; Daoud, *Al-qaḍāʾ wa al-daʿwa*, 2:125, 164–65; al-Ḥossari, *ʿIlm al-qaḍāʾ*, 1:418.

95. Al-Kāsānī, *Badāʾiʿ al-ṣanāʾiʿ*, 9:40. The English law considers that a piece of additional evidence amounts to corroboration of an existing evidence if it is relevant, admissible, credible, independent, and produces an effect in the manner consistent with the applicable statute. Keane and McKeown, *Modern Law of Evidence*, 241. On consistency of multiple testimonies, an old principle holds that "it so rarely happens that witnesses of the same transaction perfectly and entirely agree in all points connected with it, that an entire and complete coincidence in every particular, so far from strengthening their credit, not unfrequently engenders a suspicion of practice and concert." Starkie, *Practical Treatise*, 831.

96. Al-Kāsānī, *Badāʾiʿ al-ṣanāʾiʿ*, 9:41–42. See also Daoud, *Al-qaḍāʾ wa al-daʿwa*, 2:125, 164–65. Al-Ḥossari, *ʿIlm al- qaḍāʾ*, 1:417–18.

is one thousand five hundred while the other testifies that it is one thousand, the judge rules on one thousand because, as per Abū Ḥanīfa, both witnesses have uttered the common words *one thousand*, and as per his disciples, one thousand is implicitly included in the one thousand five hundred.[97] If, however, the plaintiff claims ninety dollars and one witness testifies to ninety while the other testifies to seventy, Abū Ḥanīfa rejects both testimonies because they lack express verbal agreement in any utterance, whereas his two students accept the lesser amount, seventy, because it is implied in the ninety; that is, both agreed on the seventy and so are accepted, and only one testified to the remaining amount and so is rejected.[98] Inconsistencies between two witnesses reduce the required doubly-attested testimony to two different *singly*-attested testimonies.[99] Even if the two inconsistent testimonies can be harmonized through synthesis, this is not acceptable as it amounts in effect to combining the two testimonies into a single compound testimony and reducing the two witnesses to the equivalent of one, which falls short of providing two similar testimonies by two witnesses.[100]

Differences as to kind, nature, or property of that which is witnessed annul the testimonies.[101] If two testimonies differ as to causation, they are also rejected.[102] If a witness testifies that he saw an act and another that he heard a person confess that he committed the act, both testimonies are rejected because each has testified to a different event, one being committing the act, and the other confession of committing it.[103] If one witness testifies to a fact and the second testifies to it and adds another, the judge accepts only the first fact and excludes the second because it is based on just one witness.[104]

97. Al-Kāsānī, 9:41–42.

98. Al-Ḥanafī, 9:41–43. See also al-Ḥanafī, *Sharḥ fatḥ al-qadīr*, 7:408–12; al-Ḥanafī, *Al-mabsūṭ*, 8:204–8; Ibn Nujaym, *Al-ashbāh wa al-naza'ir*, 185; Daoud, *Al-qaḍā' wa al-da'wa*, 2:125, 164–65; al-Ḥossari, *'Ilm al-qaḍā'*, 1:418.

99. Al-Ḥossari, *'Ilm al-qaḍā'*, 1:417. See also Al-Kāsānī, *Badā'i' al-ṣanā'i'*, 9:40.

100. Al-Ḥossari, 1:417.

101. Daoud, *Al-qaḍā' wa al-da'wa*, 2:167.

102. Daoud, 2:170.

103. Daoud, 2:172.

104. Al-Ḥossari, *'Ilm al-qaḍā'*, 1:421.

Islamic law allows for reconciling two seemingly inconsistent accounts where possible and if other conditions are met.[105] For example, if witnesses differ on the timing and location of a saying and agree on its contents, their testimonies are accepted, but they are rejected if the object of the testimonies is an act rather than a saying.[106] The rationale is that a saying may have been uttered more than once, each in a different time and place, thus enabling reconciliation, whereas an act happens once and so inconsistent accounts cannot be reconciled.[107] In another example, if a plaintiff claims a debt of one thousand dollars and one witness testifies for one thousand and the other for two thousand, the testimonies are annulled (unlike the aforesaid acceptable case where the plaintiff claims two thousand). The testimonies, however, can be reconciled if background explanations are revealed, such as the plaintiff's confirming that the debtor originally owed him two thousand but repaid one thousand without the witness's knowing.[108]

One important example involves theft, which is a *ḥadd* case that requires utmost attentiveness. A man files a case claiming that someone has stolen his cow. His two witnesses agree that they saw the accused person stealing the cow but differ as to its color, one saying it was light brown and the other red. Abū Ḥanīfa argues that their testimonies are accepted for two reasons. First, the two testimonies can be reconciled. Theft usually happens at night and witnesses see from a distance. They may not be able to distinguish between the two near colors. Even if one witness said it was black and the other that it was white, Abū Ḥanīfa still argues that the two accounts can be reconciled as the cow may be black on one side and white on the other, with each witness seeing it from an opposite side.[109] Second, the principal fact to be evidenced is the act of stealing a cow rather than its color. Thus, if the two witnesses kept silent on color, their testimonies would anyway be accepted. The same principle applies if the discrepant fact is the color of the thief's shirt. The point

105. Al-Ḥanafī, *Sharḥ fatḥ al-qadīr*, 7:408–9, 412. See also al-Ḥanafī, *Badā'iʿ al-ṣanā'iʿ*, 9:42.

106. Al-Ḥanafī, *Badā'iʿ al-ṣanā'iʿ*, 9:43. See also Daoud, *Al-qaḍā' wa al-daʿwa*, 2:126, 168; al-Ḥossari, *ʿIlm al-qaḍā'*, 1:420–21.

107. Al-Ḥanafī, *Badā'iʿ al-ṣanā'iʿ*, 9:43. See also Daoud, *Al-qaḍā' wa al-daʿwa*, 2:126. See also al-Ḥossari, *ʿIlm al-qaḍā'*, 1:421.

108. Al-Ḥanafī, *Sharḥ fatḥ al-qadīr*, 7:408.

109. Al-Ḥanafī, 7:415–16. See also al-Ḥanafī, al-Ḥalabī, and al-Ḥaṣkafī, *Majmaʿ al-anhur*, 3:287–88.

is that adding a secondary piece of information that was neither required nor decisive to the subject fact, even if discrepant, does not annul the happening of the subject fact, stealing.[110]

In another example also involving *ḥadd*, if the eyewitnesses agree on the act of committing adultery and the identity of the adulterers yet differ on the secondary detail of which corner of the room the act took place, their testimonies are accepted for the same two reasons. First, the two accounts can be reconciled if the room was so small as to allow for the possibility that the adulterers may have moved and covered both corners and, second, the location detail is secondary.[111] In both examples, the testimonies should be accepted without even the need for reconciliation.[112]

Abū Ḥanīfa's two students, however, differ with him. They argue that each testimony, taken as a whole, is different from the other and so fails to secure the required number of consistent witnesses.[113] This study will adopt the view of Abū Ḥanīfa, who is more authoritative than his two students, al-Shaybānī and Abū Yūsuf. In at least the above cases, Abū Ḥanīfa is stricter on formalistic adherence and more liberal on reconciliation, while his two students are more liberal on formalistic adherence and stricter on reconciliation.

Primary and secondary Islamic references give arguments and views that often involve different opinions and mostly involve hypothetical cases. Apart from the agreed general rules (e.g., number of witnesses and the need for consistency), no set rules or even principles as to details exist. These, however, can be reasonably inferred. First, *express, verbal testimonial agreement between the required number of testimonies is required while also allowing for the use of synonyms*. Second, *in case of two discrepant testimonies, a verbal common denominator between the two is recognizable*. Third, *apparent inconsistencies can be accepted upon reconciliation if plausible*, such as variations in place or time of a saying due to possible recurrence in different occasions, or variations in description due to the witnesses' viewing the event or object from different angles, or explanations involving background details not mentioned in the testimonies. Fourth, *separate accounts cannot be synthesized into one*

110. Al-Ḥanafī, al-Ḥalabī, and al-Ḥaṣkafī, 3:287–88. See also al-Ḥanafī, *Sharḥ fatḥ al-qadīr*, 7:415–16.

111. Al-Ḥanafī, 7:417. See also al-Ḥossari, *ʿIlm al-qaḍāʾ*, 1:525.

112. Al-Ḥanafī, 7:416.

113. Al-Ḥanafī, 7:415–16.

compound story as each component of the synthesis is singly attested, thus falling short of the specified number of witnesses. Fifth, *if the testimonies attest the principal fact adequately and consistently, discrepant secondary details do not invalidate the testimonies.*

A Christian reconciliation

The Gospels were written by four different authors. They contain enough apparent discrepancies in their accounts as to rule out the possibility of any collusion between the authors. Yet they have so much agreement once properly reconciled to show that they are describing the same events.[114] In demanding perfect literary consistency we forget that the Evangelists were humans not robots, and so it is only natural that machine-like consistency does not exist.[115] Their testimonies bear the marks of true ordinary witnesses in everyday life affairs such that if we reject their testimonies on grounds of these apparent discrepancies, we will have to discard most contemporaneous histories that historians hold with high confidence.[116]

Harmonizing apparently conflicting accounts is a regular endeavor in historical research, and biblical scholarship is no exception.[117] Many have suggested harmonized solutions to apparent discrepancies in the Gospels, including the accounts of Jesus's crucifixion, burial, and resurrection. This section will therefore first review examples of such solutions to show that real contradiction does not exist, while also evaluating them vis-à-vis the Islamic law. It will then give a unified account of the crucifixion, burial, and resurrection events that satisfies the Islamic law. Although some secondary details may be lost in the process as not meeting the requirements of Islamic law, the basic facts of the crucifixion and resurrection of Jesus remain intact. Before proceeding, however, a word of caution by biblical scholar Paul Feinberg is worth noting:

> A giant step forward in the quest to resolve the problems will be taken when one realizes that none of the evangelists is obligated to give an exhaustive account of any event. He has the right to

114. Greenleaf, *Testimony of the Evangelists*, 34–35.

115. Hall, *Seven Pillories of Wisdom*, 84, 86.

116. Greenleaf, *Testimony of the Evangelists*, 34–35.

117. Blomberg, *Historical Reliability*, 195.

> record an event in light of his purposes. Moreover, it must be remembered that the accounts of all four Gospel writers together do not exhaust the details of any event mentioned. There may be some unknown bit of information that would resolve seeming conflicts.[118]

Regarding the crucifixion event, Matthew, for example, records that Judas Iscariot, overwhelmed by remorse at betraying Jesus, went and hanged himself (Matt 27:3–10). According to Luke, Peter told the apostles that, "falling headlong, [Judas] burst open in the middle and all his intestines gushed out" (Acts 1:18). To reconciliate the two accounts, Judas must have hanged himself from a tree and then his body fell and burst open, probably because it was decomposed since no Jew would defile himself by burying a corpse during the feast, or because the branch of the tree broke and the body fell into a ravine below.[119] Such reconciliation may not be recognizable under Islamic law as it synthesizes two separate events, the hanging and the subsequent falling, which means that we have only one testimony for each.

The four Gospels give different wordings to the charge that Pilate wrote on the placard affixed to the cross. According to Matthew 27:37 it read: "This is Jesus the King of the Jews." According to Mark 15:26 it read: "The King of the Jews." In Luke 23:38 we read: "This is the King of the Jews." And in John 19:19 we read: "Jesus the Nazarene, the King of the Jews." One solution is to synthesize and combine all in one phrase, hence John's, but it would not satisfy the Islamic law requirement of multiple attestation. Applying the principle of common denominator, however, the phrase, "Jesus the King of the Jews" is common to Matthew and John, thus satisfying the requirement of having two testimonies. Moreover, Mark's short form is common to the four testimonies.

According to Matthew 27:54, the centurion remarked as he watched Jesus die: "Truly this was the Son of God." According to Mark 15:39, the centurion said: "Truly this man was the Son of God." In Luke 23:47, however, we read: "Certainly this man was innocent." Again, synthesizing the said statements by combining them is unrecognizable by Islamic law. Since we have three witnesses, however, we can exclude the more divergent account of Luke and still have the two testimonies of Matthew and Mark, the number required

118. Feinberg, "Meaning of Inerrancy," 302.

119. Carson, *Matthew*, 562.

by Islamic law. Both agree, with Mark adding the word *man*. Again, since a synthesis of Matthew and Mark is unrecognizable, we can only take the common verbal denominator between them: "Truly this was the Son of God," i.e. Matthew's account, which dropped Mark's *man*.

As to the resurrection event, the apparent discrepancies in the accounts describing the women visiting the tomb on Sunday morning appear to be more difficult to reconcile: Were there two women (Matt 28:1), three (Mark 16:1), more (Luke 24:10), or just one (John 20:1)? Did they go all together or in groups? Did Mary Magdalene see Jesus individually by the tomb (John 20:14) or on her way back with the other Mary (Matt 28:9)? How can we reconcile Mary Magdalene's reporting to Peter and John (John 20:2) when the Synoptics place her in the company of the other women who reported to all the disciples (Luke 24:9 and Matt 28:10), and how can we explain the content of her skeptical report of a stolen body versus the angelic tidings of a risen Jesus?

In one synthesized scenario, Mary Magdalene first came to the tomb alone while it was dark, found the stone rolled away but saw no angels, and returned to tell Peter and John (John 20:1–2). Then several women came in the dawn twilight to anoint the body but found instead two angels who told them that the Lord was not there but was risen (Luke 24:1–10). After the women returned to tell the disciples and confirm Mary Magdalene's report of the rolled stone, Peter and John ran to the tomb, saw the linen shroud wrapped orderly, and returned (John 20:3–9 and Luke 24:9–12). Then Mary Magdalene and other women came again with spices after sunrise, heard an angel telling them that the Lord has risen, and returned trembling without telling anyone (Mark 16:2–8). Mary Magdalene, however, lingered near the tomb and saw two angels, but then encountered Jesus himself and recognized him as he called her by name (John 20:10–17). The components of this synthesis are mostly singly attested and so do not meet the requirements of the Islamic law.[120]

Another attempt focuses on solving the apparent discrepancy between Jesus's appearing to Mary Magdalene alone (Mark 16:9 and John 20:14–16) and his appearing to her while she was accompanied by others (Matt 28:8–10). According to the suggested reconciliation, the Gospels describe a single event in which all the women were together at the tomb, with Mary Magdalene

120. Hailey, "Three Prophetic Days," 538–539.

standing at a distance. Jesus appeared to her first (Mark 16:9 and John 20:14–16) and then the others joined (Matt 28:8–10). Each Evangelist has mentioned what he saw as important to him. Thus, John and Peter's interpreter, Mark, mentioned Mary Magdalene alone because she was the one who reported the empty tomb to John and Peter, while Matthew had no reason to focus on her alone.[121] While such reconciling is possible, Matthew's account of Jesus's appearance to a group of women is singly attested and so does not meet the Islamic law requirement of double attestation.

New Testament scholar John Wenham makes a noteworthy book-length attempt at reconciling the crucifixion, burial, and resurrection accounts.[122] Drawing on his knowledge of Jerusalem where he had lived for some time, he gives a detailed account illustrated with roadmaps. He starts by assuming that Mary Magdalene is the sister of Martha and Lazarus, and so a resident of Bethany near Jerusalem.[123] He also assumes that the "other Mary" (Matt 28:1) is the wife of Clopas (John 19:25) and mother of Joses and James (Matt 27:56) who is himself James the Younger (Mark 15:40) and son of Alphaeus, hence one of the Twelve. He further assumes that Clopas is Cleopas (Luke 24:18), himself Alphaeus father of James the Younger and, according to tradition, brother of Joseph the legal father of Jesus. He also notes that Salome (Mark 16:1) is the mother of James and John sons of Zebedee (Matt 20:20) and sister of Jesus's mother (John 19:25).[124] The upshot is that Jesus's mother Mary, her sister Salome, and the "other Mary" were all relatives who stayed in John's family house in Jerusalem during the Passover festival.[125] Finally, Joanna, wife of Chuza the steward of Herod Antipas (Luke 8:3), must have stayed in the Hasmonean palace when in Jerusalem.[126] With this setting, Wenham describes the synthesized scene.

Upon the arrest of Jesus, the disciples fled in the opposite direction, i.e. towards Mary Magdalene's house in Bethany, and stayed there for Friday and

121. Goodenow, "Women at the Tomb," 542–543.

122. Wenham: *Easter Enigma*.

123. Wenham, 28–32. Wenham assumes that Mary Magdalene used to work in Magdala but returned to Bethany after her conversion. He stresses that this assumption is not essential to his harmonization and only aims at locating Mary Magdalene's home in Bethany.

124. Wenham, 34–38.

125. Wenham, 38.

126. Wenham, 39.

Saturday, while Peter and John followed Jesus and stayed at John's house in Jerusalem.[127] Mary Magdalene went to Jerusalem on Friday to watch the crucifixion with the other women. Luke names three women, Mary Magdalene, Joanna, and Mary mother of James (the "other Mary," wife of Clopas), and "other women" (Luke 24:10). With Salome being one of them (Mark 15:40), this leaves at least one other women. Wenham suggests she is Susanna (Luke 8:3).[128] After the hurried burial, Mary Magdalene went back to her home in Bethany, and Peter and the relatives stayed at John's house, except for the other Mary; she accompanied Mary Magdalene to Bethany to see her son, James the Younger, who was staying there with the disciples.[129] Joanna and Susanna stayed at the Hasmonean palace.[130] Such a scenario is based on synthesis between the three Synoptics and leaves Salome and the other woman, supposedly Susanna, singly attested, thus unrecognizable under Islamic law. Extra-biblical assumptions may be accepted as explanatory background details, the resulting scenario being as good as the assumptions.

Early Sunday morning, an earthquake struck, Jesus rose from the dead, and the guards fled away and later spread the stolen-body rumor at the suggestion and guarantee of the priests. An angel removed the stone, not to let Jesus out but to let in the women and disciples whom he was expecting. Mary Magdalene had left Bethany with the other Mary while it was still dark. On their way, they took with them Salome from John's house and arrived at the tomb via the Gennath Gate just before sunrise.[131] As Mary Magdalene saw the stone had been removed she immediately concluded that the body was stolen and so rushed back before the angels' appearance to tell Peter and John, while her companions were standing motionless in confusion.[132] Joanna and Susanna then arrived from the Hasmonean palace via another way, through the city's Ephraim Gate rather than the Gennath Gate, and so did not see Mary Magdalene on her way back. Joanna insisted on getting inside the tomb followed by Salome and the other Mary, where the two angels appeared to

127. Wenham, 59–60.

128. Wenham, 64.

129. Wenham, 69–70.

130. Wenham, 75.

131. Wenham, 82.

132. Wenham, 83.

them.[133] They then went back with fear, trembling, and great joy through the Ephraim Gate, not speaking to anyone on their way, until they arrived at John's house and broke the good news.[134] In this part, some details such as the earthquake, the angel removing the stone, the rumor of stealing the body, and the presence of Joanne and Salome are singly attested and so unrecognizable under Islamic law. Again, assumptions are just that: assumptions.

Upon hearing the breathless Mary Magdalene's report, Peter and John rushed to the tomb where Peter went in first and saw the grave-cloths. The shroud and headcloth were carefully wrapped, indicating that no one, friend or enemy, could have stolen the body and tidied them carefully only to carry a naked corpse through the streets of the city. Wenham here disagrees with the view that the grave-cloths collapsed as the body slipped out at the resurrection moment.[135] Mary Magdalene, however, returned to the tomb after some time when Peter and John had left, and she stood there weeping. So far, she had not heard of a risen Jesus or angelic appearances. Bowing to look into the tomb, she saw an angel for the first time. He asked her: "Woman, why are you crying?" But then she saw Jesus and, upon his calling her by name, she recognized him and held him for fear of losing him. Wenham argues that Jesus did not prevent her from touching him but rather assured her that he was not yet due to ascend to the Father and leave them, and so there was no need to cling to him. Mary then left for John's house to join the others.[136] The story of the appearance to Mary Magdalene by the tomb is singly attested and so unrecognizable under Islamic law. Peter's visit to the tomb (but not John's) is attested by both John and Luke and so is recognizable.

Joanna and the other women returned to tell the good news after their initial silence because of fear and awe. Salome and the other Mary left the group and set off to Bethany to tell the nine disciples who were there. On the way Jesus met them (Matt 28:9) and told them to tell the others about the Galilean rendezvous. They held his feet in adoration and then continued to Bethany.[137] Luke thus "telescopes" the coming of Mary Magdalene

133. Wenham, 84.

134. Wenham, 89.

135. Wenham, 92.

136. Wenham, 95.

137. Wenham, 95–96.

to Peter and John, and the other women to the rest.[138] Likewise, Matthew telescopes the angelic appearance to the three women, Jesus's appearance to Mary Magdalene, and then to the other Mary and Salome in one very succinct and abridged account. The fact is that the other Mary first went to the tomb (Matt 28:1) accompanied by others in addition to Mary Magdalene. When she returned to tell the disciples and met Jesus on the way (Matt 28:9) she had a different companion, Salome; the Magdalene had left and had a separate encounter with Jesus.

Thus, Matthew 28:1–7 describes the visit at dawn by the three women mentioned in Mark 16:1, though mentioning only two, Mary Magdalene and the other Mary, and leaving out Salome, whereas Matthew 28:8–10 *morphs* into the journey back from the tomb by the other Mary and Salome, Mary Magdalene having left earlier. This abridgment is typical of Matthew, as in Matthew 1 where he skips some names in the genealogy of Jesus, and in Matthew 21:18–22 where he tells the fig tree story as if it happened in one day rather than over two days as in Mark 11. In fact, this is also evident in the Olivet discourse when Jesus shifted, in a morph-like manner, from the impending destruction of Jerusalem all the way to the end-time great tribulation in Matthew 24:13 and Mark 13:24. Wenham argues that Matthew's account is correct: after all, Mary Magdalene did convey the good news to the disciples (those in John's house, though not the remaining nine), and the other Mary and Salome told the rest.[139] Wenham then continues with the remaining appearances with no difficulty.

Wenham, like other scholarly attempts, mostly resorts to reconciliation through synthesis based on the notion expressed by Darrell Bock that "just as a three-dimensional portrait gives depth to an image in a way that two dimensions cannot, so these four Gospels reveal a many-sided Jesus."[140] Accurate, revealing and convincing as this explanation may be, it still does not satisfy the requirements of testimony in Islamic law unless each component of the portrait is at least doubly attested. Synthesis reduces two testimonies to one compound story whose components are singly rather than doubly attested.

138. Wenham, 89.

139. Wenham, 96.

140. Bock, *Jesus According to Scripture*, 18. Bock's work aims at reconstructing a synthesized account of the life of Jesus based on the four Gospels.

An Islamic law reconciliation

This section will attempt a reconciliation of the crucifixion, burial, and resurrection accounts in the four Gospels that satisfies the requirements of the Islamic law.[141] This is achieved by juxtaposing these accounts and identifying those parts that comply with the relevant inferred principles of Islamic law in terms of testimonial consistency and excluding non-compliant parts.[142] The outcome, recognizable by Islamic law, will be evaluated for the degree of its adequacy in describing the crucifixion and resurrection of Jesus Christ.

Regarding the crucifixion accounts, Matthew and Mark are very similar and so largely cross-validate each other. Unique, uncorroborated details in Matthew include stripping Jesus (27:28), putting a staff in his hand (27:29), striking him on the head "again and again" (27:30), tasting the wine (27:34), the priestly sneering at Jesus's trust in God (27:43), the earthquake and associated resurrection of the saints (27:51–53), and the chief priests' request from Pilate to guard the tomb (27:62–66). Uncorroborated details in Mark include the names of the sons of Simon of Cyrene (15:21) and Pilate's surprise at Jesus's early death (15:44).

Regarding Luke, unique, uncorroborated details include Jesus's address to the wailing women on the *Via Dolorosa* (23:28–32), Jesus's prayer for forgiveness (23:34), the exchanges between the two thieves and between the repentant thief and Jesus (23:40–43), Jesus's committing his spirit to the Father (23:46), and the centurion's confession that Jesus was a "righteous man." (23:47).

John also has several uncorroborated contributions. These include Jesus's carrying his cross (19:17), the word *Nazarene* on Pilate's notice and the priests' objection to the words "king of the Jews" (19:19–22), the soldiers' first dividing Jesus's clothes before drawing lots for the seamless garment as related to prophecy (19:23–24), Jesus's request to John to take care of his mother Mary (19:25–27), Jesus's thirst as related to the prophecy (19:28), Jesus's words, "It is finished" (19:30), breaking the legs of the thieves and leaving intact the legs of the dead Jesus then piercing his side as related to the prophecy

141. These sections are Matthew 27:26–66, Mark 15:15–47, Luke 23:24–56, and John 19:16–54 for the crucifixion and burial events, and Matthew 28, Mark 16, Luke 24, and John 20–21 for the resurrection event.

142. See page 179 above.

(19:31–37), the secrecy of Joseph's discipleship and his accompaniment by Nicodemus (19:38–39), their wrapping of Jesus's body "with the spices" as a Jewish custom (19:40), and describing the tomb as being new and nearby (19:41–42). In sum, most of the crucifixion story as related by Matthew and Mark, with some corroborated additions in Luke and John, satisfy the Islamic law requirements of testimonial consistency. Uncorroborated details are secondary and their exclusion per Islamic law has little effect on the level of detail of a unified account.

The burial event is mentioned in the four Gospels with similar accounts. All details in Matthew's account (27:57–61) are attested by the three other Gospels in full, except that Joseph's tomb was "his own" (27:60). All details in Mark's account (15:42–47) are also attested in at least one other Gospel except that Joseph was prominent and was waiting for the kingdom of God (15:43), that he gathered courage (15:43), and that Pilate ascertained that Jesus died sooner than expected (15:44). All details in Luke's account (23:50–56) are also attested by the other Gospels except that Joseph did not agree to the Jews' action, that Arimathea was "a city of the Jews" (23:51), and that the women rested on the Sabbath (23:56). John (19:38–42) is also attested in every detail except that Joseph was a secret disciple (19:38), that Nicodemus accompanied Joseph to the tomb (19:39), that wrapping with spices was "a burial custom of the Jews" (19:40), and that there was a garden where the tomb was located (19:41). These singly-attested details are all minor. Thus, Matthew's account is a common denominator, though other details in the other Gospels are also doubly attested.

The resurrection accounts, however, are more challenging because reconciliation depends largely on synthesizing the accounts, as in the above scenarios. Many of the details are unique contributions by the respective Evangelists, especially as they relate to the women. This is expected given the state of extreme confusion, excitement, astonishment, and disbelief, and the back-and-forth movement of the women, whom Luke tells us were clearly more than three in number: "Mary Magdalene and Joanna and Mary the mother of James; also the other women" (Luke 24:10). Several groups of women must have left their homes to visit the tomb on Sunday morning. Upon discovering the absence of the body and the appearance of the angels, they were engaged in frantic talks, with some leaving one group and joining another, and some returning to the city or the tomb midway, and each reporting to the disciples and the Evangelists a true version of what happened at dawn on Easter Sunday. The challenge is that any reconciliation must be made without synthesis and must be confined to the Islamic law principles of testimonial sufficiency and consistency. Any fact must be supported by no less than two witnesses. As said, synthesis essentially reduces the testimonies to one. Likewise, the words of Jesus and the angels cannot be synthesized as the Islamic law recognizes matching words despite discrepancies in place and time, but not the opposite.

Thus, Matthew's unique, uncorroborated contributions include the number of the women as two (28:1), the earthquake at dawn and the blazing angel's rolling the stone (28:2–3), the guards' becoming like dead men (28:4), Jesus's appearing to the two women on their way back from the tomb and the women's taking hold of his feet (28:9–10), his command to tell the disciples to meet him in Galilee (28:10), the Jewish leaders' bribing the soldiers to spread the rumor of stealing the body (28:11–15), and Jesus's appearance to the disciples in Galilee and his Great Commission (28:16–20).

Mark's uncorroborated contributions include the visiting women as being three after including Salome (16:1), their discussion about removing the "extremely large stone" (16:3–4), the angel's reference to Jesus as "the Nazarene" (16:6), Jesus's command to tell Peter (16:7), and the trembling women's not telling anyone (16:8).[143]

Luke's uncorroborated materials include the two men or angels as standing rather than seated and the women as bowing their faces (24:4–5), the men's or angels' question about seeking the living One among the dead (24:5–6), their reminding the women of what Jesus predicted while in Galilee (24:6–7), Joanna as one of the women (24:10), Jesus's appearance to the two disciples on the road to Emmaus (24:13–35), the risen Jesus's eating before the disciples (24:41–43), his exposition of fulfilled prophecies and his command to

143. This is according to the short ending of Mark (16:1–8). In fairness, the long ending should be used as testimony. John Wenham argues that "in view of the fact that the last twelve verses are in any case an early witness and that they were accepted by the church to be read with the gospel, they have a standing above any of the early uncanonical writings." Wenham, *Easter Enigma*, 46.

proclaim the gospel to all nations (24:44–47), his promise to send the Holy Spirit (24:49), and his ascension (24:50–53).[144]

The longest unique, uncorroborated contribution is John's, including the surrounding darkness when Mary Magdalene went to the tomb (20:1),[145] Mary Magdalene's telling Peter and John about the stealing of the body of Jesus (20:2), John's accompanying Peter to the tomb (20:3), the detailed encounter between Mary Magdalene and Jesus (20:2–18),[146] the shut doors (20:19), Jesus's talk with the disciples about the Great Commission (20:21), his breathing the Holy Spirit on them (20:22), his authorizing them to forgive and retain sins (20:23), his entire encounter with Thomas (20:24–29), and his appearance to the seven disciples by the Sea of Tiberius (chapter 21).

Unlike the crucifixion account, which does not need reconciliation but largely follows Matthew or Mark, the resurrection accounts should be reconciled in such a manner that limits itself to the aforesaid confines of the Islamic law. This means avoiding synthesis and leaving out singly-attested details and statements that do not match verbally or synonymously. This also means allowing for reconciliation through explanation, accepting synonymous words, accepting common denominators between two accounts, and ignoring discrepancies between secondary details if the main facts are compliant.

On Sunday dawn, as the sun was beginning to rise, Mary Magdalene and the other Mary came to the tomb (Matt 28:1 and Mark 16:1–2) to anoint the body of Jesus (Mark 16:1 and Luke 24:1). They found that the stone was rolled away (Matt 28:2, Mark 16:4, Luke 24:2, and John 20:1). As they entered, they saw a man with white clothes dazzling like snow (Matt 28:3 and Mark 16:5). He told them: "Do not be afraid (amazed); you are looking for Jesus who has been crucified. He has risen; He is not here, just as he said. Here is the place where they laid him. Go and tell his disciples he is going ahead of you to Galilee; there you will see him" (Matt 28:5–7, Mark 16:6–7, and partly Luke 24:6). They left the tomb with fear (trembling) and joy (Matt 28:8 and Mark 16:8). Upon hearing the news of the empty tomb, Peter ran to the tomb

144. The private appearance to Simon (24:34), although not attested by any other Gospel, is corroborated by Paul (1 Cor 15:5).

145. Though this is reconcilable with Mark's sunrise by the time she arrived.

146. Noting that Peter's visit is corroborated in Luke 24:12, and Mary Magdalene's visits to the tomb and Jesus's appearing to her are generally corroborated by all three Synoptics.

and saw the linen wrapping alone without the body (Luke 24:12 and John 20:6).[147] Jesus then appeared privately to Peter (Luke 24:34 and 1 Cor 15:5). In the evening that Sunday, Jesus appeared to the disciples and said, "Peace be with you" and showed them his hands, and the disciples rejoiced as they saw the Lord (Luke 24:36, 40–41 and John 20:19–20).[148]

Finally, and more basically, one can view eyewitness testimony differently with respect to its object, or referent. Instead of taking each individual event as the object of examination with all its details of time, place, people, actions, and words, one can consider the basic abstract act of *seeing the risen crucified Jesus* as the object of examination and testimony. That is, instead of each event *qua* event requiring two attestations, the basic, abstract fact under examination, *seeing the risen crucified Jesus*, is what now requires two attestations regardless of the accompanying details, being secondary. This is quite consistent with the aforesaid fifth inferred principle of consistent testimonies under Islamic law: *If the testimonies consistently attest the principal fact, discrepant secondary details do not invalidate the testimonies.*[149] All that is required, therefore, is two persons' testifying that they saw the main object of examination, the risen Jesus. The New Testament presents us with at least three direct eyewitness testimonies of men who saw the risen Jesus: Matthew, John, and Paul.

Thus, limiting our search to the testimony of each direct witness about his own experience, Matthew testifies that he saw and heard the risen Jesus as one of the Eleven in Galilee (Matt 28:16–17). John testifies that he saw and heard the risen Christ at least three times, twice as one of the Eleven when Jesus appeared collectively to them (John 20:19–20 and 20:26–27), and the third as one of the seven disciples when the risen Jesus appeared to them by the Sea of Tiberius (John 21). Paul testifies that he saw and conversed with the risen Christ on his way to Damascus (1 Cor 15:3–8). These three independent eyewitness accounts attest to the *one and same object or referent* in

147. Although John 20:3 mentions that John accompanied Peter, according to Islamic law we only take the common denominator, Peter. Mary Magdalene's story in John 20:11–17 is uncorroborated elsewhere and so excluded.

148. Luke 24:40 mentions that Jesus showed them his hands and feet, whereas John 20:20 mentions that Jesus showed them his hands and side. We take only the common denominator, his hands.

149. See page 211 above.

each testimony, *the risen Jesus*, which negates the need for corroboration by further witnesses. We can even add Peter's direct testimony that Jesus has risen: "You were not redeemed with perishable things . . . but with . . . the blood of Christ . . . who through Him [you] are believers in God, who raised Him from the dead and gave Him glory" (1 Pet 1:18–21).

The same principle can be applied to secondary events, such as the account of Jesus eating before the disciples. In the first instance, he ate before the Eleven, an event attested by Luke alone. In the second instance, he ate with the seven disciples by the Sea of Tiberius, an event attested by John alone. Thus, that *the risen Jesus ate before the Eleven* is singly attested, and that *the risen Jesus ate by the Sea of Tiberius* is also singly attested. However, when the object of inquiry is the simple, abstract fact that *the risen Jesus ate before his disciples*, no matter where or when, we have a doubly-attested testimony by Luke and John, thus meeting the testimonial requirements of Islamic law.

Having met the strict confines of Islamic law, one principle employed in defense of the authenticity of the Qur'ān is worth noting here: when evidence abounds, the burden of proof falls on the party that denies.[150] The words of F. F. Bruce are also worth mentioning: "A man whose accuracy can be demonstrated in matters where we are able to test it is likely to be accurate even where the means for testing him are not available. Accuracy is a habit of mind."[151] Craig Blomberg repeats the same truth: "A historian who has been found trustworthy where he or she can be tested [or, in our case, corroborated by matching testimony] should be given the benefit of the doubt in cases where no tests are available."[152]

To conclude, the above shows that, first, apart from the limitations of the Islamic law, the four Gospel accounts of the crucifixion, burial, and resurrection of Jesus can be successfully reconciled despite apparent discrepancies, and a synthesized account gives the full picture.[153] Second, a unified picture of the crucifixion and burial events can be reconstructed to satisfy Islamic law requirements while keeping almost all details. Third, a unified

150. Sinai, *Qur'an: A Historical-Critical Introduction*, 92.

151. Bruce, *New Testament Documents*, 90–91.

152. Blomberg, *Historical Reliability of John's*, 63.

153. Richard Swinburne's argument that the discrepancies were "very small confusions easily likely to occur in the course of decades of oral transmission or fading memories" is unwarranted. Swinburne, *Resurrection of God Incarnate*, 154.

picture of the resurrection event can be reconstructed to satisfy Islamic law requirements, though at the expense of losing some singly-attested secondary details that do not affect the main event, that Jesus rose bodily from the dead on the third day.

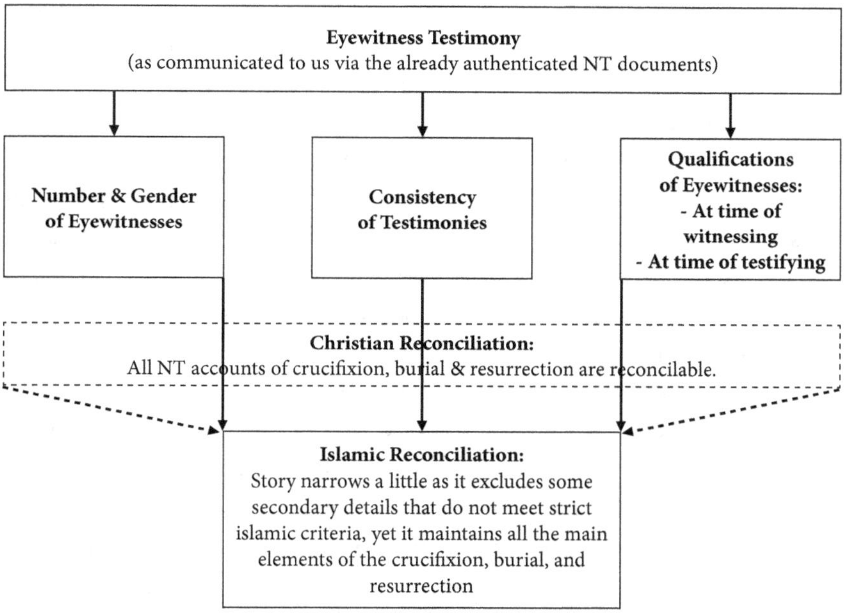

Figure 3. Eyewitness testimony

Confession

Islamic law admits confession (*iqrār*) as a primary piece of evidence. Indeed, some jurists consider it as the strongest evidence and most decisive arbiter in disputes.[154] It is even stronger than testimony by others. Bordering on certainty, it suffices as standalone evidence that needs no further corroboration.[155] Indeed, unlike testimony, it is validated and has full efficacy once it is

154. Ṣārī, *Al-bayyina fī al-Sharīʿa*, 213, 219. See also Daoud, *Al-qaḍāʾ wa al-daʿwa*, 2:5; el-Awa, "Confession and Other Methods," 112.

155. Shammouṭ, *Al-ithbāt al-qaḍāʾī*, 120.

properly uttered, even before the judge makes a verdict; it is itself a verdict.[156] This primacy of confession is even attributed to Muhammad himself: "A man's confession is stronger than the testimony of others against him."[157]

Legitimacy of confession comes from all the four primary sources of Islamic law. First, the Qur'ān: "God took a pledge from the prophets saying, 'If after I have bestowed Scripture and wisdom upon you, a messenger comes confirming what you have been given, you must believe in him and support him. Do you affirm [confess] and accept My pledge as binding on you? They said, 'We do'" (Qur'ān 3:81).[158] Second, *Sunna*, where several incidents are narrated about Muhammad's condemning an adulterer to stoning upon the adulterer's voluntary verbal confession.[159] Third, consensus, where all Muslim jurists agree that confession is affirmed by the Prophet.[160] Fourth, *qiyās* (reasoning), for two reasons: confession resolves disputes quickly and fairly, and a sober person would not confess to his own harm or loss unless he is telling the truth.[161]

Confession regarding matters of religious truth happens when an enemy of a religion or a skeptic declares that it is true. In the New Testament we find two cases of confession, by Paul and James, the half-brother of Jesus. Two other cases appear at first sight to qualify as confession and come from non-writers. The first is Thomas. He refused to believe during Jesus's first appearance to the Eleven: "Unless I see in His hands the imprint of the nails, and put my finger into the place of the nails, and put my hand into His side, I will not believe" (John 20:25). After eight days Jesus appeared to him in the presence of the Eleven: "Then He said to Thomas, 'Reach here with your finger, and see My hands; and reach here your hand and put it into My side; and do not be unbelieving, but believing.' Thomas answered and said to Him, 'My Lord and my God!'" (John 20:27–28). As powerful as this confession is, under the rigid formalism of Islamic law it cannot qualify as confession, but rather as testimony by an eyewitness, John, which also does not meet the Islamic law criterion of double-eyewitness testimony. The other case is that of the

156. Shammouṭ, 118–19. Al-Ḥossari, *'Ilm al-qaḍā'*, 2:19.

157. Al-Ḥossari, 2:14.

158. Daoud, *Al-qaḍā' wa al-da'wa*, 2:19–20.

159. Shammouṭ, *Al-ithbāt al-qaḍā'ī*, 116. See also Daoud, 2:21–23.

160. Daoud, 2:23.

161. Daoud, 2:24.

Roman centurion in command of the crucifixion who, when Jesus breathed his last and the earthquake struck, "became very frightened and said, 'Truly this was the Son of God!'" (Matt 27:54). Like the case for Thomas, this is not a direct confession per Islamic law but rather testimony by Matthew, Mark, and Luke. Thus, we are left with the two confessions of Paul and James, and they are powerful enough.

The appearance to Paul is attested by Paul alone. It does not meet the stringent Islamic law requirement of double-eyewitness testimony considering that Luke, who attests to the event in Acts, is not a second eyewitness but one who simply reported the story from Paul rather than others.[162] But then the testimony of Paul is confession rather than mere testimony. Likewise, the appearance to James is attested by Paul, who received it from James himself when he met him during his first visit to Jerusalem (Gal 1:18–19). But again, Paul is not a second eyewitness, and so such appearance also falls short of meeting the double-eyewitness testimony under Islamic law. Yet we have the direct confession of James himself: "James, a slave of God and of the Lord Jesus Christ" (James 1:1, NLT), and "our glorious Lord Jesus Christ" (James 2:1). As confessions, neither Paul nor James needs further corroboration. The confession of each constitutes legitimate, standalone evidence that the Islamic law considers stronger than the testimony of two or even four eyewitnesses. Moreover, both satisfy the rules of confession under Islamic law.

Compliance with Confession under Islamic Law

Though the original qur'anic reference concerned confession of belief, most of the particulars of confession in Islamic law have to do with financial disputes or crimes, such as adultery and murder. Nevertheless, the following rules are relevant to the case in hand. Confession must be either express, as saying, "I owe you one thousand dollars," or implicit, as when a debtor answers his creditor upon the demand of repayment: "Give me more time."[163] A gesture, however, is not accepted as a valid confession.[164] A confession must also be

162. Unless Luke interviewed Paul's companions on his way to Damascus, in which case they would be considered as eyewitnesses insofar as they heard the sound but did not see Jesus (Acts 9:7), with Luke an indirect witness reporting their testimony.

163. Daoud, *Al-qaḍā' wa al-da'wa*, 2:24–26.

164. Daoud, 2:27.

unconditional.[165] The New Testament gives an express unconditional confession by Paul: "He appeared to me also" (1 Cor 15:8), and an implicit verbal unconditional confession by James when he starts his letter by calling himself "a bond-servant of God and of the Lord Jesus Christ" (James 1:1).

The confessor must be a rational adult, though a discerning minor may be admitted in certain cases.[166] He or she must be sober, not drunk, asleep, or unconscious.[167] Confession made under duress is not valid.[168] Confession must be serious; if made frivolously or jokingly, it is invalid.[169] A valid confession must also be innocent with no hidden interest or agenda.[170] Both Paul and James were rational, sober adults who made their confessions without any duress, or indeed, *despite* duress to deny. As aforesaid, they and the rest of the apostles and Evangelists had no personal interest whatsoever but were ready to lose everything. Paul was clear when he said, "I count all things to be loss in view of the surpassing value of knowing Christ Jesus my Lord, for whom I have suffered the loss of all things, and count them but rubbish so that I may gain Christ" (Phil 3:8). James also spoke amid persecution: "Consider it all joy, my brethren, when you encounter various trials" (James 1:2). Both were serious to the degree of enduring all persecutions throughout their lives until they paid the ultimate price of life; they were "dead serious."

Moreover, the object of confession must be logically possible and legitimate.[171] Except for a confession involving adultery, armed robbery, or drinking alcohol, confession must be made with certainty, with nothing that would give room for doubt.[172] Paul and James made their confessions in certain terms. No one makes a confession and endures decades of hardship and persecution unless he is certain. And nothing in the resurrection of Jesus Christ runs against logic, reason, or law.

---

165. Daoud, 2:28, 47.

166. Al-Ḥanafī, *Badāʾiʿ al-ṣanāʾiʿ*, 10:220. See also Daoud, *Al-qaḍāʾ wa al-daʿwa*, 2:39.

167. Daoud, 2:40.

168. Al-Ḥanafī, 10:221. See also Daoud, 2:40. Likewise, confession is inadmissible as evidence in the English law if made "by oppression" and such oppression would likely produce unreliable confession. Keane and McKeown, *Modern Law of Evidence*, 407, 410.

169. Shammouṭ, *Al-ithbāt al-qaḍāʾī*, 126. See also Daoud, *Al-qaḍāʾ wa al-daʿwa*, 2:43.

170. Daoud, 2:42.

171. Daoud, 2:45–46.

172. Daoud, 2:49.

Finally, unlike testimony, integrity of character and Islam are not conditions for accepting confession, and neither is freedom.[173] Nonetheless, both Paul and James, like the rest of the apostles, were persons of exceptional integrity, and freemen.

Confession by Paul

Paul was a devout Pharisee and highly educated rabbi. In his own words: "I was advancing in Judaism beyond many of my contemporaries among my countrymen, being more extremely zealous for my ancestral traditions" (Gal 1:14). When he heard about the fledgling Christians, his zeal prompted him to lead a campaign of terror against them: "I persecuted this Way to the death, binding and putting both men and women into prisons. . . . I used to persecute the church of God beyond measure and tried to destroy it" (Acts 22:4; Gal 1:13). His wrath did not stop at Palestine, but pushed him to Damascus: "As I was on my way, approaching Damascus about noontime, a very bright light suddenly flashed from heaven all around me, and I fell to the ground and heard a voice saying to me, 'Saul, Saul, why are you persecuting Me?' And I answered, 'Who are You, Lord?' And He said to me, 'I am Jesus the Nazarene, whom you are persecuting'" (Acts 22:6–8). The risen Jesus appeared to him personally, adding him to a long list of eyewitnesses:

> For I delivered to you as of first importance what I also received, that Christ died for our sins according to the Scriptures, and that He was buried, and that He was raised on the third day according to the Scriptures, and that He appeared to Cephas, then to the twelve. After that He appeared to more than five hundred brethren at one time, most of whom remain until now, but some have fallen asleep; then He appeared to James, then to all the apostles; and last of all, as to one untimely born, He appeared to me also. For I am the least of the apostles, and not fit to be called an apostle, because I persecuted the church of God (1 Cor 15:3–8).

173. Al-Kāsānī, *Badā'iʿ al-ṣanā'iʿ*, 10:220–21. See also Ṣārī, *Al-bayyina fī al-Sharīʿa*, 272.

This direct confession comes from a letter "the authenticity [of which] has seldom been doubted even by very skeptical scholars."[174] The change in Paul was radical. He dedicated the rest of his life to propagating the very faith that he had been trying to destroy: "From Jerusalem and round about as far as Illyricum [present-day Albania] I have fully preached the gospel of Christ" (Rom 15:19). Moreover, from being a respected leader and persecutor he spent the rest of his life under persecution and hardship until he paid the ultimate price of martyrdom in Rome. He even surpassed the other apostles in laboring and suffering for the Gospel:

> Five times I received from the Jews thirty-nine lashes. Three times I was beaten with rods, once I was stoned, three times I was shipwrecked, a night and a day I have spent in the deep. I have been on frequent journeys, in dangers from rivers, dangers from robbers, dangers from my countrymen, dangers from the Gentiles, dangers in the city, dangers in the wilderness, dangers on the sea, dangers among false brethren; I have been in labor and hardship, through many sleepless nights, in hunger and thirst, often without food, in cold and exposure. Apart from such external things, there is the daily pressure on me of concern for all the churches (2 Cor 11:24–28).

This is a personal confession of an eyewitness, written in an "indisputably authentic letter,"[175] thus establishing that this event happened "beyond doubt."[176] Unlike usual conversions that are based on belief, what is special in Paul's conversion is that it was caused by a face-to-face personal encounter with the entity of belief, the risen Christ.[177] This shattered completely his hardheaded belief that Christianity was a false Jewish sect that must be destroyed. He "came face to face . . . with living proof that Israel's god has vindicated Jesus

174. Wenham, *Easter Enigma*, 51. Likewise, Habermas and Licona refer inter alia to 1 Corinthians in their "minimal facts approach" because it is "granted by virtually all scholars on the subject, even the skeptical ones." Habermas and Licona, *Case for the Resurrection*, 47.

175. Craig, *Son Rises*, 100.

176. Craig, *Reasonable Faith*, 380.

177. Habermas and Licona, *Case for the Resurrection*, 65.

against the charge of false messianism. God had declared, in the resurrection, that Jesus really was 'his son' in this essentially *messianic* sense."[178]

Confession by James

The second significant confession is by James, the younger half-brother of Jesus. According to the Gospels, "not even His brothers were believing in Him" (John 7:5). They even held him in contempt and derision: "When His own people [or kinsmen] heard of this, they went out to take custody of Him; for they were saying, 'He has lost His senses'" (Mark 3:21). Then after the resurrection and ascension we suddenly find James and his brothers with the apostles: "These all with one mind were continually devoting themselves to prayer, along with the women, and Mary the mother of Jesus, and with His brothers" (Acts 1:14). After that we find James a prominent leader of the church in Jerusalem as clear from Peter's words after he was released from prison: "Report these things to James and the brethren" (Acts 12:17). When Paul visited Jerusalem three years after his conversion, James was counted as an apostle: "I did not see any other of the apostles except James, the Lord's brother" (Gal 1:19). Then in his second visit after fourteen years, Paul notes that James was one of the pillars: "James and Cephas and John, who were reputed to be pillars, gave to me and Barnabas the right hand of fellowship" (Gal 2:9). Finally, we find James as leader of the central church in Jerusalem (Acts 21:18). N. T. Wright notes that, "since he had probably not been a disciple of Jesus during the latter's public career, it is difficult to account for his centrality and unrivalled leadership unless he was himself known to have seen the risen Jesus."[179] Indeed, Paul expressly mentions in the tradition he received from the apostles that Jesus "appeared to James, then to all the apostles" (1 Cor 15:7).[180] The confession of James that he is "a bond-servant of God and of the Lord Jesus Christ" (James 1:1) is in line with Paul's tradition.

We know from Eusebius through the early church chronicler Hegesippus (d. 180 CE) that the Jews killed James brutally by throwing him down, stoning him, then clubbing him to death, all for his insistence on acknowledging

178. Wright, *Resurrection of the Son*, 394.

179. Wright, 325.

180. Wright, 325.

Jesus as the Messiah.[181] His murder is also attested by Josephus: "Albinus . . . assembled the sanhedrin of judges, and brought before them the brother of Jesus, who was called Christ, whose name was James, and some others; and when he had formed an accusation against them as breakers of the law, he delivered them to be stoned."[182]

Indeed, being a brother of Jesus made belief more difficult, as Jesus himself experienced and said: "A prophet is not without honor except in his hometown and in his own household" (Matt 13:57). Wenham therefore notes that "to accept one's own brother (however greatly admired) as the divine Son would require a painful revolution."[183] Likewise, William Lane Craig asks: "What would it take to make you believe that your brother is the Lord, so that you would die for this belief, as James did?"[184] Paul explains: the risen Jesus appeared to him. Realizing that his brother was the risen Messiah and God himself, James called himself "James, a slave of God and of the Lord Jesus Christ" (James 1:1, NLT). No wonder Craig notes that Jesus's appearance to James is "one of the most amazing of all."[185]

Finally, one external evidence to the confession of James is an archaeological find announced in 2002. An empty ossuary was discovered in Jerusalem bearing the name of its owner in Aramaic: "Jacobus [James in Hebrew] son of Joseph, brother of Jesus." Archaeologist and historian James Hoffmeier notes that it was unusual to write the name of the brother of the deceased, except if the brother is a well-known person. This increases the likelihood that the mentioned Jesus is Christ, and the deceased is his brother James. This also suggests that James was a believer in Jesus. Hoffmeier concludes that, despite questioning its authenticity, "the weight of scholarly opinion seems to be turning in favour of the antiquity of the bone box and its text."[186] If authentic, this inscription would be the oldest mention of Jesus from a non-documentary archaeological source.[187]

---

181. Wright, 561.
182. Josephus, "Antiquities of the Jews," 20.9.1.
183. Wenham, *Easter Enigma*, 116.
184. Craig, *Reasonable Faith*, 380.
185. Craig, 379.
186. Hoffmeier, *Archaeology of the Bible*, 167–68.
187. Hoffmeier, 167.

Confessions of hardheaded enemies like Paul and James play an important role in refuting alternative theories posited to explain away the bodily resurrection of Jesus. In responding to psychological theories that attempt to explain away Jesus's bodily resurrection as a faith-motivated experience by his faithful followers, Wright refers to Paul, Thomas, and James, enemies or skeptics who had the same experience of seeing the risen Jesus as the rest of the disciples.[188] Likewise, in their "minimal facts approach," Habermas and Licona list the confessions of Paul and James as two of the five well-attested facts that meet the stringent criteria of historicity: Jesus's death by crucifixion, the disciples' belief that Jesus appeared to them, conversion of Paul, conversion of James, and the empty tomb.[189]

188. Wright, *Resurrection of the Son*, 703–4.

189. Habermas and Licona, *Case for the Resurrection*, 75.

CHAPTER 5

Expert Witness Testimony and Circumstantial Evidence

Eyewitness testimony and confession are the strongest types of evidence in Islamic law, though the latter is less common. Expert witness testimony and circumstantial evidence are secondary and so are addressed and discussed more briefly.

Expert Witness Testimony

Expert witnesses are barely discussed in both *fiqh* studies and modern research.[1] Nevertheless, Islamic law recognizes expert testimony. This is based on the qur'anic injunction: "You can ask those who have knowledge if you do not know" (Qur'ān 16:43). This recognition is also based on a *Ḥadīth* in which Muhammad was angry at a group of people who acted without seeking advice, resulting in the death of an innocent man.[2] For these reasons and other practical considerations related to the judge's need of specialized knowledge, jurists see that seeking expert testimony is inevitable.[3] The expert is knowledgeable and trustworthy, so he does not need recommendation by court-appointed witnesses, and does not have to swear an oath.[4]

1. Shaham, *Expert Witness*, 6.
2. Jaradat, *Al-niḍhām al-qaḍā'i*, 239–41.
3. Jaradat, 241.
4. Daoud, *Al-qaḍā' wa al-da'wa*, 2:329.

Moreover, one expert is sufficient, though two are safer.[5] Expert testimony is increasingly used today worldwide with the advancement of specialization, particularly in science.[6]

Luke, in addition to his role as indirect eyewitness, can be considered an expert witness. This is implied in the prologue to his Gospel:

> Inasmuch as many have undertaken to compile an account of the things accomplished among us, just as they were handed down to us by those who from the beginning were eyewitnesses and servants of the word, it seemed fitting for me as well, having investigated everything carefully from the beginning, to write it out for you in consecutive order, most excellent Theophilus; so that you may know the exact truth about the things you have been taught (Luke 1:1–4).

In stressing that he has "investigated everything carefully from the beginning," Luke assumes the role of the historian, following the rules of sound historiography. After all, he is a well-educated Greek physician who is used to the scientific approach. Bauckham notes that Luke's work belongs to the genre of Greek historiography.[7] Luke has followed everything from the beginning, meaning that "he has thoroughly understood everything that the eyewitnesses have passed on to him," and this qualification of "informed familiarity" has distinguished him as a writer of history, probably more accurately than the many traditions circulating at the time about the life and ministry of Jesus.[8] His investigation of their traditions "carefully from the beginning" describes the work of an expert. Luke's prologue shows that "just as the scope of the eyewitness testimony was comprehensive, covering the whole story [he] had

---

5. Jaradat, *Al-niḍhām al-qaḍā'i*, 241.

6. Under US common law, a witness can testify as an expert if his or her specialized knowledge will help the judge better understand the evidence or the fact, the testimony is based on sufficient data and reliable principles and methods, and the expert has reliably applied them to the case. Mueller and Kirkpatrick, *Federal Rules of Evidence*, 702. Under English law, an expert opinion is admissible if the expert is qualified and the matter requires his or her expertise, though a non-expert opinion on a matter not calling for expertise can be admissible "as a way of conveying the facts which he personally perceived," i.e. when it is "impossible to separate his inferences from the perceived facts on which those inferences are based." Keane and McKeown, *Modern Law of Evidence*, 578, 614.

7. Bauckham, *Jesus and the Eyewitnesses*, 118.

8. Bauckham, 123.

to tell ('from the beginning'), so Luke's thorough familiarity with and understanding of this testimony were equally comprehensive."[9]

Bruce notes that, in seeking the best sources he could access and arranging the events chronologically, Luke acted as a "serious historian."[10] Mark Strauss notes that such arrangement does not mean strict chronological order but a "systematical or logical account of the events."[11] With his Greek background and education, he must have "inherited the high traditions of Greek historical writing."[12] His addressee, the "most excellent Theophilus," is possibly a Roman official charged with investigating the claims of Christianity after the interest aroused by Paul's presence in Rome to make his case before Caesar.[13] After all, the title is the same one Paul used to address the Roman governors of Judea, Felix and Festus.[14] Thus, in addition to Luke's honesty as a Christian and his scientific habit of mind, this official imperial context must have added further responsibility on his part to report only upon careful investigation. Even if Theophilus is, as some argue, the patron who sponsored Luke's expensive work,[15] Luke still owed him accuracy.

Such imperial context is evident in Luke's writings. He names three emperors (one implicitly), six Roman governors, the Herodian dynasty, and the high priests who took office during the reported events. He links these with major imperial events and his reported local events, which today enables us to date many of them. Bruce notes that "a writer who thus relates his story to the wider context of world history is courting trouble if he is not careful."[16] An example of his accuracy is his identification of the proper titles of the many officials he mentions, all despite the frequent changes in titles contingent upon provincial changes between senatorial and imperial government (e.g., proconsul vs. legate). He also gives the full official titles. Although he usually calls provinces by their ethnic rather than Roman nomenclatures (e.g., Greece rather than Achaia), he refers to Gallio as "proconsul of Achaia" rather than

9. Bauckham, 124.
10. Bruce, *New Testament Documents*, 41.
11. Strauss, "Luke," 324.
12. Bruce, *New Testament Documents*, 81.
13. Bruce, 41.
14. Bruce, 80.
15. Strauss, "Luke," 322.
16. Bruce, *New Testament Documents*, 82.

Greece (Acts 18:12), in keeping with his proper official title.[17] He also keeps abreast of political changes. In Acts 19:38 he rightly refers to the *proconsuls* of Asia during the reported Ephesian riot though usually a province has only one proconsul. This agrees with the historical fact that, a few months earlier, the proconsul was murdered by two assassins. With no successor yet appointed, these two men might have been in charge.[18]

In Palestine, Herod Antipas, ruler of Galilee, was not promoted to royal status like his father Herod the Great and his nephew Herod Agrippa I. Although his subjects called him *king*, Luke keeps with the lesser official title of *tetrarch*. Some charged Luke with erroneous accounts but were refuted upon further investigation. For example, it was objected that Quirinius was not governor of Syria when Jesus was born but rather in 6 CE when he also ordered a census. However, historical and inscriptional evidence now shows that an earlier census involving the return of everyone to his or her hometown was ordered during the rule of Herod the Great, when Quirinius also held an earlier governorship over Syria.[19] Another alleged error is Luke's mention of Lysanias as tetrarch of Abilene in the fifteenth year of Emperor Tiberius when such name ruled before 34 BCE. Again, inscriptional evidence has confirmed that there was another Lysanias during the reign of Tiberius.[20] Moreover, Luke's description of local customs and atmospheres are also historically attested, such as the cosmopolitan tolerant Antioch and its first Gentile-Jewish church, the Roman pride of Philippi, the thirst for news and disputation in Athens, the lucrative superstition and magic in Ephesus, and the seamanship details of the Malta shipwreck.[21]

Bruce notes that these and many other examples of accuracy are not accidental. He concludes that "Luke's record entitles him to be regarded as a writer of habitual accuracy."[22] He argues that the church had no historian after Luke until Eusebius in the fourth century,[23] and his contribution to the history of the rise of Christianity is one of a historiographical expert. In

17. Bruce, 83.
18. Bruce, 83–84.
19. Bruce, 86–87.
20. Bruce, 88.
21. Bruce, 89–91.
22. Bruce, 91.
23. Bruce, 81.

addition to firmly anchoring the Gospel narratives and early church history to accurate historical underpinnings, his two volumes "bind the New Testament together, his Gospel dealing with the same events as the other Gospels, his Acts providing the historical background to the Epistles of Paul."[24]

Mark Strauss argues that Luke's prologue "represent[s] some of the finest Greek in the New Testament. The author is obviously an educated and skilled writer, a worthy candidate to compose the longest and most comprehensive account of the words and deeds of the central figure in human history."[25] Strauss corrects the common impression that historians in ancient times paid no attention to accuracy but were rather creative to serve their own interests. He notes that there were historians, like Polybius, who criticized those who wrote to create dramatic scenes and called upon them to objectively record factual history.[26] Thus, we find expert historians who felt the need to check the accounts written by others. The prologue shows that Luke had not simply received his information and traditions from first-generation Christians, but, as an expert, has carefully investigated these accounts to ensure their accuracy.[27] Robert Gundry notes that, "in his prologue, Luke mentions earlier written accounts of Jesus's life, oral testimonies by eyewitnesses, his own investigation of these accounts and testimonies, and his purpose to present this tradition as reliable."[28]

Leading Christian historian Earle Cairns links Luke's occupation as a physician to his role as an expert historian. Thus, Luke's "preciseness of language would grace the report of a modern scientist or physician."[29] More to the point, he notes that "we may be sure Luke quizzed [his] witnesses as carefully as he would a patient whose symptoms he was probing to make an accurate diagnosis."[30] According to his prologue, Luke obtained the material of those that have "taken in hand to set forth in order a declaration of those things which are most surely believed . . . even as they delivered them unto [him], which from the beginning were eyewitnesses" (Luke 1:1–2, King

24. Bruce, 93.
25. Strauss, "Luke," 323.
26. Strauss, 322.
27. Strauss, 323.
28. Gundry, *Survey of the New*, 216.
29. Cairns, "Luke As a Historian," 220.
30. Cairns, 222.

James Version). This means that there were two categories, the eyewitnesses themselves and the secondary compilers of accounts based on eyewitness testimonies. Cairns notes that these cannot include heretical and apocryphal gospels because they were not yet written and, furthermore, do not represent "declaration of those things which are most surely believed."[31] They also cannot be the Gospels of Matthew and John because these count among the eyewitnesses, or even the Gospel of Mark since he reflects Peter's eyewitness testimony. Cairns concludes that the accounts available to Luke were short accounts about the life and death of Jesus that are no longer available to us.[32] These were the subject of his scrutiny. Luke, therefore, interviewed eyewitnesses and, "like the best of the ancient and modern historians,[33] [he] sought to get the finest secondary accounts of those who were not contemporaneous with the event."[34] Cairns concludes that "no historian of today who is cognizant of the best manuals of historical method . . . can quarrel with Luke's methodology. Luke compresses into four short verses the best ideas of modern experts of historical methodology."[35]

Circumstantial Evidence

Circumstantial evidence, or *qarīna*, is defined as "the logical inference to be drawn from something done, or from circumstances."[36] It can also be defined as "any fact (evidentiary fact) from the existence of which the jury or judge may infer the existence of a fact in issue (principal fact)."[37] It is as an indirect evidence because it "requires the fact-finder to work with a chain of reasoning that starts with the [circumstantial evidence] and ends with an

31. Cairns, 221.

32. Cairns, 221.

33. Assuming the setting aside of the modern hermeneutic notion of historiography as "an expression of the subjective impressions of the historian" rather than as an objective investigation of facts. Van Ommeren, "Was Luke an Accurate," 69.

34. Cairns, "Luke As a Historian," 223.

35. Cairns, 225.

36. Salama, "General Principles of Criminal," 120–21.

37. Clifford, *John Warwick Montgomery's Legal*, 147.

inference."[38] Yet it may "often be more persuasive than direct testimony, since it may be far more difficult to fabricate."[39]

In Islamic law, circumstantial evidence is probably the least form of evidence that is expressly mentioned and detailed and discussed.[40] The notable *Ḥanbalī* jurist Ibn al-Qayyim (d. 751 AH/1350 CE) decried the widespread injustice in his days caused by limiting evidence to verbal testimony and oaths, and made an impassionate call to use all means available to help judges make just verdicts. Some prominent medieval *Ḥanafī* scholars and a few from the other schools followed suit and called for the use of circumstantial evidence. If God is after establishing justice, then "whatever can fulfill that purpose is what the religion requires."[41]

Islamic law scholar Wael Hallaq persuasively argues that the use of circumstantial indications is inevitable in the usage and hermeneutics of ordinary speech as language is properly interpreted in conjunction with reality and convention.[42] It was also extensively relied upon in evaluating the authenticity of transmitted *Ḥadīth/Sunna*, the second authoritative source of Islamic law.[43] Moreover, circumstantial evidence is important in understanding the implicit meanings attached to qur'anic commands.[44] In commercial daily transactions, wherever language is ambiguous in contracts, intentions of the contracting parties are determined by circumstantial evidence.[45] Circumstantial evidence thus has an undeniable "pervasive effect" in Islamic legal theory.[46] Those who accept it use it more as an indicant.[47] No matter how strong the evidence may seem to be, it cannot on its own indict the accused, though in offenses other than *ḥadd* the judge may rely on it to convict

38. Niehoff, *Evidence Law*, 209.

39. Anderson, *Lawyer among the Theologians*, 23. The common law stresses that circumstantial evidence, though contrasted with direct evidence, is no less significant. It is "particularly powerful when it proves a variety of different facts all of which point to the same conclusion." Keane and McKeown, *Modern Law of Evidence*, 14.

40. Ṣārī, *Al-bayyina fī al-Sharī'a wa al-qānūn*, 297.

41. Modarressi, "Circumstantial Evidence," 19–20. See also Jaradat, *Al-nidhām al-Qaḍā'i fī al-Islam*, 212.

42. Hallaq, "Notes on the Term,"476.

43. Hallaq," 478.

44. Hallaq, *Sharī'a*, 90.

45. Hallaq, 241.

46. Hallaq, "Notes on the Term," 480.

47. Hallaq, *Sharī'a*, 348.

the accused if he is convinced of the guilt.[48] Most jurists, however, accept it when it is "obvious and credible."[49]

The sources of circumstantial evidence are primary. The first is the Qur'ān as when it relates that Joseph's Egyptian master knew that his wife was lying in her accusation against Joseph by noting that Joseph's shirt was torn from the back rather than from the front (Qur'ān 12:26–28).[50] The second source is *Sunna* as when Muhammad recognized two murderers from the blood stains on their swords.[51] The third source is *qiyās* (reasoning), where ignoring clear circumstantial evidence would result in unfair judgement.[52] Circumstantial evidence can be either rational, i.e. inferred by reason, or customary, inferred by what is recognized by custom.[53]

While a few are still reluctant, most scholars of all schools of Islamic law today recognize circumstantial evidence as a legitimate and indispensable form of evidence, though they differ on its significance and application.[54] The *Mālikī* and *Ḥanbalī* schools are the most receptive, *Shāfiʿi* is the least, and the *Ḥanafī* takes a middle stand.[55] Circumstantial evidence thus can be either decisive with no possibility for counterevidence, or probable with the possibility for counterevidence.[56] To be recognized in the severe *ḥadd* and *qiṣāṣ* punishments, circumstantial evidence should provide decisive proof.[57] Thus, pregnancy is not sufficient to convict a woman of adultery without eyewitness testimony or confession since other causes are possible.[58] Likewise, drunkenness or the odor of alcohol are not enough to convict the drunk of drinking wine without eyewitness testimony or confession.[59] Even finding

48. Sadeghi, "Filling the Gap," 152–53.

49. Masud, Peters, and Powers, "Qadis and their Courts," 28.

50. Ṣārī, *Al-bayyina fī al-Sharīʿa wa al-qānūn*, 299–301.

51. Ṣārī, 303–5.

52. Daoud, *Al-qaḍāʾ wa al-daʿwa*, 2:225.

53. Daoud, 2:227, 232.

54. Ṣārī, *Al-bayyina fī al-Sharīʿa wa al-qānūn*, 297–98. See also Daoud, *Al-qaḍāʾ wa al-daʿwa*, 2:219.

55. Jaradat, *Al-niḍhām al-qaḍāʾi*, 212.

56. Ṣārī, *Al-bayyina fī al-Sharīʿa wa al-qānūn*, 321–22.

57. Nujaym, *Al-ashbāh wa al-nazāʾir*, 210. See also Daoud, *Al-qaḍāʾ wa al-daʿwa*, 2:249.

58. Ṣārī, *Al-bayyina fī al-Sharīʿa wa al-qānūn*, 330.

59. Ṣārī, 340.

the stolen goods in one's house is not sufficient for charging the defendant as he may have purchased them.[60]

Some scholars argue that circumstantial evidence is the weakest form of evidence, to be resorted to either when no other evidence is available or to complement an otherwise insufficient evidence.[61] Others require that circumstantial evidence, though recognizable, should be corroborated by eyewitness testimony.[62] Others, however, argue persuasively that it has "enormous bearing" on a case.[63] It can be the strongest form of evidence, even stronger than eyewitness testimony.[64] Indeed, all jurists agree that circumstantial evidence can invalidate the strongest eyewitness testimony, i.e. by four men in case of adultery, if the woman proves to be a virgin.[65] The problem with testimony is that human weakness and frailties affect it, such as poor memory and observation, bias, and intentional lying, and so circumstantial evidence can offer "substantially greater assurances of reliability."[66] Moreover, and as Islamic law scholar Norman Anderson observes, circumstantial evidence may "often be more persuasive than direct testimony, since it may be far more difficult to fabricate."[67] Even those who do not recognize circumstantial evidence often resort to it unwittingly and implicitly.[68] Notable Islamic law scholar Mohamed Selim el-Awa encourages judges today to actively seek such verifications for the sake of discovering truth. Echoing Ibn al-Qayyim, he notes that "it has been indisputably shown that Islamic law firmly upholds all methods of substantiation which assist the positive disclosure of truth or, indeed, that which comes as close to the truth as possible."[69]

Circumstantial evidence in this study means substantiating facts and indicants other than documents, testimonies and confessions. They include facts and indicants on the ground that can be examined throughout history and

60. Daoud, *Al-qaḍā' wa al-da'wa*, 2:245.
61. Shammouṭ, *Al-ithbāt al-qaḍā'ī*, 99–203.
62. Al-Bawanah, *Al-qarīna alqaḍā'iyya*, 195–96.
63. El-Awa, "Confession and Other Methods," 112.
64. Zaydān, *Nidhām al-qad ā' fī al-Sharī'a*, 188.
65. El-Awa, "Confession and Other Methods," 125.
66. Niehoff, *Evidence Law*, 209.
67. Anderson, *Lawyer among the Theologians*, 23.
68. Zaydān, *Nidhām al-qad ā' fī al-Sharī'a*, 187.
69. El-Awa, "Confession and Other Methods," 127.

today, such as the empty tomb, the rise and expansion of the church,[70] the shift from the Jewish Sabbath to Sunday as the special day of worship,[71] the influence of Christianity on civilization, and archaeology. To varying degrees, these are real-life evidences from both the past and the present that can still be tested. They are evidentiary facts that are "difficult for even a skeptic to deny. They are straightforward matters."[72]

As aforesaid, due to the secondary place of circumstantial evidence in Islamic law and its implicit recognition, little is said about it, and so it is hard to find or infer rules or even general principles. Most consulted works do not go beyond limiting or justifying its use. This limits the possibility of interaction between circumstantial evidences employed to defend the historicity of the crucifixion and resurrection and relevant provisions in the Islamic law. Nevertheless, this chapter will mention circumstantial evidences as they have a corroborative role in complementing the perspective of this study. It will mention them only briefly, however; interested readers can resort to referenced and other works for more details.

The Empty Tomb

One remarkable fact is that ever since Easter Sunday, no party has ever made a claim, let alone a substantiated one, that points to a tomb of Jesus that contains his body or bones. Several tombs of prophets and fathers are still available today and their bodies are believed to reside inside. For example, the tombs of Abraham, Isaac, and Jacob are in Hebron and the tomb of Muhammad is in Medina. The persistent absence of a tomb containing the body of Jesus, which may be the physical evidence that is most sought by enemies of the Christian faith for two millennia, is not without meaning.[73]

---

70. Clifford, *John Warwick Montgomery's Legal*, 148–49.

71. Wright, *Resurrection of the Son*, 707.

72. Clifford, *John Warwick Montgomery's Legal*, 150.

73. To be sure, archaeologists discovered in 1979 a tomb outside the old city of Jerusalem with ossuaries holding names from the first century, including "Jesus son of Joseph and Mary." This, however, did not attract any scholarly attention as similarity of names is common, and all three names were common then. In 2007, a Canadian film producer assisted by a Hollywood producer decided to utilize this find and announced in a press conference that the tomb of Jesus and his wife Mary Magdalene was discovered with their remains. Hoffmeier notes that these claims "have been greeted with considerable skepticism by biblical scholars and archaeologists alike." He gives five reasons: First, the tomb of the family of Jesus should be in its hometown, Nazareth. Second, Mary and Joseph were poor and could not have afforded such an expensive

The tomb and the crucifixion site are largely agreed to be under the Church of the Holy Sepulchre, built in the twelfth century.[74] The tomb is a Second Temple, first-century tomb, thus the plausibility that it was unused when the body of Jesus was laid in it (Matt 27:60). It also agrees with the Bible (Lev 24:14) in falling just outside the old walls of the city,[75] and on a public road so passersby can see (Matt 27:39). The church was built on an earthquake-fissured rock (Matt 28:2) that shows the remains of a Roman Venus shrine built by Emperor Hadrian in 135 CE to conceal monuments of other religions, just as he did on the Jewish Temple site.[76] Moreover, the tomb type, the *arcosolia* rather than the *kokim*, matches the Gospels' description of a seat rather than a niche, the type used by affluent Jews such as Joseph of Arimathea.[77] This location was confirmed in detail early in the fourth century by church historian Eusebius. When Helena, mother of Emperor Constantine, visited the site in 326 CE, she ordered the removal of the Hadrian pagan shrine,[78] and saw there three crosses and a placard bearing the words: "King of the Jews," in Aramaic, Greek, and Latin (John 19:10). Helena saw that the tomb lay inside the city walls yet insisted on continuing with her plans to build a church, which suggests that she felt that this apparent conflict was overruled by the other strong indicants, such as the crosses and the placard. In 1960 it was discovered that the wall had been shifted outward long before Helena's time, thus confirming her feelings.[79]

Early Christians based their belief in the resurrection of Jesus on the two main and complementary evidences of the empty tomb and his post-resurrection appearances. N. T. Wright explores the causal relation between the disciples' belief and these two pieces of evidence by the logical tool of

---

tomb. Third, the names on the ossuary are not quite legible. Fourth, residents of Jerusalem are identified as X son of Y, while non-residents are identified by their hometowns as we also find in the Gospels, e.g., Jesus of Nazareth. Five, that early Christians never paid attention to this tomb is inexplicable. Hoffmeier, *Archaeology of the Bible*, 167–68, 164–65. For more on this tomb, see Gardoski, "Usefulness of Archeology," 88–91.

74. Isbouts, *Archaeology of the Bible*, 289–90.

75. Historian Jean-Pierre Isbouts argues that tombs were located outside the walls of a city by the Romans for hygienic reasons. Isbouts, *Archaeology of the Bible*, 286.

76. Price, *Stones Cry Out*, 313–14.

77. Price, 314.

78. Archaeologist and historian James Hoffmeier argues that the pagan shrine had already been removed in the third century. Hoffmeier, *Archaeology of the Bible*, 160.

79. Ewen, *Faith on Trial*, 138–39.

necessary and sufficient conditions for an outcome to happen. A merely necessary condition must materialize for the outcome to happen, yet it is not enough to make it happen, whereas a merely sufficient condition allows for the outcome but bears the possibility of other reasons as well to cause the outcome. What is required is the combination of necessary and sufficient conditions.[80] Wright notes that neither the empty tomb nor the post-resurrection appearances evidence, by itself, is sufficient reason for the disciples' belief. The empty tomb without the appearances would be simply interpreted as grave-robbery, common in the ancient world.[81] The appearances alone without an empty tomb, on the other hand, would be explained away as hallucinations or visions, also well known to ancients.[82] Both pieces of evidence, however, provide a powerful and sufficient reason for the belief of the disciples of Jesus in his bodily resurrection.[83] Wright depicts them as the two parts of a road sign, the post and arm.[84]

Resurrection in Second Temple Judaism meant bodily, physical resurrection, and so nothing short of seeing a physically-resurrected body would convince the disciples.[85] A dead person must come back to life in the body, not just exalted or gone to heaven. The empty tomb thus *is* a necessary condition, and appearances, Wright argues, are a necessary supplement to the empty tomb.[86] This means that, other than the combination of the empty tomb and the appearances, nothing suggested by historians can explain the disciples' belief.[87] He concludes that "the combination of the empty tomb and the appearances of the living Jesus forms a set of circumstances which is itself both necessary and sufficient for the rise of early Christian belief. Without these phenomena, we cannot explain why this belief came into existence, and took the shape it did. With them we can explain it exactly and precisely."[88]

80. Wright, *Resurrection of the Son*, 687–88.

81. Wright, 688.

82. Wright, 689–90.

83. Wright, 686.

84. Wright, 692.

85. Wright, 686.

86. Wright, *Resurrection of the Son*, 694–95.

87. Wright, 706.

88. Wright, 696.

William Lane Craig bases the case for the historicity of the resurrection on the empty tomb, the appearances, and the origins of Christianity. He provides several pieces of evidence for the empty tomb. First, the Gospels' account of the burial of Jesus in a tomb is historically reliable.[89] Indeed, chapter 4 has shown that the four Gospels agree on the burial story as most details are similar, thus providing four witnesses versus the two required by Islamic law. Craig, however, uses differences among the accounts to show that Matthew and Luke each had his own independent sources versus Mark,[90] their "sporadic and uneven nature" precluding the possibility of having simply edited the Markan material.[91] The importance of burial in a tomb is that Jesus's body was not dumped and destroyed in the yard of executed criminals, but had a clear, inspectable address known to both the disciples and the Jews in Jerusalem where the crucifixion and resurrection took place.[92] Thus, Craig argues that those who deny the empty tomb also deny the burial account.[93] It is therefore impossible that the disciples, who were Jews and understood the meaning of resurrection as only bodily, would proclaim his resurrection if his body still lay in an identified tomb.[94]

Richard Swinburne refers to God's words, "I am the God of your father, the God of Abraham, the God of Isaac, and the God of Jacob" (Exod 3:6), and Jesus's interpretation that it means that God "is not the God of the dead, but of the living" (Mark 12:27). This is the only argument that may suggest that the disciples might have believed in a resurrected Christ though the tomb was not empty, i.e. a resurrection without the old body. But then one would expect the disciples to venerate the tomb and the body of their beloved master and turn it into a pilgrimage site. Yet no indications exist that they ever did,[95] at least not until Helena decided to build a church in the fourth century. Norman Anderson notes that, supposing the disciples were convinced that Jesus was raised from the dead when he was not, and so did not see the need to cling to the tomb, what about the sympathizing crowds who heard him

89. Craig, *Reasonable Faith*, 360–63.

90. Assuming Mark was their main source.

91. Craig, *Reasonable Faith*, 363–64.

92. Craig, 361, 363.

93. Craig, 362.

94. Craig, 361.

95. Swinburne, *Resurrection of God Incarnate*, 162.

and saw his healing miracles? The fact that they did not turn the tomb into a shrine means that they knew the tomb was empty and so not worth visiting.[96] People venerate tombs primarily for the bones contained in them.[97]

Other pieces of evidence include the multiple eyewitnesses' attestation to the empty tomb as per the Gospels and the early church tradition of 1 Corinthians 15. Though Paul does not expressly mention the empty tomb, his mention of the burial specifically and then the resurrection clearly implies an empty tomb.[98] Anderson notes that the fact that the Gospels mention the empty tomb and the later proclamation of the apostles (including Paul) does not can only mean that by then everyone in the city, friend and foe, knew that it was empty; the proclamation was about *why* it was empty.[99]

One nuanced indication is the awkward Greek phrase "first day of the week" as used in the Gospels, which makes perfect sense when translated into Aramaic, denoting an early Aramaic origin that supports an early tradition.[100] Moreover, the restrained and unembellished narrative of the Gospels excludes the possibility of a later legend. Another evidence is the testimony of women; inadmissible in Jewish law, it would be the last thing the author of a legend would compose.[101] Finally, the earliest claim by Jewish authorities that the disciples stole the body is itself a confession that the tomb was empty[102]

Alternative theories offered to explain away the evidentiary value of the empty tomb have all failed.[103] For example, the conspiracy theory that the disciples stole the body and claimed the resurrection does not explain the radical transformation in their lives and their readiness to face martyrdom.[104] The Islamic story of mistaking another man for Jesus and crucifying him

96. Anderson, *Jesus Christ: The Witness*, 131–32.

97. Swinburne, *Resurrection of God Incarnate*, 177.

98. Craig, *Reasonable Faith*, 365.

99. Anderson, *Jesus Christ: The Witness*, 131.

100. Craig, *Reasonable Faith*, 366.

101. Craig, 367–68.

102. Craig, 369. This confession by Jewish authorities cannot be added to the confessions of chapter 4, however, because, like the Thomistic confession, it is a testimony about the confession, thus requiring double attestation per Islamic law.

103. Andrew Ter Ern Loke links all possible naturalistic explanations to the empty tomb in one syllogism to show that they all fail, leaving the resurrection hypothesis as the only plausible explanation. Loke, "Resurrection of the Son," 579–84.

104. Craig, *Reasonable Faith*, 371–73.

instead may explain Jesus's appearances to his disciples but does not explain the empty tomb,[105] which is the strongest circumstantial evidence against the Islamic story. The wrong tomb hypothesis that the women lost their way on Sunday at dawn and located another tomb fails to account for Jesus's postmortem appearances. Moreover, it taxes credibility that the disciples or Joseph of Arimathea, owner of the tomb, would proclaim such an extraordinary event without first checking out the tomb for themselves.[106] Jews had "an extraordinary interest" in venerating tombs of their prophets and martyrs. Not expecting a resurrection, they must have paid great attention to know the tomb's location to venerate it.[107] It also overlooks the fact that the Jewish opponents would certainly point out to the correct tomb if the women had located the wrong tomb.[108] Gary Habermas believes that seventy-five percent of critical scholars on the resurrection accept the empty tomb as historical.[109] J. P. Moreland notes that "intellectual integrity" requires that one admit that the above explanations are irrational and that the only valid explanation for the empty tomb is the resurrection of Jesus.[110]

The Origin of Christianity

Craig notes that, if one denies the resurrection, the belief of the disciples in the resurrection and hence the origin of the Christian religion can only be attributable to one of three influences: Christian, pagan, or Jewish. It cannot be Christian influence because Christianity was not there yet. Nor can it be an influence of pagan mythology as none of its alleged resurrection parallels resembles the Jewish understanding of resurrection; rather, its best-known risen god Osiris ends up with a continued existence in the netherworld.[111] Finally, it cannot be Jewish influence as the Jewish concept of resurrection is eschatological, at the end of the world, and is a mass event including all the righteous throughout history.[112]

105. Loke, "Resurrection of the Son," 582.

106. Swinburne, *Resurrection of God Incarnate*, 177.

107. Craig, *Son Rises*, 63.

108. Craig, *Reasonable Faith*, 374–75.

109. Habermas and Licona, *Case for the Resurrection*, 70.

110. Moreland, *Scaling the Secular City*, 172.

111. Craig, *Reasonable Faith*, 390.

112. Craig, 392–93.

Moreland notes that first-century Judaism held at least five tenets that formed the core of Jewish identity. These were the animal sacrifice system for atoning sins, keeping the law of Moses, the strict observance of the Sabbath, non-Trinitarian monotheism, and the human nature of the awaited Messiah. The early church, which, in the early years, was predominantly composed of devout Palestinian Jews, abandoned or significantly changed these five fundamental tenets. What would have prompted them to make such a radical fracture with their old religion and risk becoming social outcasts? Why would they risk facing persecution and, worst, damnation to eternal hell, all for the sake of a carpenter from the despised town of Nazareth who had just suffered a cruel death on a cross with thieves, a death presumably accursed by God (Deut 21:22–23)? Nothing apart from the bodily resurrection of Jesus can explain this.[113]

Non-Christian historian Jean-Pierre Isbouts argues that the crucifixion of Jesus became the "starting point for a new movement, a *Christian* movement," and then notes:

> This was an astonishing development, certainly given the fact that crucifixion was reserved for those whom Rome considered hardened criminals, such as political rebels, pirates, or runaway slaves. That early Christianity was able to capture the imagination of the Greco-Roman world despite its leader's condemnation as an enemy of the state is perhaps unprecedented in the annals of ancient religions.[114]

The answer to Isbouts' wonder lies in correcting his above assumption. It was not the *crucifixion* that marked the starting point for Christianity, but another event Isbouts ignored: the *resurrection* of Jesus. Such an "astonishing" start of Christianity was "unprecedented in the annals of ancient religions" precisely because the resurrection is unprecedented in the annals of any religion.

---

113. Moreland, *Scaling the Secular City*, 179–80.

114. Isbouts, *Archaeology of the Bible*, 286.

Sunday Worship and the Eucharist

For Jews to change the day of worship from Saturday to another day is quite unusual. Swinburne observes that Sunday worship, along with the celebration of the Eucharist, replaced Saturday soon after the resurrection: "On the first day of the week, . . . we were gathered together to break bread" (Acts 20:7). He argues that early Christians had other options for their weekly worship that would sound more natural to commemorate the Last Supper, such as Thursday, the day when the original Last Supper with Christ took place. Yet this never happened. There was no veneration of Sunday from outside Christianity that the apostles might imitate or follow. The only plausible explanation for Sunday worship and Eucharist celebration is their belief that the resurrection, the central event of their faith, happened on a Sunday.[115]

Archaeology and Ancient Literature[116]

Although archaeology does not *prove* the truthfulness of the Bible, it can *validate* many of its historical claims.[117] Liberal archaeologists tend to deny even this validation role of archeology as they limit biblical truth to the theological rather than also the factual. Archaeologist Randall Price notes that this limitation fails since "many aspects of the history of the Bible have already been demonstrated to be factual. The discoveries of the places, the people, the wars, the cultural contacts, the forms of treaties, and more – down to the smallest details – have verified the accuracy of the text."[118] Archaeologist and historian James Hoffmeier notes that archaeological data can help in shedding light on the context of a biblical text so that it can be better understood, complementing its data with more details, challenging erroneous theories objectively, and confirming the historicity of its events.[119] The role of archaeology is thus to provide support, not to set a foundation. This is in line with the role of circumstantial evidence in Islamic law.

The archaeological finds that corroborated details mentioned in the Bible are numerous. This section will highlight some of those that relate to the

115. Swinburne, *Resurrection of God Incarnate*, 163–64.

116. This section will not deal with extra-biblical testimonies that were already addressed in chapter 4.

117. Price, *Stones Cry Out*, 329.

118. Price, 331.

119. Hoffmeier, *Archaeology of the Bible*, 31.

trial, crucifixion, and burial of Jesus. The resurrection and empty tomb has been covered separately above. Such finds obviously do not prove that these events happened, but that they match the corresponding details mentioned in the Gospels.

The trial

In 1990, twelve limestone ossuaries were discovered in a Jerusalem burial chamber. One of them was particularly decorated, denoting that it belonged to some wealthy or important person. On the ossuary was an inscription that read: "*Qafa* and *Yehosef bar Qayafa*." This is the full name of Caiaphas, the high priest who tried Jesus and then handed him over to Pilate demanding his crucifixion. Inside were the bones of a man in his sixties, most probably belonging to Caiaphas.[120] In 1941, a sealed ossuary was discovered in Jerusalem with the inscription: "Simon / Alexander [son] of Simon." Some believe that the bones inside belong to the son of Simon who carried Jesus's cross, and probably to Simon himself.[121] Then in 1961, archeologists discovered in Caesarea Maritima a stone plaque bearing the Latin words: "Pontius Pilate, Prefect of Judea." Pilate (r. 26–36 CE) resided in Caesarea.[122]

The crucifixion

In 1968, skeletal remains of a crucified man in his thirties named Yohanan were found in an ossuary at Giv'at ha-Mivtar north of Jerusalem. They date from the time of Jesus. Special about this find, a long nail was still piercing through the right heel bone together with traces from the piece of wood from the cross; the nail was so lodged in a knot in the wood that it could only be removed with the nail and wood. This refutes objections that crucifixion was only by binding with ropes rather than nailing. It also shows that, against objections, some of those crucified were given proper, private burial rather than dumped into a common grave.[123] Osteologists argued that his legs were broken by a single blow just prior to death. This agrees with the Gospel story of the soldiers' breaking the legs of the crucified to hasten his death before

120. Price, *Stones Cry Out*, 306–7.
121. Hoffmeier, *Archaeology of the Bible*, 158.
122. Price, *Stones Cry Out*, 307.
123. Price, *Stones Cry Out*, 309–311.

sundown in keeping with Mosaic law (John 19:31–33).[124] Later studies, however, have questioned this *coup de grâce* interpretation.[125]

In a study that captured the attention of the media, Gunnar Samuelsson reviewed numerous ancient texts that describe cases of crucifixion in Greek, Latin, and Hebrew, and then the New Testament. He concluded that there was no fixed punishment before the Common Era known as "crucifixion," though there were descriptions of execution on a pole or a crossbeam. Of interest to Muslim scholars, some major media (like CNN) reported that Samuelsson denied that Jesus was crucified. Samuelsson denies such charge, however, and explains that his study does not deny the crucifixion but concludes that ancient texts do not include many of the details depicted in post-crucifixion descriptions and artwork.[126]

Samuelsson also argues that even New Testament accounts do not support all such details. What they support is that the death of Jesus was by way of an executionary suspension on a pole (rather than post-mortem suspension), that Jesus was scourged and then he or Simon carried his tool of suspension (σταυρός) to the execution place, that Jesus was undressed "and attached to a σταυρός, perhaps by being nailed," and that a sign was affixed on the pole to indicate the nature of the crime.[127] It seems, however, that Samuelsson's scholarly skepticism is unjustified. This is evident when he states that, according to Scripture, Jesus was attached to the cross *perhaps* by nailing, despite the unequivocal biblical evidence that he was nailed, which Samuelsson acknowledges. Thus, he refers to the words of Thomas: "Unless I see in His hands the imprint of the nails, and put my finger into the place of the nails, and put my hand into His side, I will not believe" (John 20:25), and the risen Jesus's showing his hands and feet to the disciples (Luke 24:39). He also refers to the express link of Jesus's blood with the cross: "to reconcile all things to Himself, having made peace through the blood of His cross" (Col 1:20). He even refers to the express mention of nailing: "having canceled out the certificate of debt consisting of decrees against us, which was hostile to us; and He has taken it out of the way, having nailed it to the cross" (Col 2:14), which

124. Ewen, *Faith on Trial*, 130.

125. Chapman, *Ancient Jewish and Christian*, 88.

126. Samuelsson, *Crucifixion in Antiquity*, 315.

127. Samuelsson, 296–97, 312.

he admits is "the only direct indication of any nails used to attach Jesus to the σταυρός."[128] Yet all these seem not to convince Samuelsson that the New Testament does confirm that Jesus was indeed nailed. Significantly, he ignores the express mention by Jesus himself of his blood (e.g., Matt 26:28). The above references make sense only if Jesus was nailed rather than tied with ropes. Samuelsson also downplays the evidentiary value of the Giv'at ha-Mivtar remains of the crucified Yohanan in 1968, dismissing the nail piercing his heel and the remains of the wooden cross as "not a proof of crucifixion,"[129] though other scholars insist that "all are agreed that [Yohanan's] death was produced by crucifixion."[130]

In a subsequent study, David Chapman has provided a more balanced picture and corrected basic flaws in Samuelsson's argument (without referring to him by name). He shows that ancients often did not provide enough details as to differentiate between the various ways of death on a post. They "often lumped all such suspensions into a single broad category, with overlapping perceptions between the many actual forms of suspension."[131] He cautions that scholars attempting to read ancient texts through a tight modern definition of *crucifixion* err in excluding data that is otherwise acceptable to the ancients, and requiring a level of details that the ancients were not interested in.[132] Chapman also notes that the three possible ways of execution by suspension on a post are hanging, impaling, and crucifixion. Hanging (from the neck) was not known to the ancients, and impalement on an upright pointed pole caused instant death rather than the slow agonizing death that was aimed for and described. This leaves crucifixion as the method intended by their use of the term *suspension*.[133] Chapman calls modern readers to "comprehend the ancient import of a text"; translating the term σταυρός as

128. Samuelsson, 255.

129. Samuelsson, 297.

130. Chapman, *Ancient Jewish and Christian Perceptions*, 89.

131. Chapman and Schnabel, *Trial and Crucifixion*, 316. Schnabel authored the part on the trial of Jesus while Chapman authored the part on crucifixion, hence the reference to Chapman alone.

132. Chapman and Schnabel, 317.

133. Chapman and Schnabel, 317.

"a device for human bodily suspension" is too pedantic and awkward, and so *cross* is quite appropriate.[134]

Chapman, after studying extensive literary works from antiquity including, inter alia, Babylonian, Egyptian, Assyrian, Roman, and Jewish literature, concludes that "perhaps the canonical Gospels present the most detailed accounts of a crucifixion from antiquity . . . [and are] our best source on crucifixion methods."[135] To scholars who approach the Gospels with a high level of suspicion, he notes that "the level of detail in the Gospel accounts likely testifies to the profound memories the eyewitnesses had of the event."[136] He then shows that several details in the Gospel accounts are substantiated by ancient extra-biblical literature, and even where they differ, these are historically justifiable.[137] Thus, a procession like Jesus's to the crucifixion site was well known in ancient crucifixion accounts, including forcing the criminal to carry his own cross, or forcing another, like Simon, to carry it for the criminal as an act of public service. Moreover, the cross was located outside the city and in a public location to ensure public viewing.[138] According to the Gospels, the soldiers divided Jesus's clothes among them, which agrees with the fact that clothes were among the more valuable possessions to the poor.[139] Moreover, some scholars argue that the σταυρός was an upright pole and that Jesus was fixed to a pole without a crossbeam. Chapman shows that Greek and Roman sources do depict the σταυρός with a crossbeam. He notes that such a view "typically entails an etymological fallacy, by assuming that the 'original meaning' of the word remains fundamental to all future uses of the term (even centuries later)."[140] Nailing is implied in the appearances of Jesus who invited his disciples to see his hands and feet (Luke 23:49; John 20:20), and by Paul in his imagery of nailing the debt record to the cross (Col 2:14). Chapman shows that both ropes and nails were used to attach the convicted to the cross and that the Romans such as Cicero, Seneca, and

134. Chapman and Schnabel, 318.
135. Chapman and Schnabel, 670.
136. Chapman and Schnabel, 671.
137. Chapman and Schnabel, 671.
138. Chapman and Schnabel, 672–73.
139. Chapman and Schnabel, 673–74.
140. Chapman and Schnabel, 674–75.

Suetonius associated blood with the cross.[141] Chapman also shows that the pre-crucifixion abuse of convicted criminals was customary in both Roman and Jewish contexts.[142]

The fact that it was customary to humiliate, ridicule, and beat the condemned before crucifying them does not fare well with the Muslim story. The Qur'ān relates that "they did not kill him nor crucify him, but so it was made to appear to them" (Qur'ān 4:157). This, admittedly by Muslim scholars, is ambiguous and bears several interpretations. The predominant interpretation is that God sent a substitute who looked like Jesus to die in his place and exalted Jesus by lifting him up to heaven.[143] God would not allow his prophet to endure such a fate. But at which stage exactly did God make the replacement and take Jesus up to him? The Gospels tell us that the mockery, spitting, and beating started at the Sanhedrin, right upon the pronouncing of the Jewish verdict, and so any replacement would have taken place at that point (Matt 26:66–68). The substitute person would have had enough time to show that he was not Jesus, or, if the Sanhedrin insisted that he was Jesus, he would have had time to retract his teachings and repent. He would even have had another better chance to prove that he was not Jesus before Pilate, who would be only too glad to obtain such a legal reason to release him.

Interestingly, the concern that Islam shows towards God's permitting his prophet to endure the horrors of crucifixion was shared by the Jews, albeit that, instead of denying the crucifixion event, they rejected the crucified. The cross was a stumbling block that prevented them from accepting a crucified Messiah. Chapman, after surveying ancient Jewish texts, shows that the Jews, just as the Gentiles, associated the crucified with brigandage and rebellion, in addition to magic and blasphemy.[144] Worse was the charge that "he who is hanged is accursed of God" (Deut 21:22–23). To the Jews, the crucified Jesus was also "an enemy of his people."[145] Chapman notes that early Christians

141. Chapman and Schnabel, 676–77.

142. Chapman and Schnabel, 672.

143. See some interpretations in Crook, *New Testament*, 296–306. Crook is a Muslim convert.

144. Chapman, *Ancient Jewish and Christian*, 260–61.

145. Reardon, "'Hanging on a Tree,'" 409.

had to struggle to show in their proclamation that these charges did not apply to Jesus whose death was rather a "soteriological exchange."[146]

The burial

Much debate has been going on regarding the authenticity of the Shroud of Turin which, if authentic, may provide evidence for the crucifixion. Radiocarbon dating of its flax in 1988 suggested that it dates from the thirteenth or fourteenth century, yet subsequent studies cast doubt on the dating, such as the effect of bacteria sticking to the fabric, and refreshed hopes of authenticity.[147] In addition, the sample tested proved to belong to a thread used to repair the Shroud rather than to the Shroud fabric itself.[148] Moreover, analysis of the pollens sticking to the cloth shows that it originates from a dry climate, like that of Jerusalem, and traces of limestone in the fabric show similarity to the Jerusalem limestone.[149]

In 2005, a scientific analysis confirmed that the Shroud was indeed authentic in that it belongs to the first century CE.[150] Moreover, it is argued that scientists know only 5 percent of what can be known about the Shroud; 95 percent await further research and discovery.[151] The dominant view, however, is that archeology can at most determine whether the Shroud authentically dates to the first century or not, yet even if proven authentic, it cannot determine whether it belonged to Jesus or not. Hoffmeier suggests that "for the time being, it is best to be dispassionately objective and await further scientific study."[152] Others challenge this view and contend that it is quite possible, both theoretically and practically, to scientifically prove that the Shroud wrapped the body of Jesus.[153] Nevertheless, the case for the crucifixion and resurrection is well attested and does not depend on the Shroud or, indeed, any archaeological finds. They only provide additional support to a case that is already well established.

---

146. Chapman, *Ancient Jewish and Christian*, 260–=61.

147. Ewen, *Faith on Trial*, 132–=37.

148. Hoffmeier, *Archaeology of the Bible*, 163.

149. Hoffmeier, 163.

150. Fanti and Malfi, *Shroud of Turin*, 335–36.

151. Fanti and Malfi, 336.

152. Hoffmeier, *Archaeology of the Bible*, 163.

153. Casabianca, "Turin Shroud," 709–21.

Miracles and Visions

Miracles of healing and deliverance in the name of Christ are still frequently witnessed today and are undeniable. Craig Keener has investigated hundreds of eyewitness claims of supernatural events, including the healing of the blind and the crippled, the raising of the dead, and sudden changes in nature after prayer. He found the evidence overwhelming and concluded that "to dispute that such phenomena have sometimes occurred is not really possible for open-minded people."[154] He argues that "while eyewitness claims do not constitute indisputable proof, they do constitute evidence that may be considered rather than a priori dismissed."[155] He believes that such evidence of the supernatural should be "welcome on the scholarly table." As a scholar, he started his investigation with a neutral mind, but then concluded, "As the depth of my conviction about genuinely supernatural events grew cumulatively in view of some of the evidence I was finding, the burden of proof shifted so far in my mind that it became disingenuous for me to try to appear to maintain personal neutrality."[156]

Visions of Christ, while difficult to objectively prove, are well attested by the many eyewitness testimonies.[157] One missionary in Central Asia under the pseudonym Sam Martyn has examined tens of independent testimonies of believers from Muslim background who have had pre-conversion visions. He notes that these testimonies "should be taken seriously. [They] are too widespread and too numerous to be dismissed casually."[158] He adds that they "offer compelling evidence that God uses such experiences in the process of conversion."[159] What is remarkable in these visions is that they share consistent features. In most of them Jesus appears physically, clothed in white and illuminated with white light. Some see him hanging on the cross. Some hear him assuring them of his love, that he is the truth, and then inviting them to follow him. Most know him intuitively, though sometimes he discloses his identity.[160] These features reported by Martyn agree with personal

154. Keener, *Miracles*, 599.

155. Keener, 2.

156. Keener, 3.

157. Butts, "Role of Dreams," iv.

158. Martyn, "Role of Pre-Conversion Dreams," 57.

159. Martyn, 57.

160. Martyn, 61–63.

testimonies this writer has directly or indirectly encountered. According to Martyn, between 1991 and 2007, about 27 percent of Muslims who believed in Christ reported pre-conversion visions and 40 percent reported visions at the time of conversion.[161]

In his extensive investigation into visions of Jesus throughout history, Phillip Wiebe refers to the principle of credulity whereby, if a person or a figure thought to be that person seems present to a percipient, then that person or figure probably *was* present. Wiebe also refers to the principle of testimony whereby a testimony should be taken at face value unless some reason suggests that the testimony is unreliable.[162]

Christianity and Civilization

One would expect a religion proven to have come from God and spread into much of the world for two millennia to make a pronounced impact on world civilization. Indeed, *Christianity Today* devoted full coverage to this topic at the turn of the Millennium.[163] The unique impact of Christianity on individuals and on world civilization is one important evidence that is both undeniable and unmatched. Christianity has affected almost all aspects of life wherever it prevailed, and its impact is long lasting. Yet while non-Western nations and leftist multiculturalists in the West enjoy and seek the blessings of Christianity on civilization, they intentionally deny its due credit.

The first and most important Christian impact is human dignity and the sanctity of life. Michael Novak observes that "the Greeks used 'dignity' for only the few, rather than for all human beings. By contrast, Christianity insisted that every single human is loved by the Creator, made in the Creator's image, and destined for eternal friendship and communion with him."[164] The lack of human dignity was apparent in the vast chasm that separated the few powerful elite from the masses in Rome, whose homes were "cramped, dark, often smoky and unsafe, always dirty, and permeated with the stench of sweat, feces, and decay."[165] Things were no better outside homes where the average

161. Martyn, 63.
162. Wiebe, *Visions of Jesus*, 98–99.
163. Neff, "Where Would Civilization Be," 50–59.
164. Novak, "Where Would Civilization Be," 50.
165. Watts, "Christianity and the Ancient," 2.

street was "filled with refuse of every imaginable kind [with] mud, open sewers, manure, human excrement, and even the occasional body shoved outdoors and abandoned, all nicely stewing in the blazing Mediterranean sun."[166] Indeed, the Christian concept of the sanctity of life constituted a radical departure from the Greco-Roman cruelty of infanticide, child abandonment, gladiator shows, and human sacrifices.[167] Rikk Watts notes that "death was banal and the individual of little value. . . . For Homer's heroes, the ancient gods, and Greek philosophers, compassion was immoral – it was a feminine weakness and an affront to justice."[168] The chasm separating the elite from the masses even continued into the hereafter where the few elite were to enjoy the company of the gods in disembodied existence while the masses "were condemned to a shade-like wandering in the dry and dark nether regions."[169] Watts then shows how the new and radically different Christian understanding of cosmology, epistemology, theology, sociology, anthropology, and ethics had a transforming effect on the entire Western civilization.[170]

Importantly, human dignity meant elevating the status of women and liberating them from such practices as prepubertal marriage and polygamy, and stressing the sanctity of marriage and sex. Indeed, Christ endowed equal dignity to women by giving them the honor of being the first witnesses of his resurrection.[171] Watts attributes the transformation in the status of women to the Christian emphasis on sexual morality and the fact that women are partakers of the death of Christ and the gift of the indwelling Holy Spirit.[172] Once women were no longer seen as pawns of sexual pleasure, "there was to be no having of a woman's body unless you had first promised her your lifelong and self-giving commitment to her and to her alone."[173] The Christian concept of human dignity also gave rise to individual freedom and rights, religious freedom, equality, separation between church and state, and the

166. Watts, 2.

167. Schmidt, *How Christianity Changed*, 48–76. This book provides a comprehensive overview of the impact of Christianity on the various fields of Western civilization. A similar work is Kennedy and Newcombe, *What If Jesus Had Never Been Born?*

168. Watts, "Christianity and the Ancient," 4.

169. Watts, 4.

170. Watts, 6–16.

171. Schmidt, *How Christianity Changed*, 97–122.

172. Watts, "Christianity and the Ancient," 17.

173. Watts, 18.

abolishment of slavery.[174] Aristotle argued in his book *Politics* that "the slave is a piece of property which is animate. . . . Slavery is natural. . . . There are human beings who . . . are natural slaves."[175] This was reflected in the Roman society. Many slaves preferred death to their continuing misery, and their boys, if pretty enough, were used for homosexual pleasure and their girls for prostitution. While early Christians could not tear the social fabric and abolish slavery, they alone treated slaves as equal beneficiaries of God's grace, giving them dignity, respecting their private family life, and frequently granting them freedom gratis.[176] The end of slavery came after centuries, again by devoted Christians, first in Britain and then North America.[177] Christianity also protected children as God's gift, prompted by Christ's invitation to permit children to come to him. While pagan children, especially females, were often victims of abortion, exposure, and infanticide, Christian children enjoyed unparalleled safety and dignity.[178]

One important practical application of human dignity is the Christian concept of *caritas*, whereby giving is prompted by love and compassion rather than the Greco-Roman *liberalites* giving, which expected a return. Thus, Christians were the first to open orphanages, homes for the elderly, mental institutions, voluntary associations, and fraternities.[179] To Christians also goes the credit for founding hospitals and medical nursing at a time when pagans used to leave the sick and the injured, even the dearest, lying on the public roads to die without even bothering to bury the dead.[180] Christian generosity and grace were a marked departure from the pagan concept of cruel justice. As Watts put it, "for Christians, themselves shown mercy and grace even though manifestly undeserving, life was not primarily about justice, but rather love."[181] And though Emperor Julian the Apostate (331–363

174. Schmidt, *How Christianity Changed*, 248–70.

175. Aristotle, *Basic Works*, 1114.

176. Watts, "Christianity and the Ancient," 18–19.

177. Stark, *For the Glory*, 339–353.

178. Watts, "Christianity and the Ancient," 19.

179. Schmidt, *How Christianity Changed*, 125–48.

180. Schmidt, 151–67.

181. Watts, "Christianity and the Ancient," 20.

CE) tried to imitate Christians to gain popularity, "imperial dictates could not match a transformed heart and mind."[182]

A second major Christian impact on civilization is science. Scientific initiative and research were possible only due to the Christian belief in one perfect, personal, and rational God who created an ordered world with immutable principles, and rational humans tasked with discovering its wondrous order as God's handiwork, thus giving him due honor.[183] Christianity thus insisted on God's separateness from the world, contrary to the Aristotelian pantheistic thinking. Starting from the thirteenth century, major scientific discoveries were made overwhelmingly by devout Christians, and European medieval technology surpassed any other technology the world had known.[184] Science thus started with the Christian scholastics of the "Dark Ages," which, after all, were not dark.[185] They were the true owners of the scientific revolution long before the "Enlightenment," a misleading term.[186] Then came the Reformation. In de-deifying nature as God's creation, it stressed God's mandate to exercise constructive dominion over nature rather than destructive domination, thus opening the way for inquiry without charges of impiety. It also freed reason from its Greek deductive limitation and enhanced it with empirical observation.[187]

David Livingstone, while not denying the contribution of medieval Christians and Muslims, stresses the significant role of the Reformers who believed that God reveals himself in both Scripture and nature such that investigating nature reveals God's glory.[188] Indeed, "the idea that we live in a designed world whose structure carries the imprint of the Creator encouraged

182. Watts, 20.

183. Stark, *For the Glory*, 147–49, 157.

184. Stark, 134.

185. Stark, 130. Sociology of religion scholar Rodney Stark gives evidence to refute the allegations of church oppression against science. The model story of resistance to round-earth Columbus is a lie, as all then agreed that the earth was round, differing only on earth's circumference. Stark, *For the Glory of God*, 122. Moreover, the oft-told story of the struggle between the church and Galileo is misleading as Galileo was to blame for his arrogance in dealing with his old and supportive friend Pope Urban VIII and in the end losing his support. Stark, *For the Glory*, 163–165. Furthermore, the geocentric view belongs to Aristotle and Ptolemy, not the Bible. Stark, 138.

186. Stark, 166–67.

187. Sampson, *Six Modern Myths*, 42–45.

188. Livingstone, "Where Would Civilization Be," 52.

the development of a branch of learning known as natural *theology* [Italics mine]."[189]

Rodney Stark notes that, while Christian theology was essential to science, the other religious systems had a restrictive effect on it. For example, the Chinese lacked a divine basis for natural laws, and the Greeks lacked a personal God who organizes and controls and were trapped in an uncreated cyclical universe, each cycle ending with chaos and collapse.[190] While acknowledging the "significant progress" in science by medieval Muslims, Stark argues that it was limited to aspects of medicine and astronomy that did not require a theoretical basis. This is due to the limiting adherence of Averroes and his followers to Aristotelian physics and the Muslim theology of God's absolute and capricious freedom that anathemized the formulation of natural laws as limiting God's freedom.[191]

Another field of Christian impact is literacy and education. David Lyle Jeffrey notes that, while literacy was limited to the privileged elite, Christianity opened it to all classes through the distribution of the gospel in vernacular Greek and, later, in vernacular translations.[192] Christians thus were the first to open schools to both genders and all social classes and to introduce public schools, compulsory education, graded education, kindergartens, and schools for the deaf and the blind. Remarkably, Christians were the first to open universities starting from the University of Bologna in 1158, followed by Paris, Oxford, and Cambridge. Later, Cambridge bred Harvard in the United States followed by Yale and Princeton.[193]

Christianity has also influenced literature with its metanarrative of God's love and liberation. Thus, "in lieu of gory sagas of bloodthirst and power, [Christian] tales are resonant with the promise of spiritual emancipation. It is this hope for the Truth which sets us free that has charged the greatest poetry and prose of these two millennia."[194] Christianity had also a profound impact

189. Livingstone, 53.

190. Stark, *For the Glory*, 150–54.

191. Stark, 154–56.

192. Jeffrey, "Where Would Civilization Be," 54.

193. Schmidt, *How Christianity Changed*, 170–91.

194. Jeffrey, "Where Would Civilization Be," 55. *Christianity Today* also addresses two other impacts, humility and missions.

on music, where the classical forms of advanced music mostly developed in the context of church music by Christians, such as Bach and Handel.[195]

Indeed, "had Jesus Christ never walked the dusty paths of ancient Palestine, suffered, died, and risen from the dead, and never established around him a small group of disciples who spread out into the pagan world, the West would not have attained its high level of civilization, giving it the many human benefits it enjoys today."[196] These advances have only to be contrasted with the miserable living conditions and the crushing political and religious oppression that still dominate large parts of the world where Christianity is absent. The words of Christ describe it all: "The thief comes only to steal and kill and destroy; I came that they may have life, and have it abundantly" (John 10:10).

195. Schmidt, *How Christianity Changed*, 292–312.

196. Schmidt, 14.

CHAPTER 6

Conclusion

Around a quarter of the world population do not believe in the crucifixion and resurrection of Jesus Christ based on the authority of the Qur'ān. This study is directed at Muslims who, while respecting the authority of the Qur'ān, are nevertheless open to subjecting its assertions to rational inquiry and investigation. Christians claim that Christianity is based on historical evidence, particularly its foundational events, the crucifixion and resurrection of God the Son, Jesus Christ. A Muslim is not without a rational guide; the Islamic law is the ideal instrument for the examination of such evidence. It is believed to be God-given despite its composite divine-human origins, and is still revered by Muslims worldwide as God's ideal for humanity despite its rigidity and, arguably, non-applicability to modern life. The Christian finds in the Islamic law a suitable means to respectfully vindicate the historical evidence of the crucifixion and resurrection of Jesus Christ to Muslims; unlike changeable Western secular legal systems, they see it as divinely authoritative and immutable, and so trustworthy.

The Islamic law adequately provides for the examination of factual evidence. Its two foremost types of evidence, eyewitness testimony and confession, are well developed and tried over more than a millennium of Islamic theocracy. It is true that its evidentiary rules are designed to cover *contemporary* evidence with men and women personally testifying or confessing before a court of law. Nevertheless, the apostles and Evangelists who testified and confessed two millennia ago can be "brought alive" through authenticating the documents that transmit their testimonies and confessions. It is also true that documentary evidence in Islamic law deals with contemporaneous handwritten documents and, unlike common law, does not address ancient documents. Nevertheless, this study did not attempt to enforce an undue adaptation of such evidentiary rules to a procrustean bed of relevance but acknowledged that they are irrelevant to dealing with the authenticity of the New Testament documents. Although this study has found one principle vindicating the New Testament documents, that is, *iṭiṣḥāb* (the presumption of continuity), yet it acknowledged that it is a secondary source of law that may be too fragile to underpin the huge edifice of the authenticity of the New Testament documents. The study therefore took pains to examine the principles that are used to defend the authenticity of the very sources of Islamic law, the Qur'ān and *Sunna*, and apply them to New Testament documents to show that they are undeniably authentic.

In his work, *The Resurrection of God Incarnate*, Christian philosopher Richard Swinburne approaches the subject of defending the incarnation of God the Son and his resurrection in a noteworthy manner. Instead of proceeding with available pieces of evidence and then inferring a conclusion, he asks, "What would be the marks of that life which we could recognize it if it was to succeed in [satisfying God's reasons for incarnation, for example,] providing atonement, identifying with our suffering, and providing information and encouragement?"[1] He thus starts by mentioning such marks: A true God incarnate would live a perfect human life, provide us with moral teaching and guidance, demonstrate that he believed himself to be God incarnate, teach us that he came to provide atonement for our sins, and give a unique supernatural sign that no one can perform except God himself.[2] Swinburne then proceeds to show how Jesus Christ satisfied all these expectations.

This study concludes with a similar approach and asks Muslims a similar question: What kind of evidence do Muslims expect the apostles and Evangelists to provide if they were correct in their proclamation about a crucified and risen Jesus Christ? First, the documents reporting the testimonies of the apostles and Evangelists must satisfy to the same degree the very authentication principles that the Qur'ān satisfies, and satisfy to *at least* the same degree the authentication principles that the *Sunna* satisfies. Second, the testimonies of the apostles and Evangelists must be at least doubly attested as eyewitness testimonies. Third, the character of each of the apostles and

1. Swinburne, *Resurrection of God Incarnate*, 55.
2. Swinburne, 55–59, 62.

Evangelists must be one of integrity and trustworthiness, with no personal interest or gain sought from one's testimony. Fourth, their testimonies must be consistent, at least regarding the main facts in question, that Jesus Christ died by crucifixion, was buried, and then was seen alive. Fifth, for the purpose of ruling out any possibility of psychological influence, the witnesses must not all come from Jesus's disciples, but must also include former enemies. Sixth, the testimonies would be better vindicated if corroborated by expert testimony from someone who can be regarded as a historian. Seventh, the testimonies and confessions must not be contradicted by circumstantial evidence but rather be corroborated by such evidence if possible. For instance, if Jesus rose from the dead, his tomb must be shown to have been found empty. Since we are talking about a historical event, one would also expect to find some archeological remains that agree with New Testament details. Moreover, if the resurrection was known with certainty, then one would expect the witnesses to spread the news, and so a new religion must emerge despite all resistance. Finally, if Jesus rose from the dead and so his religion was from God, it is expected to influence the civilizations of all the peoples it reached in such a manner that would massively improve all aspects of life.

As this study has shown, all the above expectations have been fulfilled. What more would a Muslim expect as convincing evidence to believe a band of people who, two millennia ago, proclaimed that they saw a man die and rise from the dead? Indeed, is there any reasonable evidence at all that can possibly persuade a Muslim to believe in the crucifixion and resurrection of God the Son? If all of this evidence does not suffice, probably nothing will do so. Evidence is available and there is no need for more. Perhaps what a Muslim needs is wisdom, courage, and what J. P. Moreland calls "intellectual integrity"[3] to discern and cognitively know the truth, and then personally know the Truth, crucified and raised.

3. Moreland, *Scaling the Secular City*, 172.

Bibliography

Abdel Haleem, M. A. S. "Qur'an and Hadith." In *The Cambridge Companion to Classical Islamic Theology*, edited by Tim Winter, 19–32. Cambridge: Cambridge University Press, 2008.

Abdel Haleem, Muhammad, Adel Omar Sherif, and Kate Daniels, eds. *Criminal Justice in Islam: Judicial Procedure in the Shari'a*. London: I. B. Taurus, 2003.

Abou El Fadl, Khaled M. *The Great Theft: Wrestling Islam from the Extremists*. 2005. Reprinted, New York: Harper-Collins, 2007.

———. *Speaking in God's Name: Islamic Law, Authority and Women*. 2001. Reprinted, Oxford: Oneworld Publications, 2013.

Abualfaraj, Maha. "Evidence in Islamic Law: Reforming the Islamic Evidence Law Based on the Federal Rules of Evidence." *Journal of Islamic Law and Culture* 13, nos. 2–3 (July–October 2011): 140–65.

Ahmed, Abdelmoumin I. "The Bible and the Qur'an: A New Islamic Understanding." *Journal of Unification Studies* 10 (2009): 105–19.

Ahmed, Shahab. *Before Orthodoxy: The Satanic Verses in Early Islam*. Cambridge, MA: Harvard University Press, 2017.

———. *What Is Islam? The Importance of Being Islamic*. Princeton, NJ: Princeton University Press, 2016.

Albayrak, Ismail. "The People of the Book in the Qur'ān." *Islamic Studies* 47, no. 3 (Autumn 2008): 301–25.

Alford, Deann. "Unapologetic Apologist: Jay Smith Confronts Muslim Fundamentalists with Fundamentalist Fervor." *Christianity Today*, 13 June 2008.

ʿAlia, Samir. *Al-dawlah al-fāḍilah fī al-Islām* [Virtuous state in Islam]. Beirut: Al-Halabi Legal Publications, 2018.

ʿAllam, Muhammad Yousef. *Shahādāt al-shuhūd ka wasīlat ithbāt amām al-qadā' al-idārī bayna al-qanūn al-waḍʿī wa al-Shariʿa al-Islāmiyyah: Dirāsa muqārina* [Witnesses' testimony as a means of proof before administrative litigation between secular law and Islamic Shari'a: A comparative study]. 2nd ed. Cairo: National Center for Legal Publications, 2017.

Alwani, Taha Jabir al-. *Source Methodology in Islamic Jurisprudence: Usul al-Fiqh al-Islami*. 3rd ed. London: International Institute of Islamic Thought, 2003.

Anderson, J. N. D. *Islamic Law in the Modern World*. New York: New York University Press, 1959.

Anderson, Mark Robert. *The Qur'an in Context: A Christian Exploration*. Downers Grove, IL: Intervarsity Press, 2016.

Anderson, Norman. *Jesus Christ: The Witness of History*. Leicester, England: Inter-Varsity Press, 1985.

———. *A Lawyer among the Theologians*. Grand Rapids: W. B. Eerdmans, 1974.

Anthony, Sean W., and Catherine L. Bronson. "Did Ḥafṣah bint ʿUmar Edit the Qurʾan? A Response with Notes on the Codices of the Prophet's Wives." *Journal of the International Qurʾanic Studies Association* 1 (2016): 93–125.

Anyabwile, Thabiti. *The Gospel for Muslims: An Encouragement to Share Christ with Confidence*. Chicago: Moody Publishers, 2010.

Appleton, John. *The Rules of Evidence: Stated and Discussed*. Philadelphia: T. & J. W. Johnson, 1860.

Aristotle. *The Basic Works of Aristotle*. Edited by Richard McKeon. New York: Random House, 1941.

Arnold, Clinton E., ed. *Zondervan Illustrated Bible Backgrounds Commentary*. Grand Rapids: Zondervan, 2002.

Ashford, Bruce Riley, ed. *Theology and Practice of Mission: God, the Church, and the Nations*. Nashville: B&H Academic, 2011.

Ashqar, ʿUmar Sulaimān ʿAbdallah al-. *Al-madkhal ila al-Shariʿa wa al-fiqh al-Islāmī*. [Introduction to Sharīʿa and Islamic fiqh]. 2nd. ed. Amman, Jordan: Dar al-Nafāʾes, 2012.

Atiah al-Bawanah, Waleed A. al-. *Al-qarīna alqaḍāʾiyya wa dawruha fī al-ithbāt al-qadāʾī: Dirāsa muqārina* [Judicial circumstantial evidence and its role in judicial proof: A comparative study]. Amman, Jordan: Dar Al-Thaqafa, 2017.

Auda, Jasser. *Maqasid al-Shariah as Philosophy of Islamic Law: A Systems Approach*. London: International Institute of Islamic Thought, 2008.

Awa, Mohamed Selim el-. "Confession and Other Methods of Evidence in Islamic Procedural Jurisprudence." In *Criminal Justice in Islam: Judicial Procedure in the Shariʿa*, edited by Abdel Haleem, Adel Omar Sherif, and Kate Daniels, 111–29. London: I. B. Taurus, 2003.

Azami, M. Mustafa al-. *On Schacht's Origins of Muhammadan Jurisprudence*. 1996. Reprinted, Oxford: Oxford Centre for Islamic Studies, 2013.

Bahnsen, Greg L. *Presuppositional Apologetics: Stated and Defended*. Edited by Joel McDurmon. 2008. Reprinted, Powder Springs, GA: American Vision Press, 2011.

Bassiouni, M. Cherif, ed. *The Islamic Criminal Justice System*. London: Oceana Publications, 1982.

———. "Sources of Islamic Law and the Protection of Human Rights." In *The Islamic Criminal Justice System*, edited by M. Cherif Bassiouni. 3–53. London: Oceana Publications, 1982.

Bauckham, Richard. *Jesus and the Eyewitnesses: The Gospels as Eyewitness Testimony*. Grand Rapids: William B. Eerdmans, 2006.

Baʿyoun, Suha. *Nithām al-qaḍāʾ fī al- ʿahd al-nabawī* [Judicial system during the prophetic era]. Beirut: University Institution for Studies, Publishing, and Distribution, 2009.

Beaumont, Ivor Mark. "Debating the Cross in Early Christian Dialogues with Muslims." In *Jesus and the Cross: Reflections of Christians from Islamic Contexts*, edited by David Emmanuel Singh, 54–64 (2008). Reprinted, Oxford, UK: Regnum Book International, 2010. Kindle.

Bennett, Edmund H. *The Four Gospels from a Lawyer's Standpoint*. Boston: Houghton, Mifflin and Company, 1899.

Bergeron, Joseph W. *The Crucifixion of Jesus: A Medical Doctor Examines the Death and Resurrection of Christ*. Cumming, GA: St. Polycarp Publishing House, 2018.

Best, William Mawdesley. *The Principles of the Law of Evidence: With Elementary Rules for Conducting the Examination and Cross-Examination of Witnesses*. 9th ed. London: Law Publishers, 1902.

Blomberg, Craig L. *The Historical Reliability of the Gospels*. 2nd ed. Downers Grove, IL: IVP Academic, 2007.

———. *The Historical Reliability of John's Gospel: Issues and Commentary*. Downers Grove, IL: InterVarsity Press, 2001.

Boa, Kenneth D., and Robert M. Bowman Jr. *Faith Has Its Reasons: Integrative Approaches to Defending the Christian Faith*. 2nd ed. Colorado Springs: Paternoster, 2005.

Bock, Darrell L. *Jesus According to Scripture: Restoring the Portrait from the Gospels*. Grand Rapids: Baker Academic, 2002.

———. *Studying the Historical Jesus: A Guide to Sources and Methods*. Grand Rapids: Baker Academic, 2002.

Bonderman, David. "Modernization and Changing Perceptions of Islamic Law." *Harvard Law Review* 81, no. 6 (April 1968): 1169–93.

Bouṭī, Muhammad Saʿīd Ramaḍān al-. *Manhaj al-Ḥanafiyya fī naqd al-Ḥadīth: bayna al-nathariyya wa al-taṭbīq* [The Ḥanafī method in Ḥadīth criticism: Between theory and application]. Cairo: Dār al-Salām, 2010.

Broun, Kenneth S., ed. *McCormick on Evidence*. 7th ed. St. Paul, MN: West Academic Publishing, 2014.

Brown, Jonathan A. C. "How We Know Early Ḥadīth Critics Did *Matn* Criticism and Why It's So Hard to Find." *Islamic Law and Society* 15 (2008): 143–84.

Brown, Jonathan A. C. *Misquoting Muhammad: The Challenge and Choices of Interpreting the Prophet's Legacy*. 2014. Reprinted, London: Oneworld Publications, 2016.

Brubaker, Daniel Alan. *Corrections in Early Qur'ān's Manuscripts: Twenty Examples*. Lovettsville, VA: Think and Tell Press, 2019.

Bruce, F. F. *The New Testament Documents: Are They Reliable?* 6th ed. Grand Rapids: William B. Eerdmans, 1981.

Burns, Jonathan G. *Introduction to Islamic Law: Principles of Civil, Criminal, and International Law under the Shari'a*. Middletown, DE: Teller Books, 2013–2014.

Butts, John E. "The Role of Dreams and Visions in the Conversion of Diaspora Arab Muslims." D. Min. project, Trinity International University, 2012.

Caird, Lance D., and Wendy Cadge. "Constructing American Muslim Identity: Tales of Two Clinics in Southern California." *The Muslim World* 99, no. 2 (April 2009): 270–93.

Cairns, Earle E. "Luke As a Historian." *Bibliotheca Sacra* 122, no. 487 (July–September 1965): 220–26.

Carson, D. A. *Matthew*. In *The Expositor's Bible Commentary, Vol. 8*. Edited by Frank E. Gaebelein. Grand Rapids: Zondervan, 1984.

———. "Unity and Diversity in the New Testament: The Possibility of Systematic Theology." In *Scripture and Truth*, edited by D.A. Carson and John D. Woodbridge, 65–95. Grand Rapids: Baker Book House, 1992.

Carson, D. A., and John D. Woodbridge, eds. *Scripture and Truth*. Grand Rapids: Baker Book House, 1992.

Casabianca, Tristan. "Turin Shroud, Resurrection and Science: One View of the Cathedral." *New Blackfriars* 98, no. 1078 (November 2017): 709–21.

Chapa, Juan. "The Early Text of John." In Hill and Kruger, 140–56.

Chapman, David W. *Ancient Jewish and Christian Perceptions of Crucifixion*. 2008. Reprinted, Grand Rapids: Baker Academic, 2010.

Chapman, David W., and Eckhard J. Schnabel. *The Trial and Crucifixion of Jesus: Text and Commentary*. Tübingen, Germany: Mohr Siebeck, 2015.

Chatraw, Joshua D., and Mark D. Allen. *Apologetics at the Cross: An Introduction for Christian Witness*. Grand Rapids: Zondervan, 2018.

Clifford, Ross. *John Warwick Montgomery's Legal Apologetics: An Apologetics for All Seasons*. Bonn, Germany: VKW, 2004.

———. *Leading Lawyers' Case for the Resurrection*. 1991. Reprinted, Edmonton: Canadian Institute for Law, Theology, & Public Policy, 1996.

Cole, Graham A. "The Peril of a 'Historyless' Systematic Theology." In *Do Historical Matters Matter to Faith? A Critical Appraisal of Modern and Postmodern Approaches to Scripture*, edited by James K. Hoffmeier and Dennis R. Magary, 55–69. Wheaton, IL: Crossway, 2012.

Cowan, Steven B., ed. *Five Views on Apologetics*. Grand Rapids: Zondervan, 2000.

Craig, William Lane. "A Classical Apologist's Closing Remarks." In *Five Views on Apologetics*, edited by Stephen B. Cowan, 314–28. Grand Rapids: Zondervan, 2000.

———. *Reasonable Faith: Christian Truth and Apologetics*. 3rd ed. Wheaton, IL: Crossway Books, 2008.

———. *The Son Rises: The Historical Evidence for the Resurrection of Jesus*. 1981. Reprinted, Eugene, OR: Wipf & Stock, 2000.

Crook, Jay R. *The New Testament, An Islamic Perspective: Early Christianity and the Assault of Hellenism*. Chicago: ABC International Group, 2007.

Curry, Theodore A. "Mission to Muslims." In *Theology and Practice of Mission: God, the Church, and the Nations*, edited by Bruce Riley Ashford, 222–37. Nashville: B&H Academic, 2011.

Daoud, Ahmad Muhammad Ali. *Al-qaḍā' wa al-daʿwa wa al-ithbāt wa al-ḥukm fī al-sharīʿa al-Islāmiyyah wa al-taṭbīq al-qaḍā'i* [Litigation, suits, proof, and verdict in Islamic Sharīʿa and judicial application]. Amman, Jordan: Dar al-Thaqāfa, 2012.

———. *Al-ṣukouk wa al-tashriʿāt fī al-maḥākem al-sharʿiyya: tandhimuha wa tawthiquha wa fiqhuha al-muqaren wa nusousuha al-qanuniyya wa taṭbiqatun qaḍaiyya* [Instruments and documentation in Sharīʿa courts: Their organization, documentation, comparative *fiqh*, legal texts, and judicial applications]. Amman, Jordan: Dar al-Thaqafa, 2010.

Dembski, William, and Thomas Schirrmacher, eds. *Tough-Minded Christianity: Honoring the Legacy of John Warwick* Montgomery. Nashville: B&H Academic, 2008.

Derico, T. M. *Oral Tradition and Synoptic Verbal Agreement: Evaluating the Empirical Evidence for Literary Dependence*. Eugene, OR: Pickwick Publications, 2016.

Duderija, Adis. "Progressive Muslims – Defining and Delineating Identities and Ways of Being a Muslim." *Journal of Muslim Minority Affairs* 30, no. 1 (March 2010): 127–36.

Dulles, Avery Cardinal. *A History of Apologetics*. 2nd ed. San Francisco: Ignatius Press, 2005.

Edgar, William, and K. Scott Oliphant, eds. *Christian Apologetics Past and Present: A Primary Source Reader*. Wheaton, IL: Crossway Books, 2009.

Ergene, Boğaç A. "Evidence in Ottoman Courts: Oral and Written Documentation in Early-Modern Courts of Islamic Courts." *Journal of the American Oriental Society* 124, no. 3 (July–September 2004): 471–91.

Erickson, Millard J. *Christian Theology*. 2nd ed. 1998. Reprinted, Grand Rapid: Baker Academic, 2007.

Eshelbrenner, Derek. "The Qur'an-Gospel Resurrection Resolution." *Journal of Ecumenical Studies* 44, no. 4 (Fall 2009): 665–87.

Ewen, Pamela Binnings. *Faith on Trial: An Attorney Analyzes the Evidence for the Death and Resurrection of Jesus*. Nashville: Broadman & Holman Publishers, 1999.

Fanti, Giulio, and Pierandrea Malfi. *The Shroud of Turin: First Century after Christ*. Boca Raton, FL: Taylor & Francis Group, 2016.

Farrin, Raymond K. "The Composition and Writing of the Qur'ān: Old Explanations and New Evidence." Paper presented at the Qatar University Qur'anic Studies Conference, May 2–3, 2018. https://www.academia.edu/43294485/The_Composition_and_Writing_of_the_Quran_Old_Explanations_and_New_Evidence.

Fatima, Saba. "Who Counts as a Muslim? Identity, Multiplicity and Politics." *Journal of Muslim Minority Affairs* 31, no. 3 (September 2011): 339–53.

Feinberg, Paul D. "The Meaning of Inerrancy." In *Inerrancy*, edited by Norman Geisler, 267–304. Grand Rapids: Zondervan, 1980.

Gardoski, Kenneth. "The Usefulness of Archeology for Apologetics." *The Journal of Ministry and Theology* 17, no. 1 (Spring 2013): 79–98.

Geisler, Norman L., ed. *Inerrancy*. Grand Rapids: Zondervan, 1980.

Geisler, Norman L., and William E. Nix. *A General Introduction to the Bible*. Rev. ed. Chicago: Moody Press, 1986.

George, Timothy, ed. *God the Holy Trinity: Reflections on Christian Faith and Practice*. Grand Rapids: Baker Academic, 2006.

———. "The Trinity and the Challenge of Islam." In *God the Holy Trinity: Reflections on Christian Faith and Practice*, edited by Timothy George, 109–27. Grand Rapids: Baker Academic, 2006.

Gerhardsson, Birger. *Memory and Manuscript: Oral Tradition and Written Transmission in Rabbinic Judaism and Early Christianity*. Grand Rapids: William B. Eerdmans, 1998.

———. *The Reliability of the Gospel Tradition*. Grand Rapids: Baker Academic, 2001.

Gibb, H. A. R. *Mohammedanism: An Historical Survey*. 2nd ed. London: Oxford University Press, 1953.

Goldziher, Ignaz. *Introduction to Islamic Theology and Law*. Translated by Andras and Ruth Hamori. Princeton, NJ: Princeton University Press, 1981.

———. *Muslim Studies*. Edited by S. M. Stern. Translated by C. R. Barber and S. M. Stern. Albany: State University of New York Press, 1971.

Goodenow, Smith Bartlett. "Women at the Tomb: A Harmony of the Resurrection Accounts." *Andover Review* 6, no. 35 (November 1886): 542–43.

Greenleaf, Simon. *The Testimony of the Evangelists: The Gospels Examined by the Rules of Evidence Administered in Courts of Justice*. 1874. Reprinted, Grand Rapids: Kregel Classics, 1995.

Greifenhagen, F. V. "Scripture Wars: Contemporary Polemical Discourses of Bible Versus Quran on the Internet." *Comparative Islamic Studies* 6, nos. 1–2 (May–November 2010): 23–65.

Griffith, Sydney H. *The Bible in Arabic: The Scriptures of the 'People of the Book' in the Language of Islam*. 2013. Reprinted, Princeton, NJ: Princeton University Press, 2015.

———. *The Church in the Shadow of the Mosque: Christians and Muslims in the World of Islam*. 2008. Reprinted, Princeton, NJ: Princeton University Press, 2010.

———. "When Did the Bible Become an Arabic Scripture?" *Intellectual History of the Islamicate World* 1, nos. 1–2 (2013): 7–23.

Grotius, Hugo. *The Truth of the Christian Religion*. Edited by Jean Le Clerc. Translated by John Clarke. Edinburgh: Thomas Turnbull, 1819.

Guenther, Alan M. "Christian Responses to Ahmad Khan's Commentary on the Bible." *Comparative Islamic Studies* 6, nos. 1–2 (May–November 2010): 67–100.

Gundry, Robert H. *A Survey of the New Testament*. 4th ed. Grand Rapids: Zondervan, 2003.

Gutteridge, Don J. Jr. *The Defense Rests Its Case: A Bold Evangelism Beamed to Modern Unbelievers*. Nashville: Broadman Press, 1975.

Habermas, Gary R. "Evidential Apologetics." In *Five Views on Apologetics*, edited by Stephen B. Cowan, 91–121. Grand Rapids: Zondervan, 2000.

———. *The Historical Jesus: Ancient Evidence for the Life of Christ*. 1996. Reprinted, Joplin, MO: College Press, 2008.

Habermas, Gary R., and Michael R. Licona. *The Case for the Resurrection of Jesus*. Grand Rapids: Kregel Publications, 2004.

Hailey, O L. "The Three Prophetic Days: A Harmony of the Apparent Discrepancies in the Gospel Narratives about the Resurrection of Jesus Christ." *The Review & Expositor* 5, no. 4 (October 1908): 530–47.

Hailsham, Quintin Hogg. *The Door Wherein I Went*. Glasgow: William Collins Sons, 1975.

Hall, David R. *The Seven Pillories of Wisdom*. Macon, GA: Mercer University Press, 1990.

Hallaq, Wael B. *Authority, Continuity and Change in Islamic Law*. 2001. Reprinted, Cambridge: Cambridge University Press, 2005.

———. *A History of Islamic Legal Theories: An Introduction to Sunnī ūṣūl al-fiqh*. 1997. Reprinted, Cambridge: Cambridge University Press, 2005.

———. *The Impossible State: Islam, Politics, and Modernity's Moral Predicament.* New York: Columbia University Press, 2014.

———. *An Introduction to Islamic Law.* 2009. Reprinted, Cambridge: Cambridge University Press, 2016.

———. "Notes on the Term *qarīna* in Islamic Legal Discourse." *Journal of the American Oriental Society* 108, no. 3 (July–September 1988): 475–80.

———. *The Origins and Evolution of Islamic Law.* 2005. Reprinted, Cambridge: Cambridge University Press, 2011.

———. *Shari'a: Theory, Practice, Transformation.* 2009. Reprinted, Cambridge: Cambridge University Press, 2012.

———. "The Use and Abuse of Evidence: The Question of Provincial and Roman Influences on Early Islamic Law." *Journal of the American Oriental Society* 110, no. 1 (January–March 1990): 79–91.

Haneef, Sayed Sikandar Shah. *Islamic Law of Evidence.* Selangor, Malaysia: Pelanduk Publications, 1994.

Haykel, Bernard. "Theme Issue: Evidence in Islamic Law." *Islamic Law and Society* 9, no. 2 (2002): 129–31.

Head, Peter M. "The Early Text of Mark." In *The Early Text of the New Testament,* edited by Charles E. Hill and Michael J. Kruger, 108–20. Oxford: Oxford University Press, 2012.

Hernández, Juan Jr. "The Early Text of Luke." In *The Early Text of the New Testament,* edited by Charles E. Hill and Michael J. Kruger, 121–39. Oxford: Oxford University Press, 2012.

Hickey, Will. "Using Blockchain for Immutable Mediation and Autonomous Governance." *Harvard Kennedy School Review* 19 (2019): 143–47.

Hill, Charles E., and Michael J. Kruger, eds. *The Early Text of the New Testament.* Oxford: Oxford University Press, 2012.

Hoffmeier, James K. *The Archaeology of the Bible.* Oxford: Lion Hudson Publications, 2008.

Hoffmeier, James K., and Dennis R. Magary, eds. *Do Historical Matters Matter to Faith? A Critical Appraisal of Modern and Postmodern Approaches to Scripture.* Wheaton, IL: Crossway, 2012.

Holtz, Peter, Janine Dahinden, and Wolfgang Wagner. "German Muslims and the 'Integration Debate': Negotiating Identities in the Face of Discrimination." *Integrative Psychological & Behavioral Science* 47 (2013): 231–48.

Ḥossari, Aḥmad al-. *ʿIlm al- qaḍāʾ: Adillat al-ithbāt fī al-fiqh al-Islāmi* [The science of judiciary: Evidence in Islamic *fiqh*]. Beirut: Dar al-Kitab al-Arabi, 1986.

Howard, Damian SJ. "'Who Do You Say that I Am?': Christians and Muslims Disputing the Historical Jesus." *Neotestamentica* 49, no. 2 (2015): 297–320.

Hughes, Philip Edgecumbe. "The Truth of Scripture and the Problem of Historical Relativity." In *The Expositor's Bible Commentary, Vol.* 8, edited by D. A. Carson and John D. Woodbridge, 173–94. Grand Rapids: Zondervan, 1984.

Humphreys, R. Stephen. *Islamic History: A Framework for Inquiry*. Rev. ed. Princeton, NJ: Princeton University Press, 1991.

Hussin, Izra R. *The Politics of Islamic Law: Local Elites, Colonial Authority, and the Making of the Muslim State*. Chicago: University of Chicago Press, 2016.

Ibn al-Humām al-Ḥanafī. *Sharḥ fatḥ al-qadīr ʿala al-hidāya sharḥ bidayat al-mubtadī*. Edited by ʿAbd al-Razzāq Ghāleb al-Mahdī. Beirut: Dar al-Kotob al-Ilmiyah, 2009.

Ibn Nujaym, Zaynuddīn. *Al-ashb ā h wa al-naza'ir: ʿAla madhab Abī Ḥanīfa al-Nuʿmān*. Edited by Zakariyyā ʿUmairāt. Beirut: Dar al-Kotob al-Ilmiyyah, 2017.

Isbouts, Jean-Pierre. *Archaeology of the Bible: The Greatest Discoveries from Genesis to the Roman Era*. Washington, DC: National Geographic, 2016.

Islam, Muhammad. "The Concept of the Injīl in Ḥadīth Literature: An Analytical Study." *Hamdard Islamicus* 41, nos. 1–2 (January–June 2018): 73–106.

Janosik, Daniel J. *John of Damascus, First Apologist to the Muslims: The Trinity and Christian Apologetics in the Early Islamic Period*. Eugene, OR: Pickwick Publications, 2016.

Jaradat, Ahmad Ali. *Al-niḍhām al-qaḍā'i fī al-Islām* [Judicial system in Islam]. Amman, Jordan: Dar Al-Thaqafa, 2012.

Josephus, Flavius. *The Complete Works*. Translated by William Whiston. Nashville: Thomas Nelson Publishers, 1998.

Kahn, Paul W. "Freedom, Autonomy and the Cultural Study of Law." In *Cultural Analysis, Cultural Studies, and the Law: Moving beyond Legal* Realism, edited by Austin Sarat and Jonathan Simon, 154–87. Durham, NC: Duke University Press, 2003.

Kamali, Mohammad Hashim. *Principles of Islamic Jurisprudence*. 3rd ed. 2003. Reprinted, Cambridge: Islamic Texts Society, 2017.

———. *Shariʿah Law: An Introduction*. 2008. Reprinted, London: Oneworld Publications, 2012.

———. *Shariʿah Law: Questions and Answers*. London: Oneworld Publications, 2017.

———. *A Textbook of Ḥadīth Studies: Authenticity, Compilation, Classification and Criticism of Ḥadīth*. 2005. Reprinted, Markfield Leicestershire, UK: The Islamic Foundation, 2016.

Kāsānī al-Ḥanafī, ʿAlā' al-Dīn al-, and Abi Bakr Ibn Masʿūd. *Badā'iʿ al-ṣanā'iʿ fī tartīb al-sharā'eʿ*. Cairo: Dar el-Hadith, 2005.

Keane, Adrian, and Paul McKeown. *The Modern Law of Evidence*. 11th ed. Oxford: Oxford University Press, 2016.

Keener, Craig S. *Miracles: The Credibility of the New Testament Accounts*. Grand Rapids: Baker Academic, 2011.

Kennedy, D. James, and Jerry Newcombe. *What If Jesus Had Never Been Born? The Positive Impact of Christianity in History*. Rev. ed. Nashville: Thomas Nelson, 2001.

Kenyon, Frederic. *The Bible and Archaeology*. New York: Harper & Brothers, 1940.

Kenyon, Frederic G. *Our Bible and the Ancient Manuscripts Being a History of the Text and Its Translations*. 4th ed. London: Eyre and Spottiswoode, 1903.

Khan, Ruqayya Y. "Did a Woman Edit the Qur'ān? Hafṣa and her Famed 'Codex.'" *Journal of the American Academy of Religion* 82, no. 1 (March 2014): 174–216.

Khaṭīb al-Tomortāshī al-. *Tanwīr al-abṣār wa jāmiʿ al-biḥār*. Edited by Mohammed Abdulsalam Shahin. Beirut: Dar al-Kotob al-Ilmiyah, 2017.

Kierkegaard, Søren. *Philosophical Fragments; Johannes Climacus*. Edited and translated by Howard V. Hong and Edna H. Hong. Princeton, NJ: Princeton University Press, 1985.

Kitchen, K. A. *On the Reliability of the Old Testament*. Grand Rapids: William B. Eerdmans, 2003.

Kreeft, Peter, and Ronald Tacelli. *Handbook of Christian Apologetics: Hundreds of Answers to Crucial Questions*. Downers Grove, IL: IVP Academics, 1994.

Kubaisi, Muhammad Rajab Bakri al-. *Taṭawwor markaz al-qāḍi ʿabr al-tārīkh* [Development of the office of judge throughout history]. Beirut: Al-Halabi Legal Publications, 2016.

Kulaibouli, Abd al-Rahman bin Muhammad bin Suleiman al-. *Majmaʿ al-anhur fī sharḥ multaqa al-abḥur: lil imām Ibrahīm bin Muḥammad bin Ibrahīm al Ḥalabi*. Edited by Moḥammed Aḥmad el Mokhtār. Dar al-Kotob al-Ilmiyah, 2016.

Lahībī, Sāleḥ Muḥammad Zakī al-. *Al-qaḍāʿ fī al-ḥaḍāra al-Islāmiyya: Dirāsa tārīkhiyya* [Litigation in Islamic civilization: A historical study]. Dammam, Saudi Arabia: Dar Ibn Al-Jawzi, 1436 Hijri.

Lange, Christian. "The Judge and the judge: The Heavenly and Earthly Court of Justice in Early Islam." In *Justice and Leadership in Early Islamic* Courts, edited by Intisar A. Rabb and Abigail Krasner Balbale, 91–108. Cambridge, MA: ILSP, Harvard University Press, 2017.

Lathion, Stephane. "Muslims in Switzerland: Is Citizenship Really Incompatible with Muslim Identity?" *Journal of Muslim Minority Affairs* 28, no. 1 (April 2008): 53–60.

Lawson, Todd. *The Crucifixion and the Qur'an: A Study in the History of Muslim Thought*. 2009. Reprinted, London, Oneworld Publications, 2014. Kindle.

Layish, Aharon. "Shahādat Naql in the Judicial Practice in Modern Libya." In Masud, Peters, and Powers, 495–516.

Lazarus-Yafeh, Hava. "Some Neglected Aspects of Medieval Muslim Polemics against Christianity." *Harvard Theological Review* 89, no. 1 (January 1996): 61–84.

Levonian, Lootfy. "Christian Apologetics in Relation to Islam." *Union Seminary Quarterly Review* 7, no. 1 (November 1951): 10–14.

Lewis, C. S. *Miracles: A Preliminary Study*. New York: HarperCollins Publishers, 2001.

Lilly, Joseph L. "Alleged Discrepancies in the Gospel Accounts of the Resurrection." *The Catholic Biblical Quarterly* 2, no. 2 (April 1940): 98–111.

Lings, Martin, *Muhammad: His Life Based on the Earliest Sources*. 1983. Reprinted. Rochester, VT: Inner Traditions, 2006.

Linton, Irwin H. *A Lawyer Examines the Bible: A Defense of the Christian Faith*. San Diego: Creation-Life Publishers, 1943.

Lipka, Michael and Conrad Hackett. "Why Muslims Are the World's Fastest-Growing Religious Group." Pew Research Center. Accessed February 6, 2018. http://www. pewresearch.org/fact-tank/2017/04/06/why-muslims-are-the-worlds-fastest-growing-religious-group/.

Lippman, Matthew, Sean McConville, and Mordechai Yerushalmi. *Islamic Criminal Law and Procedure: An Introduction*. Westport, CT: Greenwood Press, 1988.

Livingstone, David N. "Where Would Civilization Be Without Christianity? The Gift of Science." *Christianity Today*, 6 December, 1999.

Loftus, Elizabeth F. *Eyewitness Testimony: With a New Preface*. 1979. Reprinted, Cambridge, MA: Harvard University Press, 1996.

Loke, Andrew Ter Ern. "The Resurrection of the Son of God: A Reduction of the Naturalistic Alternatives." *The Journal of Theological Studies* 60, pt. 2 (October 2009): 570–584.

Machen, J. Gresham. "The Scientific Preparation of the Minister." *Princeton Theological Review* 11, no. 1 (1913): 1–15.

Martindale, Wayne, and Jerry Root, eds. *The Quotable Lewis: An Encyclopedic Selection of Quotes from the Complete Published Works of C. S. Lewis*. Wheaton, IL: Tyndale House Publishers, 1990.

Mascord, Keith A. "Apologetics as Dialogue: A New Way of Understanding an Old Task." *The Reformed Theological Review* 54, no. 2 (May–August 1995): 49–64.

Masud, Muhammad Khalid, Rudolph Peters, and David S. Powers, eds. *Dispensing Justice in Islam: Qadis and their Judgements*. Leiden, Netherland: Brill, 2006.

———. "Qadis and their Courts: An Historical Survey in Dispensing Justice." In *Dispensing Justice in Islam: Qadis and their Judgements*, edited by Muhammad Khalid Masud, Rudolph Peters, and David S. Powers, 1–44. Leiden, Netherland: Brill, 2006.

Matasar, Richard A. "Storytelling and Legal Scholarship." *Chicago-Kent Law Review* 68, no. 1 (1992): 353–61.

Mattson, Ingrid. *The Story of the Qur'an: Its History and Place in Muslim Life*. 2nd ed. Malden, MA: Wiley-Blackwell, 2013.

McDowell, Sean Joslin. "A Historical Evaluation of the Evidence for the Death of the Apostles as Martyrs for Their Faith." PhD diss., The Southern Baptist Theological Seminary, 2015.

McGrath, Alister E. "Apologetics to the Romans." *Bibliotheca Sacra* 155 (October–December 1998): 387–93.

Modarressi, Hossein. "Circumstantial Evidence in the Administration of Islamic Justice." In Rabb and Balbale, 16–22.

Mohammadi, Fatemeh. "Becoming a Hijabi Now? Identity Performances of Muslim Women in Canada." *Religious Studies and Theology* 37, no. 1 (2018): 17–29.

Montgomery, John Warwick, ed. *Christianity for the Tough-minded*. 1973. Reprinted, Minneapolis: Bethany House Publishers, 1982.

———, ed. *Evidence for Faith: Deciding the God Question*. Dallas: Probe Books, 1991.

———. *History, Law and Christianity: How Does the Historic Evidence for the Christian Message Hold up against Cross-Examination?* 1964. Reprinted, Irvine, CA: NRP Books, 2014.

———. *Human Rights and Human Dignity*. Edmonton: Canadian Institute for Law, Theology, and Public Policy, 1995.

———. "The Jury Returns: A Juridical Defense of Christianity." In Montgomery, *Evidence for Faith*, 319–41.

———, ed. *The Law Above the Law*. 1975. Reprinted, Irvine, CA: NRP Books, 2015.

———. "The Legal Reasoning and Christian Apologetics." In Montgomery, *Law Above the Law*, 84–90.

———. *The Shape of the Past: A Christian Response to Secular Philosophies of History*. 1975. Reprinted, Eugene, OR: Wipf & Stock, 2009.

———. *Tractatus Logico-Theologicus*. 5th ed. Eugene, OR: Wipf & Stock, 2013.

———. *Where Is History Going?* Grand Rapids: Zondervan, 1969.

Moore, James R. "Some Weaknesses in Fundamental Buddhism." In *Christianity for the Tough-Minded*, edited by John Warwick Montgomery, 145–155. Reprinted, Minneapolis: Bethany House Publishers, 1982.

Moreau, A. Scott, Gary R. Corwin, and Cary B. McGee. *Introducing World Missions: A Biblical, Historical, and Practical Survey*. Grand Rapids: Baker Academics, 2004.

Moreland, J. P. *Scaling the Secular City: A Defense of Christianity*. Grand Rapids: Baker Academic, 1987.

Morley, Brian K. *Mapping Apologetics: Comparing Contemporary Approaches*. Downers Grove, IL: IVP Academics, 2015.

Motzki, Harald. "The Collection of the Qur'ān: A Reconsideration of Western Views in Light of Recent Methodological Developments." *Der Islam* 78, no. 1 (2001): 1–34.

Mueller, Christopher B., and Laird C. Kirkpatrick. *Federal Rules of Evidence: With Advisory Notes and Legislative History*. New York: Wolters Kluwer, 2017.

Mustapha, Nadira. "Law: Women as Witnesses: Overview." *Encyclopedia of Women & Islamic Cultures* 6 (2013): 475–77.

Naif, Ahmad Muhammad al-. *Al-bayyina al-qaḍā'iyya fī al-fiqh al-Islāmi: Dirāsa taṭbīqiyya ʿala al-qānūn al-madanī: Al-iqrār, al-yamīn, al-bayyināt al-khaṭṭiyya* [Judicial evidence in Islamic fiqh: Applied study on the civil law: Confession, oath, and documentary evidence]. Amman, Jordan: Janadria, 2013.

Nasafī, Abū al-Barakāt ʿAbdallah Ibn Aḥmad al-. *Kanz al-daqā'iq fī al-fiqh al-Ḥanafī*. Edited by Sa'ed Bakdāsh. 2nd ed. Medina, Saudi Arabia: Dar al-Basha'er al-Islamiyya, 2014.

Nasr, Seyyed Hossein, ed. *The Study Quran: A New Translation and Commentary*. New York: HarperCollins, 2015.

Netland, Harold A. *Dissonant Voices: Religious Pluralism and the Question of Truth*. Vancouver: Regent College Publishing, 1991.

Neuwirth, Angelika. "Qur'an and History–a Disputed Relationship: Some Reflections on Qur'anic History and History in the Qur'an." *Journal of Qur'anic Studies* 5, no. 1 (2003): 1–18.

Newman, Robert C. "The Synoptic Problem: A Proposal for Handling Both Internal and External Evidence." *The Westminster Theological Journal* 43, no. 1 (Fall 1980): 132–51.

Niehoff, Leonard M. *Evidence Law*. St. Paul, MN: Foundation Press, 2016.

Norman, David J. "Doubt and the Resurrection of Jesus." *Theological Studies* 69, no. 4 (December 2008): 786–811.

Novak, Michael. "Where Would Civilization Be Without Christianity? The Gift of Dignity." *Christianity Today*, December 6, 1999.

Nyazee, Imran A. K. *Islamic Legal Maxims (Qawa'id Fiqhiyyah)*. Islamabad, Pakistan: Center for Excellence of Research, 2016.

———. *Outlines of Islamic Jurisprudence*. 6th ed. Islamabad, Pakistan: Center for Excellence in Research, 2016.

O'Connell, Jake H. "Jesus' Resurrection and Collective Hallucinations." *Tyndale Bulletin* 60, no. 1 (2009): 69–105.

Patterson, Edwin W. "Logic in the Law." *University of Pennsylvania Law Review* 90, no. 8 (June 1942): 875–909.

Phillips, J. B. *Ring of Truth: A Translator's Testimony*. 1967. Reprinted, Wheaton, IL: Harold Shaw Publishers, 1977.

Plantinga, Alvin. *Warranted Christian Belief.* New York: Oxford University Press, 2000.

Price, Randall. *The Stones Cry Out: What Archaeology Reveals about the Truth of the Bible.* Eugene, OR: Harvest House Publishers, 1997.

Prothero, Stephen. *God Is Not One: The Eight Rival Religions That Run the World.* New York: HarperOne, 2010.

Qāsimī, Muḥammad Jamal al-Deen al-. *Qawā'ed al-taḥdīth min Funūn muṣṭalaḥ al-Ḥadīth.* Edited by Muḥammad Bahjat al-Bīṭār and Muḥammad Rashīd Riḍā. 2nd ed. Beirut: Dar al-Nafā'es, 1993.

Qattan, Najwa al-. "Dhimmis in the Muslim Court: Legal Autonomy and Religious Discrimination." *International Journal of Middle East Studies* 31, no. 3 (August 1999): 429–44.

Rabāḥ, Ghassān. *Al-wajīz fī al-qānūn al-Rūmānī wa al-Sharī'a al-Islāmiyya: Dirāsa muqārina* [A brief introduction to Roman law and Islamic Sharī'a: A comparative study]. Beirut: Al-Halabi Legal Publications, 2007.

Rabb, Intisar A. *Doubt in Islamic Law: A History of Legal Maxims, Interpretation, and Islamic Criminal Law.* New York: Cambridge University Press, 2015.

———. "Non-canonical Readings of the Qur'an: Recognition and Authenticity; The Himsi Reading." *Journal of Qur'anic Studies* 8, no. 2 (2006): 84–127.

Rabb, Intisar A., and Abigail Krasner Balbale, eds. *Justice and Leadership in Early Islamic Courts.* Cambridge, MA: ILSP, Harvard University Press, 2017.

Rahman, Fazlur. *Major Themes of the Qur'an.* 2nd ed. Chicago: University of Chicago Press, 2009.

Rangoonwala, Fatima I., Susan R. Sy, and Russ K. E. Epinoza. "Muslim Identity, Dress Code Adherence and College Adjustment among American Muslim Women." *Journal of Muslim Minority Affairs* 31, no. 2 (June 2011): 231–41.

Reardon, Timothy W. "'Hanging on a Tree': Deuteronomy 21:22–23 and the Rhetoric of Jesus' Crucifixion in Acts 5:12–42." *Journal for the Study of the New Testament* 37, no. 4 (June 2015): 407–31.

Reynolds, Gabriel Said. *The Qur'ān and the Bible: Text and Commentary.* New Haven, CT: Yale University Press, 2018.

Rissanen, Inkeri. "Developing Religious Identities of Muslim Students in the Classroom: A Case Study from Finland." *British Journal of Religious Education* 36, no. 2 (2014): 123–38.

Robinson, Chase F. *Islamic Historiography.* 2003. Reprinted, Cambridge: Cambridge University Press, 2004.

Robinson, John A. T. *Redating the New Testament.* 1976. Reprinted, Eugene, OR: Wipf & Stock, 2000.

Sadeghi, Hossein Mir Mohammad. "Filling the Gap in Favour of the Accused: The Approach of Islamic Criminal Law in Light of the Rule No Punishment in Case of Doubt." *Tulane European & Civil Law Forum* 29 (2014): 147–56.

Salama, Ma'amoun M. "General Principles of Criminal Evidence in Islamic Jurisprudence." In *The Islamic Criminal Justice System*, edited by M. Cherif Bassiouni, 109–23.

Saleh, Osman Abd-el-Malek al-. "The Right of the Individual to Personal Security in Islam." In *The Islamic Criminal Justice System*, edited by M. Cherif Bassiouni, 55–90. London: Oceana Publications, 1982.

Samour, Nahed. "A Critique of Adjudication: Formative Moments in Early Islamic Legal History." In *Justice and Leadership in Early Islamic* Courts, edited by Intisar A. Rabb and Abigail Krasner Balbale, 47–66. Cambridge, MA: ILSP, Harvard University Press, 2017.

Sampson, Philip J. *Six Modern Myths About Christianity & Western Civilization*. Downers Grove, IL: InterVarsity Press, 2001.

Samuelsson, Gunnar. *Crucifixion in Antiquity*. 2nd ed. Tübingen, Germany: Mohr Siebeck, 2013.

Sanad, Nagaty. *The Theory of Crime and Criminal Responsibility in Islamic Law: Shari'a*. Chicago: University of Illinois at Chicago, 1991.

Sanders, Fred, and Klaus Issler. *Jesus in Trinitarian Perspective*. Nashville: B&H Publishing Group, 2007.

Sarat, Austin, and Jonathan Simon, eds. *Cultural Analysis, Cultural Studies, and the Law: Moving beyond Legal Realism*. Durham, NC: Duke University Press, 2003.

Ṣārī, Muhammad Zakariyya Mahmoud. *Al-bayyina fī al-Sharīʿa wa al-qanūn: Dirāsa muqārina* [Evidence in Sharīʿa and law: A comparative study]. Damascus: Dar al-Moqtabas, 2018.

Sarkhasī al-Ḥanafī al-. *Al-mabsūṭ fī al-fiqh al-Ḥanafī*. Edited by Abū Abdallah Muḥammad Ḥasan Ismaʿīl al-Shafiʿī. Beirut: Dar al-Kotob al-Ilmiyah, 2017.

Satyaputra, Agus Gunawan. "The Problem of Objectivity in History and the Use of Historical Evidence in Christian Apologetic." *Evangel* 25, no. 3 (August 2007): 75–79.

Schacht, Joseph. *An Introduction to Islamic Law*. 1982. Reprinted, Oxford: Oxford University Press, 2012.

———. *Origins of Muhammadan Jurisprudence*. London: Oxford University Press, 1967.

Schaff, Philip, trans. *Creeds of Christendom*. 1931. Reprinted, Grand Rapids: Baker Book House, 1983.

Schlorff, Samuel P. "Muslim Ideology and Christian Apologetics." *Missiology* 21, no. 2 (April 1993): 173–85.

———. "Theological and Apologetical Dimensions of Muslim Evangelization." *Missiology* 28, no. 3 (July 2000): 335–66.

Schmidt, Alvin J. *How Christianity Changed the World*. Grand Rapids: Zondervan, 2004.

Shaham, Ron. *The Expert Witness in Islamic Courts: Medicine and Crafts in the Service of the Law*. Chicago: University of Chicago Press, 2010.

Shaikhy Zādah al-Ḥanafī, Ibrāhīm Ibn Ibrāhīm al-Ḥalabī, and al-ʿAlā' al-Ḥaṣkafī. *Majmaʿ al-anhur fī sharḥ multaqa al-abḥur wa maʿahu al-durr al-muntaqa fī sharḥ al-multaqa*. Beirut: Dar al-Kotob al-Ilmiyah, 2017.

Shammouṭ, Hasan Tayseer. *Al-ithbāt al-qaḍā'ī: wasā'iluhu wa ṭuruquhu fī al-fiqh al-Islāmī* [Judicial proof: Its means and methods in Islamic jurisprudence]. Amman, Jordan: Dar al- Nafā'es, 2019.

Shamsy, Ahmed El. *The Canonization of Islamic Law: A Social and Intellectual History*. 2013. Reprinted, New York: Cambridge University Press, 2015.

———. "The Logic of Excluding Testimony in Early Islam." In *Justice and Leadership in Early Islamic* Courts, edited by Rabb and Balbale, 16–22. Cambridge, MA: ILSP, Harvard University Press, 2017.

Shehadeh, Imad N. *God With Us and Without Us: The Beauty and Power in Oneness in Trinity versus Absolute Oneness*. Carlisle, Cumbria, UK: Langham Global Library, 2020.

Sherif, Adel Omar. "Generalities on Criminal Procedure under Islamic Shariʿa." In Abdel Haleem, Sherif, and Daniels, 3–16.

Sherlock, Thomas. *The Tryal of the Witnesses of the Resurrection of Jesus*. 4th ed. London: J. Roberts, 1729.

Shihadeh, Ayman. "The Existence of God." In *The Cambridge Companion to Classical Islamic Theology*, edited by Winter, 197–17. Cambridge: Cambridge University Press, 2008.

Sinai, Nicolai. *The Qur'an: A Historical-Critical Introduction*. Edinburgh: Edinburgh University Press, 2017.

———. "When Did the Consonantal Skeleton of the Quran Reach Closure?" *Bulletin of the School of Oriental and African Studies* 77, no. 2 (June 2014): 1–20.

Smith, Joseph J. "The Resurrection and the Empty Tomb." *Landas* 20, (2006): 173–99.

———. "The Resurrection Appearances and the Origin of the Easter Faith." *Landas* 20 (2006): 200–242.

Smith, Shawn C. "A Defense of Using Patristic Sources in Synoptic Problem Research." *Stone-Campbell Journal* 16, no. 1 (Spring 2013): 63–83.

Stark, Rodney. *For the Glory of God: How Monotheism Led to Reformations, Science, Witch-Hunts, and the End of Slavery*. Princeton, NJ: Princeton University Press, 2003.

Starkie, Thomas. *Practical Treatise on the Law of Evidence*. 10th ed. Philadelphia: T. & J. W. Johnson, 1876.

Stephen, Sir James Fitzjames. *A Digest of the Law of Evidence*. 4th ed. London: MacMillan and Co., 1881.

Stewart, Robert B., ed. *The Reliability of the New Testament: Bart Ehrman and Daniel B. Wallace in Dialogue*. Minneapolis: Fortress Press, 2011.

Strauss, Mark. *Luke*. In vol. 1 of *Zondervan Illustrated Bible Backgrounds Commentary*. Edited by Clinton E. Arnold, 318–515. Grand Rapids: Zondervan, 2002.

Surty, Muhammad Ibrahim H. I. "The Ethical Code and Organised Procedure of Early Islamic Law Courts, with Reference to al-Khassāf's Adab al-Qadi." In *Criminal Justice in Islam: Judicial Procedure in the Shari'a*, edited by Abdel Haleem, Sherif, and Daniels, 149–66. London: I. B. Taurus, 2003.

Swinburne, Richard. *The Resurrection of God Incarnate*. 2003. Reprinted, Oxford: Oxford University Press, 2010.

Thornton, Bruce S. *Plagues of the Mind: The New Epidemic of False Knowledge*. Rev. ed. Wilmington, DE: ISI Books, 2004.

Van Ommeren, Nicholas M. "Was Luke an Accurate Historian?" *Bibliotheca Sacra* 148, no. 589 (January 1991): 57–71.

Van Voorst, Robert E. *Jesus Outside the New Testament: An Introduction to the Ancient Evidence*. Grand Rapids: William B. Eerdmans Publishing Company, 2000.

Vansina, Jan. *Oral Tradition as History*. Madison: University of Wisconsin Press, 1985.

Wakil, Ahmed el-. "New Light on the Collection and Authenticity of the Qur'an: The Case for the Existence of a 'Master Copy' and How It Relates to the Reading of Hafs ibn Sulayman from Aseim ibn Abi al-Nujud." *Journal of Shiite Studies* 8, no. 4 (Autumn 2015): 409–48.

Wallace, Daniel B., ed. *Revisiting the Corruption of the New Testament: Manuscript, Patristic, and Apocryphal Evidence*. Grand Rapids: Kregel Publications, 2011.

Ware, Bruce A. *Father, Son, & Holy Spirit: Relationships, Roles, & Relevance*. Wheaton, IL: Crossway Books, 2005.

Wasserman, Tommy. "The Early Text of Matthew." In *The Early Text of the New Testament*, edited by Hill and Kruger, 83–107. Oxford: Oxford University Press, 2012.

Watts, Rikk E. "Christianity and the Ancient World." *Crux* 53, no. 1 (Spring 2017): 2–26.

Wenham, John. *Easter Enigma: Are the Resurrection Accounts in Conflict?* 1992. Reprinted, Eugene, OR: Wipf & Stock, 2005.

———. *Redating Matthew, Mark and Luke: A Fresh Assault on the Synoptics Problem*. Downers Grove, IL: InterVarsity Press, 1992.

Whately, Richard. *Introductory Lessons on Christian Evidences*. Philadelphia: H. Hooker, 1856.

Wiebe, Phillip H. *Visions of Jesus: Direct Encounter from the New Testament to Today*. New York: Oxford University Press, 1997.

Wigmore, John H. "Required Numbers of Witnesses; A Brief History of the Numerical System in England." *Harvard Law Review* 15, no. 2 (June 1901): 83–108.

Wilkins, Michael J., and J. P. Moreland, eds. *Jesus under Fire: Modern Scholarship Reinvents the Historical Jesus*. Grand Rapids: Zondervan, 1995.

Winter, Tim, ed. *The Cambridge Companion to Classical Islamic Theology*. Cambridge: Cambridge University Press, 2008.

Wright, N. T. *The Resurrection of the Son of God*. Minneapolis: Fortress Press, 2003.

Yamauchi, Edwin M. "Jesus outside the New Testament: What is the Evidence?" In *Jesus under Fire: Modern Scholarship Reinvents the Historical Jesus*, edited by Wilkins and Moreland, 207–29. Grand Rapids: Zondervan, 1995.

Yandell, Keith E. *Philosophy of Religion: A Contemporary Introduction*. 1999. Reprinted, New York: Routledge, 2005.

Yāsīn, Muḥammad Naʿīm. *Nathariyyat al-daʿwa bayna al-Sharīʿa al-Islāmiyya wa qānūn al-murāfaʿāt al-madaniyya wa al-tij ā riyya* [Theory of judicial case between Islamic Sharīʿa and the law of civil and commercial proceedings]. Dar al-Nafāʿes, 2011.

Zaydān, ʿAbdel Kareem. *Nidhām al-qad ā' fī al-Sharīʿa al-Islamiyya*. 3rd ed. Damascus: Resalah Publishers, 2011.

Zubair, Hafiz Muhammad and Shamanah Munawar. "Sharīʿa Ruling Regarding the Variant Readings of the Holy Qurʾān that were authentically narrated but not included in the ʿUthmānic Maṣāḥif." *International Journal of Business and Social Science* 5, no. 4 (March 2014): 1–7.

Langham Literature, with its publishing work, is a ministry of Langham Partnership.

Langham Partnership is a global fellowship working in pursuit of the vision God entrusted to its founder John Stott –

to facilitate the growth of the church in maturity and Christ-likeness through raising the standards of biblical preaching and teaching.

Our vision is to see churches in the Majority World equipped for mission and growing to maturity in Christ through the ministry of pastors and leaders who believe, teach and live by the word of God.

Our mission is to strengthen the ministry of the word of God through:

- nurturing national movements for biblical preaching
- fostering the creation and distribution of evangelical literature
- enhancing evangelical theological education

especially in countries where churches are under-resourced.

Our ministry

Langham Preaching partners with national leaders to nurture indigenous biblical preaching movements for pastors and lay preachers all around the world. With the support of a team of trainers from many countries, a multi-level programme of seminars provides practical training, and is followed by a programme for training local facilitators. Local preachers' groups and national and regional networks ensure continuity and ongoing development, seeking to build vigorous movements committed to Bible exposition.

Langham Literature provides Majority World preachers, scholars and seminary libraries with evangelical books and electronic resources through publishing and distribution, grants and discounts. The programme also fosters the creation of indigenous evangelical books in many languages, through writer's grants, strengthening local evangelical publishing houses, and investment in major regional literature projects, such as one volume Bible commentaries like the *Africa Bible Commentary* and the *South Asia Bible Commentary.*

Langham Scholars provides financial support for evangelical doctoral students from the Majority World so that, when they return home, they may train pastors and other Christian leaders with sound, biblical and theological teaching. This programme equips those who equip others. Langham Scholars also works in partnership with Majority World seminaries in strengthening evangelical theological education. A growing number of Langham Scholars study in high quality doctoral programmes in the Majority World itself. As well as teaching the next generation of pastors, graduated Langham Scholars exercise significant influence through their writing and leadership.

To learn more about Langham Partnership and the work we do visit **langham.org**

www.ingramcontent.com/pod-product-compliance
Lightning Source LLC
Chambersburg PA
CBHW051538230426
43669CB00015B/2638
9781839737909

Evidence for the Crucifixion and Resurrection of Jesus Christ Examined through Islamic Law displays a thorough understanding of the historical sources for the resurrection of Christ. What distinguishes Madanat's work, however, is how he weaves an evidential interaction of this material with the criteria of Islamic law. The result is a fascinating new way of viewing what had heretofore seemed an insurmountable epistemic problem between Muslims and Christians. I cannot recommend this work more highly.

Theodore J. Cabal, PhD
Professor of Philosophy of Religion,
Southwestern Baptist Theological Seminary, Texas, USA

Suheil Madanat's careful study analyzes available evidence for the historicity of the crucifixion and bodily resurrection of Jesus Christ and establishes that it can meet the required criteria set forth by Islamic law. A highly welcome contribution, Madanat's meticulous work sheds new light on ways for modern Christian-Muslim dialogue to go beyond traditional claims to reasonable understanding.

Ayman S. Ibrahim, PhD
Professor of Islamic Studies,
Director, Jenkins Center for the Christian Understanding of Islam,
The Southern Baptist Theological Seminary, Kentucky, USA

This is a remarkable apologetic work by an Arab Christian seeking to commend the veracity and reliability of the New Testament's witness to the crucifixion and resurrection of Jesus of Nazareth, but specifically using the evidentiary rules of Islamic law. He first applies the kind of evidence that is adduced by Muslims to determine the reliability of the Qur'an and Sunna to examine the trustworthiness of the New Testament documents. Then, leaning on an extensive dive into Islamic legal literature – both the contemporary scholarship on Islamic law in English and the classical sources of court evidentiary law in Arabic – Suheil Madanat shows how the passion narratives in the Gospels and several confessional passages in the letters of Paul, Peter, and James provide ample and reliable evidence of Jesus's death and resurrection that would hold out in an Islamic court. A very original and helpful new tool for Muslim-Christian dialogue.

David L. Johnston, PhD
Affiliate Assistant Professor of Islamic Studies,
Fuller Theological Seminary, California, USA
Adjunct Lecturer, Saint Joseph's University, Pennsylvania, USA

In this impressive work, Dr. Suheil Madanat provides a needed apologetic for the death and resurrection of Christ. It stands out as a unique contribution that serves, not only the Islamic world, but also the non-Islamic world. In Suheil's words, "available evidence for the historicity of the crucifixion and bodily resurrection of Jesus Christ can pass the criteria of sound evidence set by the Islamic law." Christians can find in this law a suitable method to vindicate the historical evidence for the Christian faith.

I enjoyed reading every page of the doctoral dissertation that provided the basis of this work. The research methodology is sound, and the flow of thought is clear and logically understandable. It is continually substantiated and aided by a wealth of supporting footnotes from references that are comprehensive, both in quantity and quality. The writing is very clear, and impressively accurate and precise.

This book will be a continual resource used by students of theology and serious thinkers who seek to promote the gospel of the death and resurrection of our Lord. I fully endorse this work with much love and appreciation.

Imad N. Shehadeh, PhD

Founder, President, and Senior Professor of Theology,
Jordan Evangelical Theological Seminary, Amman